NEVER BURN YOUR MOVING BOXES

A True Tale of a Real-Life Cowboy Wife

Jolyn Young

TRAFALGAR SQUARE
North Pomfret, Vermont

First published in 2023 by
Trafalgar Square Books
North Pomfret, Vermont 05053

Library of Congress Cataloging-in-Publication Data

Names: Young, Jolyn, author.
Title: Never burn your moving boxes : a true tale of a real-life cowboy wife / Jolyn Young.
Description: North Pomfret, Vermont : Trafalgar Square Books, 2023. | Summary: "A young woman's struggle with marriage and motherhood on some of the most remote ranches in the American West. Jolyn Young grew up in the "real" northern California-the forgotten area at the tip-top of the state with small towns, extreme poverty, and about 40 miles to the Oregonian mountains. In a childhood defined by a subdivision, she decided she wanted to be a cowboy, and two years out of college, she saw that dream through, taking a job at a Nevada ranch in the search for a lifestyle subsisting of horses, cattle, and the wide open range. Falling in love was never part of the plan. Jim Young was tall, strong, and could ride a bronc and rope a steer like no one's business. And before she knew it Jolyn found her cowboyin' dreams overtaken by a new and intoxicating cowboy reality. With long days side by side in the saddle, nights sharing a bedroll, and the deep satisfaction that came with hard physical work in a place filled with natural beauty, it seemed life was all a strong-willed young woman might want it to be. But when a baby-to-be suddenly spun her wild romance into a very practical marriage, and one decrepit ranch trailer home led to the next, Jolyn found her young family desperately seeking stability in what is by definition a transient lifestyle that moves with the seasons. Often hours from the nearest grocery store and half-a-day from the closest hospital, pregnancy, childbirth, and illness required a do-it-yourself mentality. With days, sometimes weeks on her own as Jim worked the farthest reaches of whatever ranchlands they currently called home-and first with one child to care for...and eventually with three-Jolyn fought profound loneliness, finding comfort in writing and company in her camera. As the cowboy lifestyle pulled them further toward the brink of civilization and Jim's drinking became a liability, losing him jobs and sending them packing, again, to yet another, different, distant cow camp, Jolyn struggled with the knowledge that she was choosing a life of scrubbing filthy mobile home floors and bunkhouse bathrooms in order to keep her family together. It would take leaving it, and Jim, for her to determine whether a world built on risk could coexist with the responsible mother she had needed to become. With a memoir that is brave, honest, and heartbreakingly funny, Jolyn Young has written the story of every young adventure-seeker, every new mother, and every partner who has loved an alcoholic in a whole new light-that of a campfire, on the edge of the desert night, miles away from cell phone reception"-- Provided by publisher.
Identifiers: LCCN 2023014692 (print) | LCCN 2023014693 (ebook) | ISBN 9781646011766 (paperback) | ISBN 9781646011773 (epub)
Subjects: LCSH: Young, Jolyn. | Ranchers' spouses--United States--Biography. | Horsemen and horsewomen--United States--Biography. | Mothers--United States--Biography. | Marriage--United States. | Ranch life--West (U.S.). | West (U.S.)--Biography.
Classification: LCC F596 .Y68 2023 (print) | LCC F596 (ebook) | DDC 978.0092 [B]--dc23/eng/20230418
LC record available at https://lccn.loc.gov/2023014692
LC ebook record available at https://lccn.loc.gov/2023014693

Book design by Maria Mann
Cover design by RM Didier
Typefaces: Amasis MT Light

Printed in the United States of America

10 9 8 7 6 5 4 3 2 1

For everyone who thought they couldn't
but did anyway.

CONTENTS

✳

"Slap some bacon on a biscuit, we're burnin' daylight!"
— John Wayne

CHAPTER 1 ✳ **More Than a Conversationalist**

The wind blew down from the mountains in an icy blast. I tucked my silk wild rag into the top of my down jacket and buckled my chaps around my waist. We had a photoshoot to do regardless of the frigid air and spitting snow. A few feet away, Dano and Jim zipped their heavy coats and pulled on cotton gloves.

"Just think, somewhere out there, thousands of people are water skiing and basking in the sun," said Jim. Beads of hail stuck to his handlebar mustache. The tapered ends flailed wildly in the wind, alternating between hitting him in the eyes and darting up his nostrils with the changing gusts.

"Yeah, those people definitely don't live in North Fork," Dano replied.

Tayler and I giggled and walked to the back of the horse trailer to retrieve our mounts for the day. Come spring snowstorm or sunny skies, I couldn't think of a single way I'd rather spend Memorial Day weekend. Or any other day, for that matter. Ever since I was twelve, all I'd wanted to be was a full-time cowboy. And now here I was at age twenty-four, drawing ranch wages and riding along with two guys who had never done anything besides ride and rope for a living. They'd brought each of us a horse to ride, since Tayler was from out-of-state and I didn't own one.

I had a sorrel mare of Dano's named Dirty Girl. I bridled her, tightened my cinch, and hitched up my chaps to step on. Jim and Dano readied their own mounts while Tayler threw her reins over one arm and snapped pictures left and right. The assignment was to document Dano for a magazine article, but she pointed the lens at all of us equally. Photos were her artistic medium of choice; words were mine.

We rode down the gravel road to a scenic pond. Dano loped circles on his palomino colt near the water while Tayler took pictures. Jim sat off to the side, turning his horse in small circles to improve his mount's lateral flexion. I waited on Dirty Girl and watched it all.

The country was huge. We were in a Bureau of Land Management allotment that encompassed hundreds of square miles of towering mountains, ice-cold creeks, sagebrush flats, falling-down homesteads, dirt roads, wire fences, antelope, elk, cougars, and domestic livestock. There was a boundary line somewhere, but its presence didn't alter the vastness. On the other side of this allotment was another allotment, and another, all across northern Nevada. They joined together to form an enormous swath of wildlife habitat and ranch country that was occasionally interrupted by a ranch headquarters or a small town consisting of little more than a gas station and a bar. There was always a bar. A man didn't want to risk getting too thirsty this far out on the desert.

When Dano's yellow horse was loped down and Tayler was satisfied with her first set of pictures, we rode on to find another location. Dano's dogs jumped a bunch of yearling steers within a few minutes. We all stepped off to tighten our cinches before we took our ropes down and built a loop.

Tayler hung back with her camera to her eye while Dano ran up and roped a steer around the neck. Jim stopped his horse with his rope in his hand, a loop built and ready to swing.

"Go ahead, get in there and take the first shot," he told me.

I kicked Dirty Girl up to heel the steer. I swung my rope with the tip of my loop pointed down over the steer's hip, followed a few strides until I felt confident of my shot, threw my loop, and missed. I reined in my horse to coil my rope and rebuild a loop, just in case Jim missed his shot. He rode up swinging with authority and picked up two feet on the first try.

I wasn't sure if I should dismount and work the ground like the person who misses usually does when doctoring cattle outside. I hung back with my rope in my hand and looked from Dano to Jim to pick up a hint. I wanted to stay out of Tayler's pictures for magazine purposes, but I dang sure didn't want to be accused of shirking my duties.

Dano turned his horse to face his partner and stepped off when Jim's rope came tight. He tied the rope to his saddle horn and walked to the steer's head to set his own rope. His yellow colt perked his ears forward and leaned his weight back, holding the rope tight so the steer couldn't get up. This was how the pair of cowboys and their equine partners worked all day, every day.

Tayler furiously snapped pictures from various angles. As a joke, the guys drew a smiley face on the steer's side with a fat chalk stick before turning it loose. Ordinarily, they would mark the animal on the back or forehead with a line to indicate it had been doctored, but this time, they were roping solely for photographic purposes.

Halfway through the day we trailered to a new location. Jim and Dano taught us how to tie our horses in the trailer like real cowboys, wrapping the lead rope around the closest vertical bar once, then running it back and securing it with two half hitches tied to a different bar. There were no slip knots and daisy chains on real working ranches. Dano and Jim were everything I aspired to be—minus the mustaches and Copenhagen rings in their shirt pockets.

I'd wanted to work as a full-time cowboy since I was in sixth grade. When I trained backyard horses during summer breaks from college, I warmed up my favorites by trotting down the bank of the irrigation canal behind my dad's house as the sun came up. I was in a rural subdivision in northern California, but I pretended I was trotting to work on the range. Two years out of college, I got a job on a ranch in Nevada.

I loved riding and roping for a living, but, like most jobs you love so much you'd do them for free, it didn't quite pay the bills. I'd started picking up freelance writing assignments here and there—as long as they were close by, I didn't have to travel far and could keep expenses down. That's how I wound up writing a story, to be accompanied by Tayler's photos, about Dano, aka Dan Lock, and his unique summer job. He lived in a wall tent with fellow cowboy Jim Young from May to September each year, taking care of yearling cattle for Mitch Goicoechea.

I was glad for an excuse to hang out with these guys, ride good ranch horses, and ask dozens of questions. I still couldn't quite believe I was really out there, living my twelve-year-old self's dream. I wrote the story, filed it with my editor, and didn't think too much about either Dano or Jim again.

I sat in the living room of the single-wide trailer I shared with my coworker and friend, Tilly. It was late afternoon, and we were done with work for the day. The couch was small and ancient. Corded brown upholstery hid the worst of its stains. (Sometimes, it's better to just not know.) A multitude of fly specks were splattered across the low ceiling. They were brown on white and there was no hiding those spots. I'd discovered it was best to slay as many as I could with a plastic swatter first thing in the morning, when they were too cold and sluggish to move quickly.

But at least the trailer was warmer than the cold spring air outside. And I only needed to clean up and change my clothes before I headed to Elko.

I was headed for the door when the phone on the end table rang.

"Hi, is this Jolyn?" a male voice asked when I picked up the receiver.

"Yes," I answered cautiously. Usually only my roommate's friends and family called on the landline. Was this a telemarketer? A bill collector? I didn't owe anybody and wasn't in the mood to switch my auto insurance, so it would probably be a short call.

"This is Jim Young," the voice said.

I knew right then that he would make small talk for a few minutes and then ask me for a date, which he did.

"Sorry," I said. "I can't go. I'm headin' to town this afternoon to order a saddle."

Ordering a custom saddle is a big deal. Cowboys often spend more time designing a saddle than they do choosing a spouse, and rightfully so. The average American marriage dissolves after about eight years. A well-made saddle can easily last for decades.

After my polite refusal, Jim countered with an offer of dinner the following Saturday.

"Sure," I said. "That would work."

I didn't have high hopes the date would lead to anything. Jim looked about twenty years older than me. But I operated under the basic dating principle that a man who asked a woman out on a proper date deserved at least one yes, no matter how unlikely the prospect of a second date seemed.

The sound of a diesel engine coming up the driveway to Reed Station, the name of the division of the ranch where I lived, reached my ears before the truck came into view. It was seven o'clock, and I was dressed and ready for Jim to pick me up. He stopped in front of the single-wide and turned off the engine. The sight of his face through the driver's side window shocked me.

He'd shaved off the huge mustache and looked his actual age (which I later found out was thirty). A crisply shaped straw hat replaced his sweat-stained felt one, and he wore boots as a matter of course. A long-sleeve button-down shirt was neatly tucked into his blue jeans. Both were heavily starched and pressed. A trophy belt buckle lay flat against his stomach.

I blushed hard and quickly turned back down the hallway. I fanned my face with my hand, stirring the artificially sweet smell of hair gel through the air. I breathed deeply and hoped the redness would leave my cheeks by the time Jim knocked on the front door. In my outfit—a fitted purple t-shirt and blue jeans—I suddenly felt a bit underdressed. I was glad I'd taken two minutes to swipe on some mascara before he arrived. At least my jeans were skintight.

"Hi," Jim said when I opened the door. "You look nice."

"Thank you," I replied. "You, too."

At least I didn't stutter or say, "Ditto." Now I just had to make it down the steps without tripping.

Jim walked me to the passenger side of his old brown Ford and opened the door. I wasn't sure if the gesture was modern chivalry or because only he knew the secret combination of "lift and twist." Dents of various widths and depths decorated both sides of the pickup bed. The tailgate was missing and the tags were expired. The interior of the single cab featured stained cloth upholstery and the original AM/FM radio.

I liked everything about it. That worn-out pickup told me Jim was a real cow-boy, not a data analyst with a shiny new crew cab and heated seats who had no clue how to step on a horse that might buck. I scooted onto the bench seat and fastened the seat belt. The cab smelled like dirt, oil, and leather. I also smelled something unfamiliar, masculine, and sprayed from a bottle, but I couldn't tell what brand the cologne was. I wasn't even sure if it was cologne, body spray, or aftershave. I didn't grow up with brothers and had only dated a handful of guys before Jim. Like, a small handful. Probably not even a whole hand. All I knew was that his scent made me want to lean in and inhale deeply. Whatever marketing ploy made him buy it was definitely working.

"Where would you like to eat?" Jim asked politely.

"How about Biltoki's?" I suggested. "You can't go wrong with Basque food."

The food was always good at Biltoki's. Garlicky, but good. The restaurant was in Elko, a full forty-five minutes away. It was a short drive by Nevada ranch standards but a long time to chitchat with a first date. Between his clean-shaven face and alluring scent, I could hardly look around or breathe without feeling flustered. I rested my right arm on the cracked brown Naugahyde of the pickup door and reminded myself to act normal.

At dinner I ordered a filet mignon and tried not to get lettuce stuck in my teeth. Afterward, we walked down the street to the Silver Dollar Club, a dive bar surrounded by more dives, several all-night casinos, and a couple yuppie eateries. The Saturday night party crowd was still on their first round and starting to get noisy. The career drunks had been at it since yesterday morning, hunched on their barstools and not making eye contact. Cigarette smoke spiraled up from along the bar and the shuffleboard tables. Pockets of white fumes were trapped against the ceiling while swirling clouds escaped out the door to vanish into the night sky.

I suggested we play a game of pool. Jim dug in his pocket for some quarters and racked up the balls. I fancied I knew a little more about the game than the average girl, since I'd taken billiards as an elective in college. My break was weak, but I calculated angles and called my shots well enough to beat Jim (barely) in our first game of eight ball. He consistently sunk what he aimed at, but every time I thought he was going to pull ahead, he fumbled a shot just enough that I regained my lead.

We started another game as I took the first sip of my second gin and tonic. I rested the end of my pool stick on the floor and stood with one leg slightly bent at the knee. I saw Jim look at me out of the corner of his eye from across the pool table. I stood up straight and sucked in my stomach. I knew my small waist was one of my best features, and I wanted to make sure Jim noticed, too.

A middle-aged woman with the wrinkled tan face of a smoker who had spent too much time in the sun approached Jim. Her shirt was synthetic and too tight, but her smile was genuine.

"You know, I just have to ask—are you on the city council?" she asked him.

"City council? No, not me," said Jim, taken aback.

"Oh, well, you just look like an upstanding pillar of the community." The woman laughed and waved her arm in an airy gesture. Jim pondered his open beer for a few seconds.

"I've been called a lot of things, but 'pillar of the community' has never been one of them," he said. He caught my eye over her head and I laughed. I was pretty sure city councilmen didn't live in canvas range teepees and drive pickups with expired tags and missing tailgates. But in his crisply pressed pearl snap shirt, I could see where the woman had gotten the misguided notion that Jim voted on parking meter policies and listened to concerned citizens argue about their need for more public drinking fountains. Or maybe she was just drunk.

After I barely beat Jim at our second game of pool, it felt like time to go. A logical second stop would have been to walk one block south to Stockmen's and its slot machines, blackjack tables, and live band. But the bigger casino meant a bigger party crowd that likely included people one or both of us knew. I wasn't ready to face any of our friends with my date just yet, and I for darn sure wasn't going to stay out all night alone with him, so I asked him to drive me home.

I sat on the passenger side of the bench seat, but I didn't lean my arm on the door this time. I didn't need to remind myself to breathe normally. The cover of darkness and two (or was it three?) gin and tonics had calmed my nerves and loosened my tongue.

"Do you have any brothers or sisters?" I asked.

"No, I'm an only child."

"Where do your parents live?"

"Colorado."

"Do you have any kids?"

"No."

"Do you do any illegal drugs?"

"No."

"Okay. Good. That would be a deal-breaker."

Relieved that we'd cleared the air on my primary dating hang-up, the conversation progressed easily as Jim drove north on Mountain City Highway.

"I was married for five years," he said.

"Oh."

I hadn't expected that. I instantly imagined five years' worth of matching Christmas stockings. Five years of homemade birthday cakes, Fourth of July fireworks, and dinner for two every night. He could probably still smell her freshly baked chocolate chip cookies.

"After my divorce, I just have a few ground rules," Jim continued. "For example, no sleeping with my friends."

I looked at him and laughed. That seemed reasonable enough.

The more he told me about his first marriage, the less it bothered me. He'd only lived with his ex-wife for a handful of nonconsecutive months over the course of their union. His family had never liked her, his friends hadn't attended their wedding, and she'd Maced him at court-ordered counseling. Jim had finally signed divorce papers when he'd learned that his estranged wife had propositioned his close friend in a text message.

I was glad that his longest and most serious prior relationship was a dysfunctional firestorm that had left no smoldering embers. Jim was good-looking, funny, polite, and shaped his cowboy hat to perfection. I was beginning to think I wanted him all to myself.

Jim asked me for a second date before he drove away at the end of our first one. I knew this was a good sign because I had read *The Rules,* a dating book from the late 1990s that was considered by many to be anti-feminist because it encouraged women not to chase men.

Once again, he picked me up on time and took me to dinner.

We decided to see a movie after dinner and had some time to kill before it started, so we stopped at Raley's and bought a pack of cherry-flavored Swisher Sweets. It was my idea; I'd loved cigars since I was fifteen and my dad offered me one at his then-girlfriend's Easter party. Jim and I sat in the back of his pickup in front of the strip mall and smoked, with our legs dangling over the edge of the bed where the tailgate should have been. The summer night was dark and cooling, the parking lot mostly empty. An occasional shopper hurried into Raley's for a late-night frozen pizza or box of beer. Engines roared and faded down the nearby interstate in a steady stream of diesel exhaust and screeching jake brakes.

We puffed and talked as we waited to see *Bad Teacher*. Suggesting an R-rated comedy about a sleazy teacher was a bold move for a second date, but I did it anyway. We probably weren't compatible if he didn't appreciate a girl who laughed at the f-word in public.

Jim and I laughed at all the same parts of the movie.

When he drove me home, I sat on the opposite end of the bench seat. I wasn't moving any closer than the passenger side just yet. Before he opened my door in the driveway, however, I glanced at him just long enough. He instantly leaned across the seat and kissed me, his chin warm and smooth against mine. I kissed him back for a quick second. Then he walked me up the rickety wooden porch steps and asked if he could take me on a third date.

"Yes," I said.

Then I smiled. I could hardly believe that a man had lined me up for a date before finishing the one we were on not once, but twice. I knew this was a really good sign, and not just because of *The Rules*. I didn't need to read a dating book to know he was interested in getting to know me better, and not just as a conversationalist.

Jim turned to face me when we stopped on the porch in front of the door. He put his arms around my waist and kissed me again, longer this time. He didn't need to remove his cowboy hat or even tip it back. I stood so much shorter than him that I raised up onto my toes to meet his lips and our bodies pressed together for a brief moment. His muscles were hard and flat against my soft, compact curves. I smelled his cologne clinging to my shirt after he walked back to his truck. Or was it aftershave? Body spray? I still wasn't sure. All I knew was I couldn't wait to see him again.

———————————

We went to dinner in Elko again for our third date. Afterward, we walked around the Biker Rally in a light rain. I slipped my hand in his back pocket on the sidewalk and didn't care who saw.

On the way home, I once again sat on the passenger side of the bench seat, but I laid down and rested my cheek on Jim's leg once we were a few miles out of town. I wanted to be closer to him, and it made me feel safe, like when I was a little girl, riding home from team ropings with my dad in his white '75 Chevy pickup with step sides and a manual transmission. I'd always get tired partway home and fall asleep to the rise and fall of the gas engine as he shifted up through the gears.

Jim kept one hand on the steering wheel and his eyes focused on the road ahead. He laid his other hand on my hip, over the rounded curve where the front pocket rivet meets the outer seam. I closed my eyes and listened to the diesel engine's rhythmic hum as he drove forty-five miles through the midnight desert to my doorstep.

The engine slowed as Jim turned left off the paved road onto the dirt lane leading to the trailer house. I knew the slowing engine and crunching gravel meant our date was almost over, so I didn't sit up until Jim got out of the cab to open the horse pasture gate.

"Thanks for dinner," I told him when he parked in front of the trailer. "I had a really fun time tonight."

"Me, too," he said.

I smiled but was on edge, sensing the unspoken expectation of a third date. I was extra careful not to invite Jim inside the trailer. There was no telling what that oversized cowboy would talk my body into doing if I let him cross the threshold. Once again, we parted with a warm kiss under the porch light.

CHAPTER 2 ✳ **Don't Call Me Sweetheart**

Jim asked me to go away with him to a three-day rodeo the week after our third date. The thought of spending two nights alone with him unsettled me, but I packed a suitcase and ignored my growing apprehension. I knew Jim expected—or at least anticipated—certain things. I also knew I wasn't ready to do those things. I assumed he'd had sex before, but I still hadn't told him that I hadn't. Of course, we didn't talk about any of these things because I don't like to talk about things that make me uncomfortable.

The drive to the McDermitt Fourth of July Ranch Hand Rodeo took four hours. McDermitt was a middle-of-nowhere town on the Oregon/Nevada border—half of it on the Fort McDermitt Indian Reservation. Jim warned me to stay away from the "rez side" of town at all costs. That was where "people get stabbed and nice girls just don't go." He said that if I was ever alone in our motel room, I should lock the door and not open it for anyone, no matter what. I believed him, and that's why his friend Hezzie slept in the parking lot that night after banging on our door when Jim had already passed out. I knew

Hez and probably should have opened the door for him, but rules are rules, and I wasn't about to get stabbed.

Jim and his friends drank two cases of beer on the way to McDermitt. By the time we hit the rodeo grounds, the guys were pretty well tuned up. Cowboys rarely get a day off, so the prospect of three days at a rodeo without adult supervision had everyone in a party mood. I wasn't a big drinker and never did like beer, so I stayed sober and smiled a lot. (Which was also how I'd gotten out of several speeding tickets during my teenaged years.)

The guys unloaded their horses at the arena in a dirt parking lot full of dried weeds and gopher holes. Kyla, a friend who'd ridden over with us, and I applied sunscreen and painted our nails by the horse trailer. I was the only woman at the rodeo wearing a dress and sandals. I knew I'd probably get a sunburn and that walking through the stickers and weeds would make my feet itch, but I wore Levis and a cowboy hat most days. I wasn't about to pass up a chance to look cute in public.

I only knew a handful of people at the rodeo, so I was extra glad for Kyla's company. It was nice to have someone to sit with in the grandstand while Jim roped. "Grandstand" might be a bit of an overstatement. The bleachers were old and wooden, paint peeling and mostly gone—too steep to be safe for little kids and too wobbly to be safe for old folks. Most spectators packed an ice chest and pitched a shade canopy just outside the arena fence.

I spectated with Kyla the next morning, too. As the female member of her team, her presence was necessary for entry into the rodeo, but she was only required to saddle up and throw a rope once, during the ladies' steer-stopping event. By contrast, the men on each team competed in four events. The guys all liked going to McDermitt because there were no events that involved manhandling a bovine into a stock trailer or wrestling an animal three times their body weight to the ground. They got to keep a rope in their hand and their butt in the saddle at all times, just like cowboys should.

Later in the day, Kyla and I stood in the dirt just outside the arena fence, behind someone else's shade canopy and a pickup bed full of overweight locals wearing shorts and asking too much of their lawn chairs. The announcer called Jim's name and the chute gate swung open. He rode a black bucking horse across the arena with one hand gripping his rope and his other hand lifting on the bronc rein. He rode for the full eight seconds, then jumped off on the pickup man when the buzzer sounded. I cheered and smiled, glad he was my brand-new boyfriend.

My smile faded as I began to realize how Jim planned on celebrating his successful ride. Or maybe he was celebrating the Fourth of July, or his first weekend trip with his new girlfriend, or a weekend off from work, or who knows what. Whatever his reason, he celebrated it with a beer in each hand and one in his pocket for later. He'd prepared for the ride the same way, then he drank the rest of the case for good measure. He appeared to be racing his buddies to the bottom of the beer cooler. And if he wasn't in the lead, he was a close second.

Back in Elko County, Jim only drank two beers each time he took me out to dinner. He opened my doors, removed his hat at the table, said thank you to the waitress, and told clean jokes. I liked the earlier version of Jim a lot better than this drunken cowboy, the one with bloodshot eyes whose words were turning mushy and who rode his rope horse with one hand on the reins and the other holding two beer cans stacked on top of each other. When we'd first showed up at the rodeo, I was proud when people realized I was with Jim. On his arm. As his girlfriend. A "taken woman." Claimed by him. But as he got drunker, I became less enthusiastic about thinking of myself as "his."

I slipped away while Jim and his friends were distracted with the rodeo. I walked behind the pickup truck with the overloaded lawn chairs. I passed by pens full of broncs and roping steers at the far end of the arena to avoid the crowd of contestants at the main gate. I didn't want to run into anyone who would ask where I was going. I just wanted to put some distance between myself and Jim.

The hot air assaulted me from all sides during the walk back to the motel. It shot down from the sun and radiated up from the blacktop as I marched a quarter mile back to the cheap, crappy room. My short cotton dress and back-less sandals offered little protection from the sweltering elements, but I was too mad to care about the possibility of obtaining a moderate to severe sunburn.

All I could think about was that good-looking, bronc riding, no-good Jim Young.

I stormed down the pavement like a one-woman thundercloud wearing shimmery pink eyeshadow and Insta-Dri nail polish. The Diamond A Motel sat at the south end of the parking lot from McDermitt's main attraction, the Say When Casino. The carpet was dirty and the bathtub was covered in a grimy film that made me wonder if taking a shower actually made me cleaner. I perched on the edge of the motel bed with my legs crossed and tried not to touch anything.

What should I do? I'd driven to a rodeo halfway across the state with a man I really liked but didn't know very well. His friends were nice, but they were *his* friends, not mine. I was in a sketchy town in the middle of the desert where drug deals went down in the lobby of my motel every night. I might be stabbed at any moment. And now the man I really liked but didn't know very well was completely wasted, which was a major bummer because one of the reasons I really liked him was because he always seemed so sober.

I left the grungy motel room and walked over to the Say When after Jim and the rest of the crowd made it back to town. Jim put his arm around my shoulders and tried to buy me a drink. I told him no thanks. Then he called me sweetheart, which really pissed me off.

The music was loud and the small casino was crowded with dusty cowboys, women wearing halter tops, and slot machines. Kids ran through the crowd, darted between legs, and dodged elbows to find their parents, then ran back outside to toss water balloons and run relay races in the street for candy prizes. It was easy to slip between bobbing shoulders and sloshing drinks to stay on the opposite side of the room from Jim. Our mutual friends gave me questioning looks and the mean girls casually stepped over to block for me when he tried to catch up.

Out back, a band played on a stage directly across the street from a faded pink crack house, which was next door to another crack house in a more neutral color. Straw bales corralled slow-dancing couples into a potholed parking lot, along with little kids who spun and jumped to their own beat. All the stars came out in the summer sky while the band played Brooks & Dunn and Lynyrd Skynyrd covers.

Jim and I left the Say When about the time all the single people had paired up for the night and the glassy-eyed drunks started telling the same story for the fourth time. Tension hung in the air of our motel room, dangling in the fluorescent light alongside the dust mites and mildew spores. Loud shouts sporadically burst into the night when someone opened a door to the Say When. Spurs clanked unevenly down the sidewalk in front of our room, stopping every few strides as some cowboy tried to match the number on his key tag to the number on a door.

I stepped into the bathroom and closed the door. I changed into a t-shirt and pair of cotton panties, then huffed over to the double bed without looking at Jim. I climbed in and pulled up the covers.

"I'm not having sex with you," I stated.

"I don't remember asking you to," Jim replied.

He kicked off his boots, undressed and climbed under the covers. I was suddenly hyper-aware of his nearly naked body so close to mine. His chest was broad and his arms were long. I wanted to feel his skin against my skin. I wiggled my foot until it found his calf. He reached for me and I rolled over, pressing my back against his chest. Then he slipped a hand beneath my t-shirt and cupped my breast for the rest of the night.

The next morning, Jim asked me to reach into his duffel bag and hand him a pair of spurs. I unzipped the side pocket and found a daily devotional book and a box of condoms. I had read the Bible from Genesis to Revelation, but I had never even held a box of rubbers before.

"Which one of these were you planning to use?" I asked.

"Well, right now I just need the spurs so I can get on my horse and rope," he said. "Could you please hand them to me?"

I handed him the spurs and decided he was a total jerk. What kind of man brought a safe, effective, noninvasive form of birth control on an overnight trip with a woman who he didn't know was a virgin because she was too emotionally immature to talk about sex? I had a hunch that other couples routinely bought and used birth control on weekend getaways, but not me.

I didn't set out to become a twenty-four-year-old virgin. It all started when I failed to switch from horse-crazy to boy-crazy in high school. When the other girls were putting on makeup and spaghetti-strap tank tops for a drive-and-park session on the hill behind the high school, I was still wearing a waterproof canvas barn coat and loping circles on my barrel-racing horse. I made it through four years at a state college still holding my V-card because I was determined to earn a bachelor's degree before my four-year scholarship ran out. I knew the biggest threat to accomplishing that goal was an unplanned pregnancy.

Saying no was just a part of me by the time I graduated with a Bachelor of Science in Agriculture Business at twenty-one, like my gray felt cowboy hat and brown chaps with the flanky spot on the right thigh. I brought all three, along with a used bedroll my neighbor gave me, when I left California for Nevada at twenty-three to be a professional cowboy. I needed the experienced cowboys to teach me what I needed to know in order to keep a job in the working cowboy world. I wanted them to respect me, not trade stories about what I was like in the sack. Nobody respects the bunkhouse whore.

My few romantic relationships before Jim hadn't been serious enough for my chronic virginity to become an issue, but now here I was in a motel room with a full-grown, red-blooded man who—until the rodeo road trip, anyway—treated me right by day and wanted me by night. And maybe I wanted him to want me.

It was all too much. I had to pull the ripcord.

Jim and the crew dropped me off at Reed Station after the rodeo ended. I barely looked at him as I marched up the gravel driveway carrying my duffel bag. I'd already decided what I was going to do. I didn't look forward to doing it, but I wanted it done.

The next day, I set off to fix a wire gate on the ranch. I took the fencing pliers, a roll of smooth wire, and my cell phone. I knew there was a little patch of service at the top of the hill.

I stood in the warm sunshine on a little sagebrush-covered knob not far off Mountain City Highway, holding a roll of wire in one hand and my shiny blue slide-out phone in the other. I cradled the phone between my shoulder and ear so I could end things with my boyfriend while I mended the fence.

"I'm just not ready for a steady relationship," I said. The words came easier than I expected. "I still want to have some more adventures."

I went on for a few minutes about wanting to start racehorse colts in Kentucky, work on a different ranch in Nevada, maybe go on a mission trip to South America and care for disadvantaged orphans. Jim listened quietly.

"Okay, if that's what you want," he said when I finished talking.

I hung up the phone, relieved that it was done. No more daily phone calls, no more Saturday night dates, no more look of desire in his eyes when he leaned in for a kiss.

CHAPTER 3 ✳ **Elko County Summer**

I lay on a twin bed shoved into the small bedroom at the end of the trailer house and looked up at the ceiling, spotted with yellow rings and splotches of water stains in addition to the fly specks. The bed was there when I moved in. The whole room was filled with books nobody read anymore, outdated clothes, worn-out shoes, broken toys, nonworking oscillating fans, funeral programs, framed pictures, loose pictures, and Lord knows what else crammed into the closet and shoved into dresser drawers. But if I wanted a bit of privacy to talk on the phone, read, or write in my journal, I had to shut myself in with other people's clutter.

And I needed privacy to talk on the phone because even though I'd broken up with Jim, I couldn't resist the pull to be near him. He hadn't ever casually texted at one in the morning. He never suggested we maybe meet up at Stockmen's and then flaked because he saw a blonde. Jim had guided me through doorways with his hand on the small of my back. He could rope a maverick bull and spur a full-grown bronco until it quit bucking.

He was everything wild and reckless in life that I wasn't, yet still craved.

"Hey, it's Jolyn," I said casually into the cordless house phone.

"Hi," Jim replied. "How are you?"

"Good. Just wondering what you've been up to." *You know, since I broke up with you and all.*

"Oh, just ridin' the bad and ropin' the wild," Jim said. "Nothin' too exciting. Me and Dano been kickin' some yearlings around the Perkins. How about you?"

"I've been riding my sale colt and getting Banner ready to show at the Fair."

"That will be good for you."

"Yeah, it should be fun. Did you ever show horses when you worked for Ellisons? I thought I'd heard that they used to send the cowboy crew to the town with show horses every year."

"Ellisons? No, they didn't have show horses when I worked there. Not in my string, anyway."

"Oh, I see. Did you ride the rough string?"

"Nah, I didn't have anything that was too bad. I mean, you had to saddle 'em out in the yard with a hind leg tied up so they didn't kick down your stall, but they weren't too scary."

Yikes. If that's his definition of "not too scary," then he must be...fearless.

The conversation turned from bucking horses to mothers, as it so often doesn't. I was beginning to think of Jim as a friend and ally, and I needed a bit of support.

"My mom is coming to visit next month and I'm nervous," I said. "I haven't seen her in over two years."

"My mom calls me almost every day and won't shut up," Jim countered. "Wanna trade?"

I chuckled. I hadn't met Jim's mom, but he'd told me about phone calls during which she complained about how broke she and his dad were from hauling him to high school rodeos fifteen years ago. She went on long enough for him to set down the phone, walk across the house, get a beer out of the fridge, drink half of it, ponder which horse to ride for work the next day, drink the rest of his beer, walk back across the house, and pick up the phone in time to reply, "Uh-huh," when she whined as expected, "Are you even listening to me?"

After a while, Jim and I said goodbye and hung up the phone. I'd gotten the "Jim fix" I wasn't fully aware I'd needed, so I felt satisfied. Jim had gotten a friendly call from an ex-girlfriend, so he probably felt confused. Regardless, I knew I'd get to see him again soon when my boss and I helped the Holland Ranch gather yearling cattle off the summer country.

Ty Van Norman and I stopped our horses on a little sagebrush-covered hill. Ty was my boss, mentor, and one of the few local ranchers willing to hire a woman. We looked up the mountain toward the rest of the crew—a combination of cowboys from his ranch and Mitch's. I swung my leg over the back of my saddle and stepped down to air out my horse's back at the same time Ty did.

I unbuckled the back cinch and let the thick piece of leather dangle beneath my horse, Jubilee. I loosened the front cinch so it hung several inches below his belly, then stood at Jubilee's hip and lifted the back of my saddle. I'd already turned him so that the slight breeze blew directly underneath the wool saddle blanket and cooled the sweaty surface beneath. I rested my elbow on the gray gelding's hindquarters and leaned on him, cocking one leg at the knee.

It was mid-summer in the high desert. The grass was still mostly green but turning brown and crunchy. Thistles had passed full purple bloom and dispersed their fluffy white seeds into the air to drift and replant elsewhere. The mountains in front of us rose up like a great earthen wall, full of jagged canyons and rocky cliffs. Below us lay the foothills, and beyond them were native meadows and creeks still running with snowmelt. Another line of jagged mountains formed the far side of the valley to the west.

Ty was the first to break the silence.

"I feel bad for Jim," he said. "It must be hard to do a day's work with blue balls."

My head snapped around to look at my boss in surprise. He didn't usually make jokes, especially off-color ones. Suddenly I felt like I did in second grade when Chris Clark passed me a love note on the school bus and all the other kids made fun of me. I'd naively thought that no one else had paid attention to my and Jim's attempted, failed, and now maybe-on-again romance. But at age twenty-four, I should have known that full-grown adults could tell when a full-grown man was interested in a woman.

I forced a chuckle to mask my embarrassment but couldn't think of a witty retort to deflect the attention. Ty and I stood beside our horses for another few minutes, then pulled our cinches tight and remounted to join the rest of the crew. I adjusted my carefully coiled rope over my right thigh and smiled to myself. Maybe I'd tell Jim about Ty's joke when we talked later. He might get a kick out of it.

I nudged my horse into a run and started swinging my rope. Jubilee was known to buck when riders leaned out to throw a loop to catch them off balance at the exact moment they were most vulnerable. The other cowboys told me this, but today I didn't care about the risk of personal injury. I was hot, thirsty, and determined to catch that runaway steer.

I was also tired of not "necking" stuff outside. If you're going to be a cowboy, you need to be able to rope cattle around the neck or by both hind feet as needed. Roping an animal's feet after somebody else has necked it is physically easier on your horse and less mentally stressful for the roper, since you don't have to move at breakneck speed to catch the animal. So far, I had been a full-time "heeler," too timid to run up behind a fast cow and throw my rope at a full gallop. So many things could go wrong—my horse could step in a badger hole and fall down, I could get bucked off, or (worst of all) I could catch the cow but lose my rope and look dumb in front of the crew.

Then one day I overheard Ty tell someone that he seemed to be the only person on the ranch who was able to neck stuff outside. The shame at possibly being considered a coward was worse than the potential danger. It was time to step up my roping game.

That day at the Holland Ranch was my chance to prove myself. I kicked Jubilee until he brought me into position directly behind the fat Hereford yearling, my left hand steering the reins and my right arm swinging my rope as hard as I could. A semi-truck and trailer roared past barely twenty feet away as we ran full-tilt down the shoulder of the highway. I stood in my stirrups, leaned over the saddle horn, and launched my rope. The loop circled around the steer's neck on the first try. I quickly dallied my rope around my saddle horn and reined the big gelding to a stop. Through no skill of my own but to my great fortune, he never once tried to buck.

The steer stopped to face me when my rope came tight. Now what? Determination had helped me catch the steer, but I had no clue what to do with him after that. I glanced behind me toward the rest of the cowboy crew. Hopefully one of them would come help.

Just then, Jim rode into view. He crested a swell in the sagebrush flat with his hat pulled down tight and his rope in his hand, loop built and ready to swing. He saw me right away and trotted over, riding tall and straight in the saddle. His horse carried his head up with his ears pointed forward.

"Good job," Jim said. "Now, to lead him, just kick your horse up right beside the steer. Keep a little slack in your rope. If that steer wants to trot, you just trot with him."

I followed Jim's instructions and we headed toward the wire gate on the other side of the highway. When the steer walked in the direction I wanted him to go, I gave him some slack in the rope so he could catch his air and be rewarded for going the right way. When he stopped, I stopped my horse and waited for the steer to move toward the gate. Then I steered Jubilee beside him so the loop around his neck would loosen and he could get some more air and another positive reinforcement. I didn't say a word, just followed Jim's instructions and led the steer across the blacktop like I roped and led cattle every day.

As we approached the gate, Ty rode his horse up alongside me and threw another head loop on the steer to offer additional support leading the captured escapee to his new home. I looked straight ahead and kicked the gray horse onward.

Jim rode up behind us and started swinging his rope. I didn't look back like an experienced cowboy would have. I was sick and tired of acting timid and being the backup help, so I locked my eyes on the wire gate up ahead and spurred Jubilee with both feet. Nobody was gonna have to tell me to hurry up that day.

Suddenly shouts of "Whoa, whoa, whoa!" rose up behind me, followed by laughter. I turned in the saddle to look back. Jim had his rope dallied to his saddle horn, firmly attaching him and his horse to the steer I was leading. His horse had assumed a crouched position as he tried to stop the steer, but he wasn't able to since I was still forging ahead in the lead. I stopped my horse just before we pulled Jim through an H-brace made of two upright railroad ties with a horizontal piece wedged between them in the fence corner.

"Don't forget to look back once in a while!" someone called out. I laughed along with the crew. I was also secretly impressed with Jubilee. He'd never faltered or lost stride even while dragging a fat red steer *and* a horse ridden by a tall cowboy. That horse was a powerhouse. (And he hadn't sent me flying.)

It was Saturday night, and Jim and I were eating dinner together. We were at Lone Mountain Station this time, a solitary outpost consisting of a restaurant/bar/RV park thirty miles north of Elko. Jim bought my dinner even though we weren't on an official date. He'd also bought dinner for the rest of the crowd because he was generous whether drunk or sober. I liked sitting beside him at the bar while we ate salty tomato-encrusted prime rib and garlic-studded Basque beans.

Jim pounded whiskey, I sipped wine, and we both downed a shot of bourbon when Rolly bought a round for the bar. It looked dark and beautiful in the clear glass, but it tasted like regret and exploding campfires. I had no idea how anyone in Kentucky managed to sell that stuff by the barrel, much less turn a profit and attract repeat customers.

Jim and I slipped out to the parking lot together after a while and left our friends to shoot pool and slide empties across the bar for a refill. The soft yellow light from inside the restaurant slipped out the windows and fell onto the wooden porch, but the icy white starlight took center stage this far from town. There were no other buildings for miles in any direction. There was nothing but pale green sagebrush desert unfolding into the night around us, the Milky Way above, and the two of us below.

We sat side by side on the edge of his pickup bed, with our legs dangling over the missing tailgate. We didn't touch or make eye contact. I gazed across the parking lot and highway into the rolling hills that I knew lay tucked behind the inky wall of darkness.

The conversation turned to when I'd roped and led the steer alongside the highway a few weeks before.

"You did a good job," Jim slurred. "I's so fuckin' proud of you."

"Really?" I said. I sat a little straighter on the cold metal of the pickup bed. "Thanks. And thanks for your help, too."

I knew Jim was drunk, but the compliment still glowed in the dark. His words affirmed my decision to leave my hometown and ride for my wages. Because while money in the bank was nice, everyone knew that earning the respect of your fellow cowboys was the true reward of a saddle tramp.

Before the warmth of his praise had time to cool, Jim dropped another bomb I wasn't expecting.

"I'm just gonna go ahead and say this," he announced. "I'm in love with you."

"Oh?" I said and looked down. "Thank you."

I knew it was cliché to express gratitude when someone said he loved you, but it was all I could think to do. I was still mostly sober, a condition not generally conducive to midnight-parking-lot confessions of love. I wasn't even sure if Jim's profession was a reflection of his true feelings or just a sappy side effect of too much beer and bourbon. At this point, his brain was basically that exploding campfire.

I stared into the darkness beneath our feet. Somewhere down there was gray gravel and desert sand, probably a few cigarette butts. I smiled. I'd never swapped the L-word with a man before and suddenly found myself halfway there with Jim. I wondered if he would remember saying it the next morning.

A few weeks later, Tilly and I headed to the Holland Ranch to help Mitch and his crew for the day. It was August twenty-fourth, my birthday. It also marked the first ride in my brand-new saddle.

We parked by the wooden corrals in front of the big red barn behind Mitch's house and unloaded our horses. Next, we changed a flat tire on the trailer. We could've hollered at the guys and they would have willingly helped us, but changing a flat on a double-axle trailer is pretty easy when you have that little "ramp thingy." You just drive the remaining good tire on the side with the flat up onto it and start loosening lug nuts. Actually, first you slightly loosen the lug nuts with a tire iron, then you drive up on the ramp. Then you finish removing the lug nuts, remove the flat tire, pop the spare tire onto the axle, replace the lug nuts, drive off the block, fully tighten the lug nuts and bam—you've changed the tire and impressed the guys who didn't even know you needed help until after you'd handled the situation yourselves.

Jim and Dano didn't know we had a flat because they were inside the barn, saddling and graining the horses they'd caught for the day. A cowboy usually gives his horse a scoop of grain to munch on while being brushed and saddled in the morning, sort of a friendly gesture to get the workday off to a good start.

Jim appeared in the barn doorway when we were loading the flat tire into the stock trailer. He stopped and leaned his shoulder against the wide plank door frame while he lit a cigarette. The collar of his denim jacket was turned up and his cowboy hat was pulled down low. He wore off-white chaps covered in dirt, blood, and scars. He took a drag on his Marlboro Red and sent swirls of white smoke rising toward the sky in the gray morning light. He looked sexy as hell.

Tilly and I jumped our horses into Mitch's trailer alongside his crew's. Besides Jim, Dano, and Mitch, a day worker named Moe was also cowboying with us that day. We drove a ways out on the desert and unloaded our horses.

After moving my horse out of the way, I held my lead rope and looked at my saddle. It was the first time I'd seen it strapped onto a horse. The leather was clean and bright, untarnished yet by hours of friction with denim, dirt, and sweat. The shiny stirrups were unscratched by tree limbs and sagebrush.

The horn wrap was clean and fresh, with no dark grooves worn into the fuzzy mule-hide leather by the dallies of a nylon rope. The only features that stood out against the medium red-brown of the thick leather were my grandpa's brand, Slash JL, stamped onto the horn cap and the inscription "John 3:16" carved onto the back of the cantle. I'd spent my first nine years of life on Grandpa Joe's ranch in a remote corner of northern California, and its river and canyons were always with me still.

I couldn't decide if I wanted everyone to look at my new ride or if I hoped no one noticed. I'd spent thousands of dollars and many hours selecting and second-guessing my order specs. I couldn't wait to ride a horse in it but was afraid I'd discover I'd goofed up a major element and the whole thing was an unusable piece of junk. Either way, I had a job to do that day. I checked my cinch, gathered my reins, and swung aboard.

The saddle seat fit perfectly and was just as comfortable as when I'd tried it out on the saddle stand. The new sheepskin lining underneath was full and springy, making my seat a bit higher on my horse's back than it would be after thirty or forty rides, once the wool fibers had packed down. The stirrup leathers were perfectly molded to my legs and twisted at the bottom so they wouldn't sore my ankles.

"How's the new wood?" someone asked.

"So far, so good," I replied.

"Hope it don't leak!"

"Me, too!" I called back. A saddle was said to "leak" if a cowboy was bucked off while riding in it. I hoped my new ride would prove to be watertight.

Owyhee was my mount for the day, and he was not a bronco by any stretch of the imagination. He was a middle-aged sorrel from the nearby Owyhee Indian Reservation. Ty had bought him as a "cavvy horse." Ranches in that region called their saddle herd a "cavvy" and kept it stocked with horses, generally geldings, for their hired hands to ride. Owyhee was tall and gentle with the unusual habit of swinging his head side to side and looking at his rider with alternating eyeballs. It was a bit unnerving, as I wasn't used to making direct eye contact with a horse while riding him in a forward motion.

Mitch dropped the crew off in a line to gather yearlings. We strung out and trotted down the dirt road, cowboys reining in their mounts and turning toward the general direction of the steers as we went. I was dropped off on one of the shorter inside circles.

I rose and fell with Owyhee's rhythmic stride. My saddle creaked as all new leather does and I turned off the road to trot through the sagebrush. My left hand held my rawhide reins just in front of the saddle horn. I bent my right arm at the elbow and loosely held the romal, or end of the reins, near my ribs. I scanned the country ahead of me for cattle and breathed evenly so my muscles could keep up with the aerobic work of posting to Owyhee's long trot. I sat down in my saddle and slowed to a walk when I hit cattle.

"Hey, steer; hey, steer," I called, urging them forward. I slapped my chaps with the end of my romal. Some cowboys could whistle real loud to help cattle move. It sounded cool and I wished I could do it, but I could only ever whistle loudly enough for myself to not quite hear it.

We reached the stock pond and held up our horses to let the cattle drink before the final leg of the drive. I rode Owyhee to the edge of the muddy water and slid my hand forward on his neck to put slack in the reins so he could drink. Cattle spread out around me, forming a continually moving tapestry of black hide, brown dirt, green sagebrush, and splashing water. We still had many miles of wide-open desert country to cover that day without a paved road or motorized vehicle in sight. The other cowboys spread out to water their horses on either side of me, some calling a wisecrack over their shoulders and others looking silently at the pond.

I relaxed in my saddle and looked around, then inward, while we rested the stock. I thought about it all: I sat on a cavvy horse that belonged to an historic Nevada ranch. I rode in my first custom saddle, one purchased with money I'd earned by riding and roping. Grandpa Joe's old rawhide reins hung from my bridle and his brand was just a glance away on my saddle horn. My horse stood on iron shoes that I'd personally nailed on. It was not a bad way to spend my twenty-fifth birthday.

I was most proud of shoeing my own horse. Horseshoeing was a difficult yet necessary skill that I'd recently learned through hours of sweat and aching muscles. I didn't outright know how to shoe a horse when I left for Nevada, but that didn't stop me from stretching the truth a bit and saying I could. I didn't feel that bad for my white lie. I was hardly the first cowboy to claim false shoeing expertise in order to get a job, then figure it out later. Besides, it was partly true. My dad had worked as a farrier for years and gave me a crash course before I left home. I also had a hand-me-down shoeing outfit made from Dad's old tools and a hoof knife I'd received as a Christmas present.

Ty was particular about how his horses were shod and didn't grant me permission to go at one with a pair of nippers right away. So, I volunteered to help him shoe every horse on the place until I could trim, level, shape, nail, and clinch a set of horseshoes with confidence, or at least a minimal amount of bloodshed. Ty still seemed reluctant to turn me loose as an independent shoer, even though he often mentioned how handy it would be if someone else on the ranch besides him could shoe a horse.

One Friday afternoon, I decided I was done waiting for permission. I knew I could do the job. I waited until Ty left for the day and caught Jubilee. I tacked front shoes on the big gray gelding in the same amount of time it takes an experienced farrier to shoe two horses all the way around. Then I lay down on the floor and died. Horseshoeing was a total body workout that personal trainers knowledgeable in the science of muscle oxygenation and metabolic rates could only hope to achieve for their fittest clients.

The next day, Ty saw what I'd done and didn't fire me. I then shod Jubilee's hind feet and moved on to Owyhee. Women would hardly ever shoe their own horses, but now that I'd demonstrated competence in that area, my confidence grew in my ability to hold a ranch job—maybe even on a new ranch—and keep my adventure going.

After the yearlings watered at the pond, we pushed them across the desert to a fresh pasture and doctored another bunch using medicine carried in our saddle bags. When the last yearling was taken care of and our horses were tied to the trailer, we all gathered around the long dining table in Mitch's house. His family embraced Basque customs of hospitality and cooked traditional meals his forebearers had carried over from the homeland. Many people of Basque ancestry had immigrated to northern Nevada from the Spanish/French border region. They were known for herding sheep, ranching cattle, and cooking amazing dishes with a heavy hand on the garlic cloves.

Like his father Larry, Mitch was an excellent cook. A perk of helping the Holland Ranch was the delectable feast laid out each day for the crew. Homemade lasagna, lamb chops, fresh garden salad with creamy dressing, and pan-fried venison steaks were standard fare. I looked from one heaping dish to the next while my hollow belly grumbled. The table was silent while everyone wolfed down a few bites, too empty from the day's work to chat. The only sounds were forks scraping on plates and tall glasses of ice water and cold bottles of Coors clunking down on the thick wooden tabletop.

"So, how are things going with Megan?" Mitch asked Jim after a while. "Do you have another date with her?"

I looked up from my salad. *What was this now?*

"It's good," Jim replied. His face looked red, but that was probably just from the beer and heat.

I crunched Romaine lettuce and looked down at my plate. Jim was taking another girl out?

"Is she going back to Washington?" Mitch asked.

"Yeah, I think she's headin' back in a couple months," Jim said in between bites of steak.

Jim was seeing a new woman and had talked about her enough that his boss knew her name and upcoming travel plans? Shoot. And here I thought that he and I might slowly, possibly be heading in the general direction of probably restarting the relationship we'd begun earlier that year. But now it looked like some hussy had beaten me to the punch.

This news was especially hard to digest after the flirty afternoon we'd had. After moving yearlings all morning, we'd trailered to another allotment to check a different set of cattle. Etiquette dictated that the boss loaded his horse in the trailer first, followed by the next most senior guy on the crew, on down to the newbies and neighbor girls. I saw Moe load his horse first (out of order, by the way), so I stood off to the side and pretended to check my cinches until Tilly loaded her horse next to Moe's. I knew we'd be dropped off in pairs to rope and doctor, and I wanted to be paired with Jim.

Jim let me go first when we trotted up a narrow trail, and I suspected it was just so he could look at my butt. And he was a gentleman and let me throw the first loop at the gimpy heifer we needed to doctor.

But now I didn't know what any of it meant. The phone calls, my wanting to be near him, the L-word in the Lone Mountain parking lot—did it mean we'd get back together, or had I missed my chance completely when I'd broken up with him earlier in the summer?

———✦———

I settled into my saddle and looked up between my horse's ears. The morning air was still pleasantly cool, and I was alone in the warm-up pen at the fairgrounds. I kept my lower back loose and relaxed my shoulders, allowing my body to merge with the rhythm of Chili's lope. He was a three-year-old colt Ty and I had started that spring and I'd ridden all summer to prepare him for the Van Norman and Friends Production Sale held each fall in Elko. Chili was my special project, and he was loping balanced circles with his head down, just like I'd hoped he would for his first trip to town.

I also hoped Jim would be at the sale. I wanted him to see how good Chili looked. I also wanted him to see how good I looked—slim and trim from riding horses all summer in the heat and working many hours between meals. Ty was a devout Christian who believed in a lot of things, but eating lunch was not one of them. I wore my go-to-town pearl snap shirt, a purple plaid with retro red-and-white piping on the yoke, and the Cruel Girl jeans I'd worn on our first date. My sweat-stained gray felt hat was mashed down on my head like always, because I wasn't affluent enough to afford a specially designated "town hat."

After I loped Chili both directions and felt his coltish energy settle down, I slowed to a walk and rode out of the warm-up pen. I headed toward the barn where the Van Normans stabled their sale horses for the two-day event. My interest level perked up when I saw Dano standing in the wide barn aisle. If Dano was here, Jim was likely nearby.

"Hey, Dano," I said as I swung out of the saddle. "How are you today?"

"I'm good," he replied. "How's your colt doing?"

"He's feelin' pretty good. I'm just riding him around to get him used to all the town stuff."

I scratched Chili beneath the browband of his headstall while I talked. He lowered his head and bobbed it toward me in appreciation for itching his sweaty spots.

"Perfect," Dano said with a smile. It was tough to catch that guy in a bad mood. He held up a headstall. "Jim asked me to give this to you. He went to Vegas with Mitch this weekend."

"Oh. Thanks."

I reached for the headstall and hoped I didn't look as disappointed as I felt that Jim wouldn't be at the horse sale, but I've never been able to hide my emotions from anyone except myself.

"Wow, that looks really nice," I managed.

I turned the headstall over in my hands and admired Jim's quality workmanship and attention to detail. It was a simple, solid, split-ear headstall with beveled edges and "bleeder knots" to tie the cheekpieces around a bit. The bleeder knots made a fishtail design with the leather thongs and lay flat, holding the bit on to the headstall without adding extra bulk. I was impressed he'd finished it so quickly. We'd only just arranged the trade: He would make me a headstall for the new Myler bit I'd recently bought, and I'd make him dinner. I guessed I'd better figure out a menu.

Jim came over and ate syrupy mashed sweet potatoes, cucumber-and-tomato salad with congealed olive oil dressing, and mostly cooked chicken. I'd tried baking an entire chicken in a Crockpot, but it took forever and the dang thing was still pink near the bone by the time Jim showed up. He politely suggested I pop it in the oven to finish the job, then asked for seconds. (I later learned that he hated chicken in all forms and refused to eat it as a general rule.)

During that summer, Tilly had gotten married and moved out of our shared single-wide at Reed Station. This afforded Jim and me more privacy when he came over, although he still slept on the living room floor in a bedroll. But he drove ninety miles round trip to bring me flowers when I got my wisdom teeth removed, and Meg the apple-picker from Washington was no longer in the picture, so it seemed like forward progress was being made.

Jim's seasonal job at the Holland Ranch ended in early October when Mitch shipped the last load of yearlings to their cold-weather homes elsewhere. Jim headed to Texas for the winter and got a job on a preconditioning outfit that operated on outside pasture with an old buddy of his, Joe Harper. In layman's terms, he took care of just-weaned calves and helped them transition from living with their mamas and drinking milk to frolicking with their buddies and eating grass. He liked it because the weather was warm and he got to rope a lot.

I worked for Ty until the first week of October before heading to Elko for the winter. The Van Normans ran pasture cattle, so they also shipped everything each fall, and I was laid off for the winter. I hated to leave the wide-open sagebrush country of the ranch, but I consoled myself with knowing I'd be back again in the spring. I didn't want to return to my hometown in northern California, so I moved to Elko and worked as a substitute teacher in the local school system. I rented a basement room from local legend Allie Bear, "The Knower of All Things," as Jim and I called her. She was divorced, in her sixties, and an outrageously successful cattle buyer for Superior Livestock Auctions. She traveled all over the state of Nevada, connecting ranchers with buyers for their calf crops. She knew everyone and their business.

Allie had a beautiful two-story house on a hill on the edge of town with horse pastures, a barn, and an arena. It seemed like the Taj Mahal after living at Reed Station. Rent was cheap and utilities were included. I often had the place to myself because Allie traveled a lot.

I set out for the hills across the road from Allie's house one cold December day. The wind blew into my face in a series of blasts straight from the coldest glacier in the Arctic. I hunched forward and pulled the hood of my jacket farther over my ears and face. Too much wind always hurt the inside of my ears, made them ache way down deep where I couldn't do anything about it.

I kept walking as fast as I could despite the frigid weather and impending inner ear pain. After all, I had calories to burn. I rode horses all day and stayed in shape without even making a conscious effort in the spring, summer, and fall when I worked for the Van Normans. But my winter job had me sitting behind a desk most hours of the day, so I walked five miles each afternoon after work.

Earlier that day, I'd driven a hundred and twenty-five miles to Winnemucca and interviewed for a full-time staff writing position at the *Nevada Rancher,* a regional ranching magazine. Writing for a living was my second dream job, after cowboying. I'd kept a journal since I was six and once wrote in it that I wanted to be an author when I grew up. I ducked my face toward the desert sand and pushed on into the wind. I pumped my arms to help establish a fast rhythm and hustled through the sagebrush and rocks.

I wondered what the editor and publisher had said about me after I left the interview. I thought I'd answered their questions with intelligence and confidence, but it was hard to know for sure.

My phone rang from my jacket pocket. I pulled it out with a gloved hand and saw the magazine office's phone number on the screen. A good sign? Or maybe they were just calling to thank me for my time.

"Hello, Jolyn?" came Carmen Kofoed's voice through the cell phone. She was the editor of *Nevada Rancher.*

"Yes, hi, Carmen. How are you?"

"Good. I'm calling to make your day, hopefully. Holly and I would like to offer you the writing job if you want it."

I smiled and forgot about the cold.

"Definitely," I said without hesitation. "When do I start?"

"We'll have you start January second. We'd like you to come into the office the first week for training. Then you can work from home, since you live a long way away."

"Great! Looking forward to it. Thank you."

Carmen said she'd see me in a couple weeks and ended the call.

So that was that—I was officially a magazine writer.

I dialed Jim's number as soon as Carmen hung up. He had been my boy-friend again since about three days after he left for Texas, and he was the first person I wanted to tell my good news.

"That's great!" Jim exclaimed. "I'm proud of you. Good job."

"Thanks," I replied, still warm from the news, despite the unrelenting wind. "I know it means I won't get to cowboy as much, but I can still come hang out with you and Dano at the Perkins this summer, right?"

"Yep, you can rope and doctor yearlings with us anytime you want."

My happiness at getting a real writing job dimmed a little as I realized that I wouldn't be a professional cowboy anymore. What any of us do for a living defines a large part of us, whether we like it or not, and I really liked being defined as a "cowboy." Being a writer sounded pretty cool, too, but typing articles wasn't nearly as tough as riding horses that might buck and roping runback calves.

I reminded myself that at least I'd already gotten a cowboy job on my own merit, not because I was dating someone on the crew or I was the manager's daughter. I could check that life goal off the list. It would be weird to move from that lifestyle to sitting in a padded chair within walking distance of the snack box all day, but I could get used to it.

Plus, I was with Jim. That meant I could get out of town and cowboy regularly. I'd seen what it was like to be the girl on the crew; now I'd get to experience what it was like to be the girlfriend on the crew. I knew I couldn't cowboy for a living forever, anyway, because I wanted to have babies eventually. I knew my days as a full-time cowboy were numbered. Jim was the first man who made me think maybe that number was getting pretty small.

A glow of satisfaction repelled the cold by the time I hung up the phone with Jim. I had a great new job, a supportive boyfriend, and the holidays were just around the corner. Within a month I'd be down in Texas to spend New Year's Eve with Jim. The wind could blow until the thermometers burst for all I cared. Right then, everything felt rosy.

Jim was the only man who'd made me think about engagement rings—what they looked like, how much they cost, where they came from, how one would feel on my left hand. I didn't know what width of band or cut of diamond I wanted, but I found myself glancing at the jewelry counter at JC Penney on my way to the clearance rack to pick out a new shirt for my trip to visit Jim in Texas.

I definitely wanted a diamond that was ethically sourced. Wearing a blood diamond mined by a child in Africa would take all the fun out of flashing some bling on my left hand. Maybe I didn't even want a diamond…. Most girls had a diamond. They were a bit overdone, really. I'd always liked emeralds. They were unique and green like my eyes.

I wondered how Jim would propose. Would he ask my dad first? Would he take me to dinner at a restaurant with a real tablecloth and I'd suspect he was going to propose but I wouldn't be totally sure, just wondering why he seemed so distracted and growing more nervous by the minute? Would he deliver a prepared speech or just wing it? Would we kiss afterward, once he'd slipped a ring that was somehow just my size onto my finger?

The ring itself would be a delicate yellow gold band topped with an emerald stone. The whole thing would be a complete surprise, yet somehow exactly what I wanted. Because that's how it happened in the few Hallmark movies I'd watched.

I realized I better figure out my ring size so I could somehow nonchalantly slip it into a conversation with Jim. I hoped he had a pen ready during our next conversation.

"How are the calves doing? Staying pretty healthy after weaning?" I could say during one of our two-hour phone calls.

"Yeah, pretty good. Havin' to doctor a little handful every day or so, but nothin' too major."

"Glad to hear. I wear a size seven ring. Have you been to any team ropings lately?"

He could pretend he didn't hear me but write it down to make sure he got it right. I only had one opportunity to be proposed to. I didn't want him to screw it up.

CHAPTER 4 ✴ Texas, Where Everything Changed

My heart beat faster as the elevator descended. Standing at the bottom was the man I had raved about to my friends and told my dad about. I'd fallen asleep thinking about him every night and woken up to his "Good morning" texts for the past three months, ever since we'd officially become boyfriend and girlfriend over the phone on October ninth. I hadn't seen him in person for the entirety of those three months. I briefly wondered if the real, actual human could possibly live up to the fantasy version of him I'd concocted in my head. Then I looked over the railing and saw him standing with his thumbs hooked in his jean pockets, wearing a faded denim jacket and black felt cowboy hat.

Jim had gained at least twenty pounds. He'd left Nevada with a board-flat stomach, but those defined abs were now hidden underneath a paunch built from deep-fried Twinkies and second breakfasts. But no matter. When he kissed me at the bottom of the elevator and reached for my hand, my body registered the familiar feel of his calloused fingers. They were twice as thick as mine. I easily tucked my thumb inside our clasp against his palm, just like before he left for Texas. I looked up at him and saw that his eyes looked every bit as nervous as I felt.

"It's good to see you," he said. "You look pretty."

"Thanks," I replied. I was still too reserved to tell him I thought he looked handsome, especially in public.

We walked toward the baggage claim hand in hand. I felt like each and every one of the thousands of people in the sprawling Austin International Airport were watching our every move. I didn't feel comfortable walking through a crowd with a boyfriend yet, even though I was twenty-five. Just holding his hand in public felt like a brazen display of affection. It gave me the flutters, but they were the kind that made me want to feel more of them.

It was true that Jim and I turned heads as we walked through the airport, but not because of our G-rated PDA. Jim stood out in the crowd of urban travelers because he wore a cowboy hat like always. His steady stride soon eased my nerves and I relaxed beside him. By the time we collected my huge black suitcase from the conveyor belt, I leaned into his shoulder and welcomed the curious glances with a nonchalant smile.

Jim and I exited the airport building and headed for the parking lot. The night was black and the air brisk. December nights can bring a chill even to central Texas. Jim turned up the collar on his denim jacket. I zipped up my down coat that was more suited to the snowy winter I'd left behind. He walked me to the passenger side of the shiny white pickup owned by the ranch he worked for.

"The starter went out on my truck," he explained.

He closed my door and hefted my suitcase into the back. I had overpacked. I always overpacked. A girl never knows what outfit and shoe combination will suit the weather and her moods while on a trip to a distant locale. I had also crammed a full-sized afghan I'd crocheted for Jim as a Christmas present into my giant suitcase. It might have been warm and made with love, but it was not lightweight.

We drove north through the darkness to Jim's temporary home in the tiny town of Schwertner. He was crashing with his buddy Joe, who rented a little house with a pasture and horse barn. Jim typically unrolled his bed on the couch, but he'd moved into a one-room clapboard shack next to the little house for the duration of my stay. The story went that Diane Lane, who played Lorena on the epic western *Lonesome Dove*, had once owned the shack. But half the population of Texas claimed to have personally known a cast member or sat in a saddle that was used in that movie, so who knew.

There was no porch light to illuminate the scene when we arrived, but I could see that the shack was weathered gray and constructed from thin slabs of wood. The whole thing appeared to be leaning to one side and looked like one strong wind would knock it over. Jim wheeled my suitcase across the uneven lawn and opened the front door.

"Well," he intoned, "this is it."

I stepped through the paintless door and looked around. Not surprisingly, the shack was just as run down on the inside as the outside. It was crammed with discarded household furnishings. Broken end tables, old lamps, cast-off chairs, and dusty oil paintings were piled high in one half of the room. Jim's bedroll was laid out in the other half, tucked into a back corner with the blankets pulled up over two pillows and the canvas tarp neatly folded at the bottom. The entire room, including the walls and windowsill, was covered in a thick layer of dust. The only exception was a path that Jim had swept from the door to his bed.

Jim had also placed a low table, no doubt borrowed from the other side of the room, at the foot of the bed. It held a bottle of pinot noir and two red plastic keg cups.

"Ah," I said. "Now I know why you asked what my favorite wine was the other night."

Jim gave a small smile. "I just wanted to make sure."

He parked my suitcase near the edge of his bedroll and opened the bottle of wine with a pocketknife. I took a drink, then set down my cup and reached up to wrap my arms around his neck. His kisses were every bit as persuasive as I remembered. His bedroll smelled like canvas and dirt, just like I'd expected.

I wiped the grease from my lips and returned the napkin to my lap. I took a tiny sip of gin and tonic and set my drink on the wooden table. I dabbed the napkin to my mouth again. I took another nibble of my cheeseburger, then gave up and tried a French fry.

I looked across the table at Joe. I wondered if he could tell how nervous I felt. He and his flavor of the week were eating dinner with me and Jim at a diner in Schwertner. They thought we were just four friends out for a cheap meal, but Joe and his date had unknowingly joined us for my last meal as a virgin.

Earlier that day, I'd told Jim I was ready.

"Are you sure?" he'd asked.

I'd nodded.

"Okay," he said. "But I'm not doing it if you're drunk."

I thought of his cautionary words as I sipped my drink. The cocktail was crisp and juniper-fresh. I took tiny, frequent sips and gave myself a strict two-drink max. Jim was serious about what he said. So was I.

We finished dinner and someone paid the bill. I had no idea what the check's total was, who left the tip, or if the pickup was pointed north or south when we drove out of the parking lot. All I could think about was what waited in the electrifying darkness beyond.

<hr>

Jim was late for work the next morning. From our cocoon inside the shack, we heard the horse trailer door open with a screech of the metal latch. It was soon followed by the dull thud of a horse jumping inside. Joe was already loading up for work and Jim wasn't even dressed. He stepped out of the bedroll and pulled on his boots, then shoved his shirttail into his jeans. His belt was already threaded through the denim loops. All he had to do was shove the trophy buckle into the hole with the most wear marks and he was ready to go.

"See you after work," Jim said.

He pushed his hat onto his head and headed for the door, then turned back with his hand on the doorknob. He crossed the room in three steps, knelt on the dusty wooden floor with a clang of his spurs, and gave me a quick kiss. Outside, Joe fired up the diesel engine with a loud roar.

"Okay, I really have to go now," Jim said. He glanced out the window toward the barn, where the horse trailer door was still open and waiting for his uncaught, unsaddled horse.

"Bye," I called after him as he strode across the room.

I snuggled down and pulled the blankets up around my bare shoulders. Tucked in among the faded comforters and fleece blankets was the afghan I'd given Jim. I was tempted to pull on my own boots and rope calves with Jim all day, but I wasn't ready to look the rest of the crew—or anyone else—in the eye just yet.

I felt like I had a big sign on my forehead that read: "I had sex last night! For the first time ever! And I liked it!" Or maybe I wanted to make that sign and wave it high for everyone to see. Either way, the new development was too much to process in front of other people. I wanted time alone to marvel at the changes it brought to me and my relationship with Jim.

It didn't take long for the first big change to materialize. Back in Elko a few months later, I sat on the lid of the toilet seat and waited. The instructions on the box said that results would appear in five minutes. I held the plastic stick in front of me and stared at it. I wanted to watch the results appear in real time.

A liquid line moved swiftly across the clear plastic window in the middle of the stick. It left two distinct pink lines in its wake.

Cool, I thought. *Two pink lines, just like in the commercials. This pregnancy test totally works!*

Then, *Wait a minute. If this pregnancy test is positive, then that means I'm pregnant. Like, going-to-have-a-baby pregnant.*

I smiled. Because I was going to have a baby with Jim. He loved me and I loved him and we were in love. Now I just needed to tell him about our love child.

I still lived in Allie's basement, and Jim lived in the bunkhouse at the TS Ranch forty-five miles to the east. It was April, and he'd come back from Texas early to be closer to me until his regular summer job at the Holland Ranch started. I couldn't just call to tell him the news because his cell phone was temporarily out of commission.

I decided to drive my Ford Ranger out to the ranch that very instant. News like this couldn't wait. But first, I stopped at a gas station to fuel up and buy a pack of gum. I smiled extra big at the cashier and wondered if he could smell my

Chapstick. It was all I could think about, how fruity and extra fragrant this particular batch was. I wanted to remove the cap and inhale it straight from the tube.

I parked in front of the TS bunkhouse and turned off the engine. Jim wasn't expecting me and the gas engine was quiet, completely concealing my arrival. I walked through the front door without knocking. Jim looked up and saw me from his seat on the couch where he was watching a DVD on the communal television. He met me halfway across the room and hugged me in greeting. Without saying a word, I handed him the positive pregnancy test. I figured he could find out the same way I did, by staring at those two pink lines in surprise.

Jim looked at the white plastic stick and smiled.

"I never thought I'd have to drive to a bunkhouse to tell someone this kind of news," I said.

"I never thought I'd get this kind of news in a bunkhouse," Jim retorted, but as he looked at me, he smiled. He hugged me again and smiled some more. He couldn't stop smiling.

"I'm glad you're happy about this," I said into his shirt, my cheek pressed against his chest.

"Of course I'm happy," Jim replied. "We're going to have a baby."

"Isn't it crazy to think that right now the baby is either a boy or a girl? I mean, right now we have either a son or a daughter."

"I know, that is wild," Jim agreed. He rested his chin on top of my head and we stood in the middle of the living room for a long minute, arms around each other but looking different directions.

We sat down on the couch and he put his arm around my shoulders. I curled up next to his side, and he pushed play to finish the movie. We'd have to tell family, friends, and employers the pregnancy news at some point. But for that first night, we were the only two people in the world who knew our special secret.

⸎

I lay on the double bed in Jim's room at the TS bunkhouse and stared at the ceiling. I'd hid in the room earlier that morning when Jim cooked bacon for breakfast. The smell of sizzling seasoned pork bellies had brought on such an overwhelming wave of nausea that I'd had to leave the room. Pregnancy hormones had heightened my sense of smell to the point where a bag of flour smelled offensive.

Now, I was waiting out a different set of first trimester problems. Gas bubbles burbled back and forth through my intestines. Jim had indicated his interest in becoming romantically entangled later that evening, if I was also similarly inclined, so I decided to take care of my issues beforehand like the discreet lady I hoped to be.

The knob turned and the hinges creaked as Jim opened the door.

"Don't come in," I said. "I have to fart."

"Does your stomach hurt?"

"Yes, and I'm just so bloated and miserable for half the day. And the other half of the day, I feel like puking and can't eat anything. Our baby's going to starve."

I turned my face away from him and pressed my cheek against the pillow so he wouldn't see me cry.

"Isn't the baby the size of a poppyseed right now? I'm pretty sure it doesn't eat much."

"It's not just that," I moaned. "How can I go to church now? Everyone will know I'm not perfect. I've ruined my life."

In my mind, I walked up the steps of Grace Baptist Church in Elko with my baby bump just beginning to show. I imagined all the other worshippers looking at me, the unmarried pregnant girl. A neon sign hovered over my head, flashing, "Neither a virgin nor a wife, please point and laugh." The women in their Sunday dresses raised their eyebrows and walked past without saying hi. Their husbands looked away in solidarity with their wives, but they wouldn't really care because guys just want to get laid.

I rolled over to my side, away from Jim. He walked across the room and sat down by me on the bed.

"I'm pretty sure everyone already knows you're not perfect." His voice sounded amused, but his hand on my shoulder felt comforting.

I was mortified that people would know that I was no longer pure. My perimeter had been breached and my womb overtaken by the seed of a man.

Jim, on the other hand, had been overjoyed by our baby news and told anyone who would listen that he was going to be a dad. I'd always assumed I would get married and have kids in that order. It was a rude awakening to realize that the universal laws of biology weren't just for "those other girls" who didn't think things through. They applied to me, too.

I had eventually told my mom when I was about nine weeks along. She had gotten pregnant with my older sister when she was twenty-two and single, then married the baby's father, who was also my dad. I didn't want her to think I was following her path, which had ended in divorce fourteen years later.

It was even harder to tell my dad, who thought I was pure as driven snow. (His words, not mine.) I eventually emailed my dad's girlfriend and asked her to tell him. I couldn't bear to deliver the news myself. I just wanted to keep quiet about the whole pregnancy issue until I was more used to it, or maybe until the baby was born and looked all cute and squishy. Lots of people judge an unmarried pregnant girl, but nobody can stay mad at a baby.

We stood just inside the doorway of the TS bunkhouse in the mudroom with the low table and Swiffer sweeper. Jim loved to Swiffer the bunkhouse floor when it got dirty. I knew this because he often told me or anyone else within earshot how handy the Swiffer system truly was. But on that cool April afternoon, I could tell he wanted to talk about something important. He was drunk but serious.

"If we're gonna do this, you need to know something," he began. "I'm a cowboy. I've always been a cowboy. I'm never going to stop being a cowboy. I'm not going to change my mind and go work in the mines. The money isn't important to me."

We'd talked about getting married before I got pregnant, but the baby's impending arrival had bumped the topic to the forefront of our conversations. I knew he was giving me fair warning, one last chance to back out if I wanted. But I looked up at him and nodded.

"Okay," I said. We kissed, then walked into the bunkhouse.

I propped my legs on Jim's ankles to escape the heat radiating up from the floor-boards of Clayton's ancient pickup. Clayton drove, I sat in the middle, and Jim sat in the passenger seat. It was hotter than hell, which seemed to be located directly beneath my feet. There was no point in complaining to Clayton, though. He was too young and broke to know any better.

I was tired, cranky, and four months pregnant. I'd been the only sober person hanging out with the rowdy drinking crowd for three days, and I was over it. We three were on our way back to the TS Ranch from the McDermitt Ranch Hand Fourth of July Rodeo. I'd made my ranch rodeo performance debut as our team's steer stopper. A combination of light but steady nausea and being a rookie caused me to miss my first loop and fail to earn any points for my team. But at least I could still tuck in my shirt and button my jeans at sixteen weeks along. That was more than I could say for some of the other non-pregnant contestants, both female and male.

We drove home slowly with the windows rolled down since the pickup didn't have air conditioning and couldn't go much faster than fifty-five pulling a trailer on the highway. An hour into our drive, we stopped in Winnemucca to fuel up. Clayton and Jim both got out at the pump but I stayed in the cab. I was too cranky to actually do anything to improve my situation, like get out and risk cooling down in the fresh air.

It was Jim's turn to buy a tank of diesel. I watched him walk up to the card reader at the pump. He looked at it, looked at his card, pushed a button, looked back at his card, tried another button, then asked Clayton for help. The younger guy walked around the pickup to assist the older cowboy. Two cowboy hats bowed together over the card and pump for a brief conference on how best to proceed.

"Um, you go like this," Clayton offered politely as he demonstrated how to swipe the debit card.

I rolled my eyes and vowed to not get out and help my boyfriend. He'd always paid cash for our dinner dates and road trip purchases prior, but I hadn't realized that was because he didn't know how to operate a debit card. Who didn't know how to use a debit card? The man was thirty-one years old, for crying out loud. He could stand at the gas pump and look confused till hell froze over for all I cared.

After both men had punched the appropriate buttons on the card reader, the fuel was somehow paid for and pumped into the pickup. We began the last leg of our journey home. That stretch of I-80 between Winnemucca and Beowawe held two formidable mountain passes and several lesser but still noteworthy hills to climb. The floorboards beneath my feet grew hotter with each additional hill. I put my feet up on Jim's legs once again. He squirmed under my body heat but didn't say a word.

We were halfway up Golconda Summit when a white crew cab pickup towing a shiny aluminum trailer zipped past. The rig pulled up alongside us and the windows rolled down to reveal several cowboys. They waved and cheered as they lifted cans of beer into the air and yelled their hellos. Clayton and Jim dutifully jerked their chins up in a nod and I waved in response. It was the YP Ranch cowboy crew and some of their buddies, mostly Indian guys from the Owyhee reservation. We knew Junior Kelly and his wife Crystal. She was white and had worked for the Van Normans like me. She was also pregnant like me. Crystal smiled and looked comfortable in the climate-controlled cab going seventy-five, like she was enjoying herself. So rude. I forced a smile and then resumed staring at the highway directly ahead of us.

We finally made it back to the TS. Jim unloaded our horses while I collapsed onto the blue couch in the bunkhouse living room and sank into the cushions beneath the ceiling fan. My irritation at the long, hot drive and the debit card difficulties decreased as my body temperature lowered.

So what if my boyfriend/baby daddy didn't know how to pay for things with plastic? He could ride a bad horse and rope anything with hair. That was way cooler than keeping up with the latest technology anyway.

The door slammed shut when Jim walked in from the horse barn. The jingling of his spurs paused as he removed his cowboy hat and carefully set it upside-down on a table so the brim shape wouldn't get messed up. He stopped again at the fridge before handing me the large bag of assorted Hershey's miniature chocolate bars I kept in the kitchen.

"Here's your nose bag," he said.

"Thanks," I said and unwrapped a square of Special Dark, my favorite.

I had been slightly offended at being likened to a horse at feeding time when he first made the nose bag reference, but that had been several weeks ago. It was like being called a "first-calf heifer" and being compared to a "tight-bagged cow." You just get used to it after a while.

———

I stayed overnight at the TS bunkhouse a lot that summer. Ranch rules stated that girls weren't allowed in the bunkhouse, but for once in my straightlaced life I openly flouted the rules. What was the worst that could happen? I'd get pregnant? I think ranch managers made those rules to discourage guys from having women stay the night and cause jealousy and drama on the cowboy crew. Most big outfits had that rule, and most cowboys broke it on the regular.

One night, we watched a movie called *The Grey* in the living room of the bunkhouse. The nausea had mostly subsided, but Jim still brought my nosebag from the fridge because he was thoughtful like that. I opened my first square of the night and scooted over to make room for him on the blue couch. He sank into the cushions beside me. The movie recommendation had come from a friend of his in Texas, Mickey Steed, and I still haven't forgiven him for it. In the film, a plane crashed in Alaska and the handful of survivors—all male—ended up being picked off one at a time by a pack of vicious wolves. It was awful. Horrifying. Devastating, even though you knew how it was going to end within the first ten minutes.

All the death followed by more death made me realize that I, too, would die one day. I might even die during childbirth, which was tentatively scheduled for the end of that very year.

I made Jim promise that if I died during delivery, he wouldn't give the baby away.

"Of course I wouldn't do that," he declared. He looked at me with an expression that was part wonderment at my suggestion he might do such a thing and part not wanting to know why it might occur to me. "I would never do that. Why would you think I'd do that?"

He took a drink of his Keystone Light and continued to give me the side eye while I dug through my nosebag looking for the last piece of dark chocolate. I was going to need a lot more chocolate to get through this pregnancy.

CHAPTER 5 ✳ **Shacking Up**

I pushed open the glass door and walked inside. I'd never been in a pawn shop before, but it wasn't as scary as I'd imagined. There were no bikers lurking in the corner smoking cigarettes and eyeing women up and down as they stepped inside. Huge speakers weren't blaring Metallica and the lights weren't dimmed. I had long equated a pawn shop with a dive bar: similar customer base, different service.

Instead of the Hells Angels' clubhouse I'd pictured, the lights inside the Sierra Jewelry & Loan of Nevada were bright and the air was clean.

"Hi," a round, middle-aged woman called from behind the counter at the back of the store.

"Hello," I replied with an automatic smile.

The woman returned to her conversation with a younger, similarly round version of herself. *Must be her daughter.* Looked like this pawn shop was a family business. I walked past a rack of used DVDs and a handful of guitars to the jewelry counter on the left side of the store. Rings, necklaces, bracelets, and watches were arranged in tiny rows on black velvet. I searched for the ring section and wondered why the precious stones had ended up here. Had the original owners pawned their rings because of a divorce? Were they here after a death in the family—maybe an aunt no one liked much but who'd had some nice jewelry and no direct descendants to inherit it? Were they family heirlooms pawned to pay for a son's medical school tuition or to buy groceries when times were hard?

"Can I take something out for you to look at?" the older round woman asked.

"Um, sure. Can I see these two?"

I pointed to a slender yellow gold band with three small diamonds set in a row along the top and a more traditional-looking single-stone ring. Both were yellow gold. The only thing I knew for certain about my ring was that it had to be yellow gold. That was the kind of ring worn by my grandma, aunt, Mama Bev, Mary Ann Fitzgerald—all the women I knew who'd had decades-long marriages.

The three-stone ring was simple, understated, and didn't scream "engagement ring." I didn't get a typical proposal, so I didn't want something that looked like a typical engagement ring.

My naked left hand really bothered me. I wanted a ring ASAP, to show people that someone had made a commitment to me and the baby who was making my belly stick out. I'd initially wanted an emerald ring, but that was back when the future was still a daydream. Now that I knew what was going to happen, I wanted a traditional stone set in an untraditional arrangement. I'd also realized the chances of Jim getting my ring size right on the first guess and reserving a table at an exclusive restaurant to pop the question while a string quartet played in the background were slim to none, leaning toward none. For one thing, there were no exclusive restaurants in Elko. The Star was the fanciest eatin' place in town, and they served everything family-style.

Jim claimed I'd proposed to him, but here's what really happened: One day while driving down Interstate 80, I asked him if we were going to get married or what. He said, "Sure, pick a date and let's do it."

Not quite a Hallmark movie, but it would get the job done.

Brand-new engagement rings were expensive, though, so I'd suggested we buy one from a pawn shop. That's what had me here looking at the rings the round woman handed over the glass counter. I turned my favorite one, the one with three small stones all in a row, over in my hands. The handwritten paper price tag read "$750." That was half a month's paycheck from Jim's job at the TS.

It seemed doable.

I was vaguely aware of some formula for calculating the amount of money a man should spend on an engagement ring—a percentage of his salary or four months' wages or something like that—but I was pretty sure those rules didn't apply to pregnant cowboy-girlfriend-type people.

"Thank you," I told the woman. I handed back both rings. I decided to come back with Jim after his next payday. If the three-stone ring was still there, we'd get it.

It was mid-July when we walked into the shop together. He checked out the firearm display while I walked straight to the jewelry counter. My ring was still there.

"This is the one I like the most," I told Jim after one of the round women set its case on the counter. "What do you think?"

Jim walked over and glanced at the ring.

"Looks pretty. If that's the one you want, let's get it."

We left the pawn shop with the small velvet box in my purse. We decided to hold off on purchasing a wedding ring for him indefinitely. You don't actually need rings to get married, and his bare left hand didn't eat away at his insides like mine did. We got in the pickup and I started the engine to get the A/C going.

"Wait," Jim said. He pulled the ring out of its case and reached for my left hand. "Here," he said as he placed the ring on my finger.

It wasn't a champagne proposal with violin music playing in the background, but my man put a ring on the hand that mattered. I looked down and smiled. The diamonds sparkled and shined in the sunlight, just like I thought they would. I didn't even ponder the potentially unhappy story of how the ring had ended up in the pawn shop in the first place. None of that mattered now—the ring and I were on a new adventure together.

We drove east on Interstate 80 in a used Dodge Ram we had bought a week before to replace Jim's old Ford. The odometer read 118,000 miles and the green paint was faded and patchy from too many summers in the desert sun. But it pulled a stock trailer loaded with all seven of our horses and the bank agreed to loan us the full purchase price, so it was ours.

I found an FM radio station while Jim drove. Don Williams and Loretta Lynn were my favorites, but I tuned into a hard rock station because I knew that Jim liked it. He reached over and turned up the volume.

"This is a good tune," he said. "Quick—who sings this?"

"I have no idea," I answered. "Guns 'N Roses?"

"No."

"AC/DC?"

"No."

"That's it. Those are the only two rock bands I know."

"This is Rob Zombie," Jim chided, pretending to be miffed that I didn't share his love for heavy metal.

"Ah-ha, that was my next guess," I said with mock chagrin. "I totally knew that."

"No, you didn't," Jim said confidently (and correctly). "But you better study up, because this is the best music ever."

I rolled my eyes and scooted a little closer. We had been together less than a year, and the novelty of sitting in the middle while my boyfriend/fiancé manned the wheel hadn't yet worn off. I never called him my fiancé or introduced him to anyone as such. I thought of him as both and neither; Jim was simply the man I was going to marry and have a baby with.

Jim steered the pickup off Interstate 80 at the small town of Battle Mountain and pointed it toward the Rafter J headquarters. The sagebrush desert stretched out on either side of the road, extending north to the foothills and mountains behind the ranch.

We were meeting the Rafter J's cowboss, Chris McSharry, to discuss a job and check out the housing situation. I had always sworn I'd never live with a man before we were married, but I also never envisioned myself a pregnant girlfriend/fiancée without a firm wedding date—so things change.

Jim had to call Mitch and tell him he wouldn't be returning to his job at the Holland Ranch because I was pregnant and it was a seasonal position with no benefits. We needed Jim to land a job on a ranch that offered both married housing and health insurance. Expectant mothers are advised to see a doctor once a month, and so far I had only been to one appointment at nearly five months pregnant.

The August heat was bright and the sun glared through the windshield. I adjusted my black sunglasses, turned the A/C dial to "HI," and pointed the vents directly at my body. Pregnancy made me extra warm all the time.

Jim turned the driver's side vents toward the floor.

"I hate when the Freon blows right into my face," he said. "It gives me a headache."

I closed my eyes and let the cold air dry the sweat that dripped from my hairline. The desert heat was intense, but we were about to see the place where we would hopefully make our first home together. I nestled my leg closer to Jim's.

We made a sharp left turn at the fifty-five-gallon barrel that marked the entrance to the Rafter J. Huge old trees lined the lane leading up to the housing area. The temperature dropped as we entered the cooling shade of the thick canopy. When we drove out the other end, I saw a red double-wide mobile home. Directly across from it and to my left was a narrow lane. We turned down it and passed two run-down single-wide trailers. Jim pulled into the parking area in front of a third trailer that was in even worse shape than the first two.

"This is it," Jim said. He shifted into park and let the pickup idle for a full two minutes before turning it off. He was a stickler for engine maintenance.

I dropped down from the passenger seat and followed Jim to the front yard. Chris showed up a few minutes after we arrived. He only had a short walk down from the red double-wide, where he lived with his wife and two kids. His wife was the ranch manager's daughter, and he had been the cowboss for several years. Chris was short, blond, and smiled a lot between sentences.

"This is it," he said. "It's not much, but it's all we have available right now."

Jim and I followed Chris up the rickety wooden steps. I walked through the front door and looked around. I had already made up my mind that this house was going to work. It had to work. Woody Harney, cowboss at the TS and Jim's boss all summer, had promised him a house on the TS once we were married. Then one night he got drunk and rescinded his offer at the last minute. Jim called around for a job and found out that the Rafter J was the only ranch in the area with an open spot for a married man.

Directly through the front door was a tiny living room that held an old navy-blue couch with lumpy cushions. The once-white carpet was covered with splotchy stains of assorted colors and sizes. A dark brown table and two grimy chairs looked cramped in the dining area. Cabinet doors hung precariously from their hinges in the kitchen. Plastic grocery bags stuffed tight with more plastic bags sat on shelves next to old coffee cans and boxes of rodent bait. Yellow water stains crawled across the ceiling and down the walls. Several holes were punched into the faux wood paneling, and the back door was tied shut with a piece of frayed rope. A small, noisy swamp cooler perched in the kitchen window. The open space around it was covered with a piece of bent cardboard tacked to the wall with horseshoe nails.

The air was warm and stuffy and the whole place smelled like dirty laundry. Previous occupants, presumably lovers, had written their names on the bathroom wall and drawn a heart around them.

"Looks good," I said. "We'll take it."

Jim and Chris shook on it, and we set a date to move in. As we left, the cowboss made one request.

"I just ask that you water and mow the lawn," he said. "My daughter has been coming down here every day and taking care of the grass, so it'd be nice if you could keep it up."

"Sure," I said. "I can mow the lawn."

At the time, I had no idea that pushing a lawnmower through the late summer heat while pregnant would be by far the easiest part of moving into that house. The old trailer should have been demolished. But I was full of second-trimester energy and thrilled to finally be living with my future husband.

We had to empty out all the junk before we could move into the decrepit single-wide. Jim and I hauled yellow-stained mattresses, broken clothes hangers, and tubs of trash to the ranch dump. My growing midsection limited my ability to lift and carry, but I pushed and slid anything I could out the front door. Our few moving boxes sat stacked in the living room while we worked. I owned just a few household furnishings, and the bulk of Jim's belongings hung on the bridle rack and saddle stand in the barn.

The day after we arrived, Jim left for cow camp.

"Are you sure you have to go?" I asked. I folded my arms over my maternity shirt, a blue and white striped cotton top that flared in the front and tied in the back.

"Well, the boss said I need to go to Stampede and I'm the new guy, so I better go," Jim replied. "You'll be okay. I'll see you in five days."

He loaded his horse and bedroll into the ranch rig and kissed me goodbye. Back at the trailer, I laid my own bedroll on the least dirty patch of carpet in the master bedroom. When I lay on the foam mattress, I had an optimal view of the dark clots of spiderwebs that filled each corner. Each gray mass extended across the ceiling along the wall and down toward the floor. I closed my eyes tightly and rolled onto my side.

I drove into Battle Mountain the next morning to buy cleaning supplies at the small town's only grocery store. The selection was limited and everything was overpriced, but it was quicker than driving another hour to Winnemucca to go to Walmart for just a few items. I bought a bottle of bleach, a pack of sponges, a scrub brush, and another bottle of bleach. Then I drove home to launch my attack on decades' worth of grime.

I threw dirt out the door by the shovelful. I scrubbed the linoleum in the kitchen until all the grease and grime were gone. Removing the dirt revealed several holes in the flooring, so I strategically placed cheap throw rugs over the biggest ones. I decided to just ignore the smaller holes, which were numerous. I emptied an impressive collection of coffee cans, trash, and expired food from underneath the kitchen sink. I found a Pampered Chef stoneware cookie sheet in excellent condition. Those things were expensive, so I washed it and sorted it off into the "keep pile." (It remains one of my go-to kitchen tools.)

In the bedroom, I stabbed at the thick gray cobwebs with a broom handle, then smashed the spiders with a sponge mop when they ran along the wall. I vacuumed a thick layer of dead flies out of the windowsills. I shampooed the living room floor with a carpet cleaner I'd borrowed from a friend until most, but not all, of the brown and gray stains were lifted or at least lightened. We didn't own a couch or chairs, so I washed the slipcovers on the blue couch, put them back on the lumpy cushions, and tried not to think about all the cowboys who'd gotten drunk and pissed on them.

I cleaned for four solid days. On the fifth day, I woke up discouraged. My back ached from bending and scrubbing. My arms were tired from lifting and moving. My legs were sore. I didn't mind sleeping in a bedroll, but I realized that it would become significantly harder to get up off the floor as my pregnancy progressed.

My almost-husband was still at camp, the windows were still covered in fly specks, and I was exhausted. I climbed into the green Dodge and drove down the road to find cell phone service. I needed to call my mom.

"I don't want to complain, but it's so bad," I cried when she answered.

I bent my head over the steering wheel and closed my eyes to squeeze back the tears.

"Well, you're cleaning and making it better," Mom reassured me. "I'm sure it will be fine once you're all moved in."

"Yeah, you're right," I agreed with hesitation. I sure hoped she was right.

"Just take it easy today," Mom continued. "You need to rest and take breaks. Make sure you're eating and drinking lots of water. You have plenty of time to get everything done."

I knew she was right. I also knew everything would seem better once Jim got home. I allowed myself to sit in the pickup and cry into the phone for a few more minutes. Then I drove back down the narrow lane to the shitty trailer and picked up a sponge, driven by an inner sense of urgency fueled by pregnancy hormones and Pine Sol. My baby would be born in four months, whether or not the nursery was brought up to World Health Organization sanitation standards.

I concentrated my efforts on the small bedroom at the end of the hallway. In the middle of the floor was what looked like dried dog poop. I attacked the pile of feces with a stiff brush, but it didn't budge. I brought out the big guns: my fabric scissors from the sewing box my mom had given me for Christmas when I was eight. I cut the crap out of the carpet, cleaned the scissors with rubbing alcohol, and put them back in my sewing box. They weren't just my "good scissors," they were my only scissors. Then I dragged the borrowed carpet shampooer down the narrow hall to finish scrubbing any remaining bits of dog poop from what was intended to be the baby's room.

While I scrubbed, I wondered if bleach could be a nursery theme. No whimsical wall hangings, no colorful mobiles, just bleach, bleach, and more bleach, covering all porous and nonporous surfaces.

After it was clean, I assessed the space I had to work with. The closet still had a clothes bar, but the sliding doors had been ripped off. The window had no screen. It matched all the other windows in the house, which also did not open. The east wall had separated from the floor and left a narrow opening between the faux wood paneling and old brown carpet. I peered at the rocks and dirt below. This seemed a bit much.

When I pointed this gap out to the ranch manager, he handed me a caulking gun. In my roomy t-shirt and shorts that wouldn't quite button anymore, I squatted on the worn carpet and tried to compensate for a major structural flaw in my home's integrity with what basically amounted to construction-grade hot glue. I decided not to ask about the complete lack of insulation underneath the trailer.

By the time Jim got back from Stampede, the house was clean enough that we could walk barefoot and not worry (too much) about catching a viral disease. Now, all we had to do was get married.

"Hi, honey," I said when he climbed out of the company pickup in front of the trailer. I stood on my toes to give him a kiss, my cheek brushing against his five-day beard. His shirt was covered in dirt smudges and he smelled like stale sweat. "We need to go to Reno. When can you get a day off?"

CHAPTER 6 ✳ **Could Have Been Worse**

We drove to Reno on a Thursday afternoon after Jim's boss gave him a long weekend off work.

"Should we go through a drive-through chapel?" I asked. "That sounds kinda fun."

"But we're taking the trailer so we can pick up furniture from your dad's house," Jim said.

"Yeah, that's true. And it doesn't have brakes or a left turn signal. Better just go to a regular wedding chapel. Driving through Reno will be stressful enough as it is."

Halfway between the Rafter J headquarters and the Biggest Little City in the World, Jim turned to me in the front seat of the pickup and said, "Hey, did you pack my ID?"

"No, I thought you grabbed it."

I held the steering wheel with both hands focused on the highway ahead. Road construction narrowed the road to one lane, and I focused on not hitting orange cones with the wheel wells of the horse trailer. I was driving because Jim didn't have a driver's license. He'd gotten four DUIs in the years before we'd met, and the state of Colorado had placed a restriction on him getting a license until he took care of some business that he'd never returned to clear up.

Jim turned in the passenger seat and began rummaging through the luggage in the back seat. He checked the door pocket, the glove box, and the console.

"I must have accidentally taken it to Stampede and lost it," he said.

If Jim didn't have his ID, we couldn't get married. I'd already bought him a tie and ironed my dress. The sixteenth of August was an even number, which was my favorite kind, and "8-16-2012" was eight days before my twenty-sixth birthday. There were so many even numbers. I didn't believe in numerology, but I really wanted to get married on that day.

I stared straight ahead and held my breath. I thought that if I didn't breathe, I wouldn't cry.

I was wrong.

The tears came hot and fast, in gasps and sobs. I was ugly crying in a construction zone, everything a bride doesn't want on her wedding day.

"I'm sorry, I don't want you to feel bad," I said without turning to look at Jim. Even from the corner of my eye, I could see that he looked miserable. "It's just that I wanted to at least have a fun story for our wedding. Staying the night in Reno, going to a wedding chapel, that would have been really fun. But it's okay, we'll still stay the night in Reno, we just won't get married. And then we'll go to my dad's tomorrow and get all that furniture."

I didn't want to be a pregnant girlfriend anymore. I wanted to be a pregnant wife.

Jim turned around once more and unzipped a side pocket on his old red duffel bag, the one with a hole in it.

"Hey, I found my wallet!" he exclaimed.

I smiled and the tears stopped. We exited the construction zone and drove seventy-five the rest of the way to Reno. If all went as planned, we'd be married by midnight.

I sat next to Jim in a padded maroon booth at a casino. We'd checked into the Grand Sierra Hotel and Resort on the east side of Reno away from downtown, chosen primarily because it had a parking lot roomy enough to accommodate our three-quarter-ton pickup and twenty-foot stock trailer. The receptionist upgraded us from a regular one-bedroom to a suite when we told her it was our wedding day. I made a mental note to always tell receptionists it was our wedding day when traveling in the future.

We ate dinner at the onsite steakhouse for the sake of simplicity.

"How's your lobster?" Jim asked.

"It's delicious," I replied. "How's your ribeye?"

"It's good," he said and took a sip of his Coors.

I took another bite of the sweet, light lobster meat dipped in melted butter. It was the first lobster tail I'd ever eaten, and I was thoroughly enjoying every morsel. I wished I'd ordered lobster while on dates with guys before marrying Jim, since I'd be jointly paying for every expensive shellfish I ate from here on out.

I took a sip of white wine and glanced around to see if any of the other restaurant patrons would notice me drinking alcohol and frown in my direction, even though I knew research showed an occasional glass of wine did not cause fetal harm. My pregnant belly was barely noticeable to the casual onlooker, but to me it felt like wearing a sandwich board that screamed, "Lady with a baby!" The wine tasted sweet and sparkly going down. It was just how I imagined my wedding dinner beverage would taste.

That glass of chardonnay was about the only thing that matched my mental image of my ideal wedding day. I looked around and realized none of the other diners knew this was the big night for us, the night we would become Mr. and Mrs. James Lee Young III. Our attire hardly gave us away: Jim wore a white long-sleeve button-down shirt and blue jeans, and I wore a yellow sundress from the bargain rack at Maurice's. In front of us, a twenty-something man with spiky black hair and a black long-sleeve shirt with the cuffs turned up laughed while drinking a beer. Our waiter stopped by the table and asked if we needed anything. He smiled patiently while he waited for our answer.

I needed something all right, but it was something the waiter couldn't help me with. I needed my mom. And my best friend. Maybe a sister or two. I suddenly felt an acute ache for the physical presence of people I'd known longer than fifteen months. My soon-to-be husband was a good man and the father of my unborn baby, but he didn't know me like my family and lifelong friends did. I wished I had a handful of people who loved me to smile and share the joy of the occasion, to squeeze my hand until I wasn't nervous and clap when my husband kissed me after we said, "I do."

I'd always imagined I would ask my older sister Lacy and my college room-mate Theo to be my bridesmaids. Maybe I would ask my half-sister Sara to be a bridesmaid, too. We hadn't lived together growing up and weren't close, but it might be a nice gesture to bond the extended family. My best friend Casey would be my maid of honor, of course. I had been hers when she'd gotten married two years earlier. I never imagined my own wedding day without her smiling beside me.

"Everything was great, thank you," Jim told the waiter.

We split a piece of cheesecake for dessert and asked for the check. Once the tip was calculated and the dinner bill paid, there was nothing left to do but become man and wife.

We took a cab downtown and walked into the chapel. It was now after nine o'clock. No matter—it was just the two of us, so I thought we could head back to the resort and find a band to dance a few songs to after the deed was done. We approached the receptionist behind the counter and learned that we needed a marriage license, purchased separately, before we could utilize the chapel's services.

Back out into the dark night we went. Hand in hand, we walked two blocks to the courthouse. Jim walked on the streetside of the sidewalk, and I got whistled at by a car full of guys driving by. I blushed slightly at the unwanted attention. Couldn't they tell I was clearly taken, as indicated by the man walking beside me and holding my hand? But then again, I was five months pregnant and felt pudgy. I was flattered that someone besides my baby daddy thought I looked attractive.

Or maybe they were whistling at Jim. You never knew in the big city.

We bought the marriage license and I signed "Jolyn Laubacher" for the last time. Back at the chapel, we found a spot on a wooden bench along the wall and waited our turn. Two other couples waited on a longer bench along the opposite wall. I made Jim press his face close to mine and smile while I turned a camera around in my palm and pressed the shutter, hoping we were somewhere near the middle of the frame. I snapped a few of us kissing. Taking selfies helped pass the time and calm my nerves.

I wasn't nervous about marrying Jim. I was one hundred percent, sign-it-in-ink, take-it-to-the-bank certain I wanted to marry him. He was a tall, handsome, honest, hardworking, God-fearing, dang good cowboy.

But I was nervous about all that could happen after we were officially married. One minute I would be Miss Jolyn Laubacher, single woman, and the next I would become Mrs. Jolyn Young, fully half of one whole legally binding partnership.

I told myself that all about-to-be-married people probably felt like that. It was completely normal, and I shouldn't let last-minute anxiety stop me from going through with my (thoroughly) premeditated decision. Sure, I would have preferred an October wedding in an outdoor venue with crisp colorful leaves and golden light, but expectations change when you have a baby on the way.

The receptionist called our names at half past ten. She escorted us down the hallway to a room on the left.

"Would you like to walk down the aisle to music?" she asked.

"Um, sure?" I stammered.

"Okay," she replied. She closed the door with a warm smile and the traditional wedding march began playing from speakers somewhere in the room.

Jim bent his arm at the elbow, and I placed my hand on his forearm. Together, we started down the aisle. The procedure felt a tad formal for a ceremony devoid of attendants or guests. Three steps in, I stumbled in my three-inch wedge sandals and clutched Jim's arm. He reflexively reached for me with his other hand. I giggled nervously. He smiled and helped me regain my footing.

We made it the rest of the way down the aisle without further incident. A smiling, stocky, dark-haired man wearing a clerical robe greeted us at the altar. With better planning and advance notice, we'd been told he would have styled his hair and attire just like the King of Rock 'n Roll's, allowing us the full "married by Elvis" experience. But instead, we'd settled for Almost-Elvis.

"Do you have rings to exchange today?" the officiant asked.

I looked down at the three small diamonds on the gold band already on my hand.

"No," I said.

"Okay, then, let us begin," he continued. He flipped to the "No-Ring Ceremony" page in his binder.

Almost-Elvis led us through our vows, which reminded me of the prewritten vows of every wedding movie I'd ever seen, minus the "place this ring on her finger." We kissed at the end, right on cue, and Almost-Elvis smiled wide like he was truly happy for us. I appreciated the kindness from a stranger who was the sole witness to our wedding in a faraway city late at night.

We walked back down the hallway and into the reception area hand in hand, just like we'd arrived. I didn't feel any different. I thought I might feel some strong emotion—happiness or excitement, contentment or even regret—but I just felt tired and pregnant.

We approached the desk to pay and the receptionist asked if we'd like to add a "professional photo package" onto our bill. I didn't see anyone else around so I assumed the woman also served as the photographer. I was growing wearier by the minute and the thought of staying long enough for five different poses (eight if we bought the premium package) didn't sound appealing.

"Would you mind snapping a few quick pictures with my camera?" I asked. It probably sounded like I was trying to be cheap, which I was.

She obliged and took a couple shots of Jim and me with a white lattice arch as a backdrop. I stood in front of Jim while he encircled my waist and placed his hands on my belly with my hands on top of his. "Make sure you get a belly picture!" my mom had told me before we eloped. My yellow sleeveless dress and his necktie made it look like we were at the senior prom.

We caught a cab back to our room at the Sierra. We again held hands and walked through the casino floor between clanging slot machines and tourists wearing stiletto heels and barely-there sequined cocktail dresses. All I could think about was sitting my pregnant butt down on the king-sized bed and taking off my high-heeled sandals. The left one had chewed a blister onto the outside of my foot. I felt puffy—was probably retaining water like a camel in the Sahara—and out of breath.

I didn't remember my plan to go dancing until the next morning, when we were already Mr. and Mrs. Young, and it didn't matter anyway.

The alarm clock shrieked on the nightstand beside our bed at four in the morning. I leaned over and slapped the button to make the terrible sound stop before it woke up Jim. The clock was boxy and outdated, with a huge numerical display and an AM/FM radio. It sounded like every abrupt morning wakeup of my childhood, because that's what happens when you furnish your newlywed home with hand-me-downs from your dad's homemade storage unit.

We'd driven to my dad's house in northern California the day after we eloped—the real northern California, not the misnomer that is San Francisco and wine country, which is actually pretty much the middle of the state. True northern California is the forgotten area at the tip-top of the state with small towns and extreme poverty. It's where I grew up, roughly forty miles from the border, with Oregon mountain ranges visible on a clear day. Most days were clear, because while we didn't have any money, we also didn't have any smog.

Jim and I had spent the weekend in the rural subdivision of Big Springs so we could load up his—now our—horse trailer with secondhand furniture and host a spontaneous post-wedding barbeque in the backyard of my childhood home. My dad met my husband for the first time the day after I married him.

I'd texted friends and family near my hometown two weeks before we drove out. We knew for sure that we were making the trip, because we needed furniture, but since our actual wedding date was a moving target until the morning of, we didn't announce our marriage until the guests showed up at my dad's. It was a surprise wedding reception in reverse.

I hadn't had a bridal shower or wedding registry, but I got to experience the fun of opening a stack of presents from people who loved me as several guests brought baby or wedding gifts. Dinner was potluck. Only the guests my dad invited brought dishes because I hadn't known it was a potluck so I hadn't told my invitees. There wound up being just enough food to go around, plenty of beer, and a mismatched assortment of popsicles and ice cream cups for dessert. My favorite dish was a sweet and vinegary salad made from homegrown cucumbers brought by a family friend who'd been a guest at my parents' wedding years ago.

After the whirlwind weekend, we'd returned to real married life at the Rafter J. I silenced the alarm clock and slipped out from beneath the covers. They were made of polyester and circa 1987 because my family of origin didn't believe in throwing anything away. I headed for the kitchen, where I started the coffee pot and turned a burner on the stove to medium. Eggs and bacon were soon frying in cast-iron skillets while I made pancake batter from scratch. Dinner entrees weren't my thing, but I'd always been a good breakfast cook.

The food was ready at a quarter to five and I woke up Jim. He was groggy but happy, like he was every morning when he staggered into the kitchen to a plate full of steaming food. I sat with him while he ate at our table, which used to belong to my great-grandma Ethel.

When Jim sopped the last sunny-side-up egg yolk from the stoneware plate, which was part of the same set I'd eaten off as a child, he placed his dishes in the sink and put on his coat and cowboy hat.

"Thank you for breakfast," he told me. "That was delicious." Jim thanked me after each and every meal I cooked for him. It was a habit he'd learned in ranch cookhouses and maintained out of adherence to a strict personal code of politeness.

"You're welcome. I'm glad you liked it."

"Have a good day. I love you."

"Love you, too. See you after work."

He leaned down to kiss me, then headed for the door while I fell back into bed to sleep until the sun rose fully over the eastern horizon. Then I'd rise once more, change out of my nightgown, and clean up the breakfast mess in the kitchen before starting daily housework and writing articles for the *Nevada Rancher*. I still could hardly believe my name appeared on the masthead of a real magazine and that I got paid to read and write.

I didn't write every day. Some days I scanned the AP newswire for story ideas or read through other industry publications to see what else was going on in the world of agriculture. Other days I went for walks down the ranch lane, sewed headbands and throw pillows out of fabric scraps, or read the giant Mark Twain autobiography I'd picked up on a side trip to Virginia City over the summer. My job was laidback and the expectations were easy to meet—as long as I turned in six articles by deadline each month, all was good.

One day, Jim and I walked hand in hand beneath the big, old trees that lined the lane and shaded us with overhanging green leaves. I wore a black jersey knit dress that expanded over my baby bump and a pair of platform flip flops. The September afternoon was warm with a hint of autumn. We headed for the barn in no particular rush.

"What are we going up here for again?" Jim asked.

"Ty wants my saddle horn measurements. He's either ordering a new saddle or wants 'em for a friend, I can't remember."

We passed Chris's house at the top of the lane and made our way across the gravel parking area. When we walked around the corner of a metal storage container that held extra tack and supplies, we came face to face with a black Angus bull standing in front of the barn. I stopped short and laughed in surprise. I didn't expect to see a bull this far from the pasture. But then it became apparent the bull was trapped by the barn door, a corral gate, and the storage container. We had unwittingly blocked his only exit.

The bull immediately and unexpectedly put his head down and charged. Jim and I turned on our heels, grabbed hands, and ran as fast as we could. I made it three strides before a flip flop slipped in the loose gravel and I tripped over my own feet.

"Jim!" I yelled as I fell.

Two thoughts crossed my mind as I braced with my free hand and hit the hard ground: *I'm falling on my baby,* and *I'm about to see what it feels like to have an Angus bull step on my back.*

Jim grabbed his cowboy hat and whipped the bull on the head. The bull tossed his head to throw off the hat and jumped over me, then ran out of the parking area and down the lane.

I stood up and brushed the dirt from my dress. My elbows and knees were bloody. I looked down at my belly in horror. Could the baby survive a fall like that? There was no blood running down my legs. My stomach wasn't aching or cramping. I felt my abdomen with both hands. Nothing felt hard or hot to the touch. My own body seemed to be unbroken, so maybe—hopefully—the baby's was as well.

The bull was now pacing along the fenced lane between the barn and our trailer house. He had his head up and was looking for something else to fight. There was no way I was walking past him in that narrow area. Jim held onto my arm and walked me to an old white company pickup that was parked nearby. He shut the passenger door after helping me into the seat, then turned the keys that were always in the ignition and drove down the lane to our home.

I walked up the steps and sat on the couch holding my belly with both hands. Jim sat down and placed his hand beside mine. We stayed that way for what felt like a long time until we both felt a kick. It was a regular kick, just like the ones we'd marveled at, then grown accustomed to, over the past few weeks.

"I wonder if I should go to the hospital just to get checked out, but at this point I feel like everything is fine and they'd just send me home," I said, moving my gaze from my belly to Jim's concerned face.

Jim nodded. "Yeah. I don't know."

I wanted to go to the hospital, to have the doctors ask what happened and palpate my abdomen and officially determine if the baby was injured or safe. But we didn't have health insurance yet—Jim still had to fill out all the "new hire" paperwork and get me added to his benefits—and we were paying cash for all medical expenses. I knew a trip to the ER would run at least a thousand dollars just to walk through the door. That was half a month's paycheck for a cowboy, and it didn't even include the expensive tests and diagnostic imaging they would undoubtedly require.

I made myself think calmly. The baby was moving and kicking, so I was re-assured she was okay. I had known for a full month we were having a daughter because my best friend Casey was as an ultrasound technician and had sneaked me into the hospital where she worked for a fetal exam and gender confirma-tion. So now I was not just worried about our baby, but about our baby girl.

Common sense told me an acute injury would be apparent right away with blood or intense pain. Neither of those symptoms were present. Once my mental shock had eased and I'd felt normal baby activity for about twenty minutes, I decided to stay home and not go to the hospital.

Jim took the ranch pickup back to the barn, herding the bull into his pasture along the way. I sat on the couch and focused on the steady bump, bump, whoosh of baby kicks. Jim came back and told me Chris had been surprised when he told him about the charging bull. The black Angus belonged to Chris' family and was named Ferdinand.

"He must have gotten whipped out of the pasture by the bigger bulls and was looking for somebody's ass to kick," Jim rationalized.

"I guess it was just our bad luck to walk around that corner and trap him like we did," I said.

"Yep," Jim agreed. "Just bad luck. At least nobody got hurt."

We ate dinner, watched a few episodes of *The Big Bang Theory* on DVD and went to bed, unsettled and relieved at the same time. Things could've been so much worse.

CHAPTER 7 ✳ **Childbirth,
for What It's Worth**

Jim and I opted not to take a childbirth class. It would mean several more hour-and-a-half trips into town, which would be a hassle to coordinate with Jim's work schedule. Cowboys officially work six days a week, but they usually work seven. I didn't think it was necessary to do all the extra driving to study birthing techniques when I would end up giving birth no matter what. Why study for a test you know you're going to pass?

Jim and I had, however, agreed that our upcoming childbirth experience would take place in a hospital. There would be none of that hippy-dippy, "pop the kid out in your bathtub and hope for the best" business. We decided this very early in my pregnancy and didn't mention the subject again after that.

As my due date of December twenty-sixth grew closer, the prospect of actually giving birth became increasingly more magnified and detailed. I didn't like what I saw. For my particular situation, I was looking at a scheduled C-section.

One evening deep into the holiday season, I sat across the small dining table from Jim and cried. We were supposed to be eating dinner, but I was too upset to even think about the food I'd cooked. Jim stared down at his plate and poked at his garden salad with a fork. His bushy winter beard concealed the bottom part of his face, but I could still see his green eyes. They looked miserable.

"I don't know what to do," I said. "I'm scared to try and turn her, but I can't even handle the thought of having a C-section."

A fresh wave of tears rolled from my eyes when I heard myself say the dreaded "C-word" aloud. I was nine months pregnant and recent sonograms showed that our baby was breech, or positioned feet first. Babies usually flip head-down when delivery draws near. When the head and shoulders are pushed through the birth canal first, the baby can breathe while the rest of the body slips out. Attempting to deliver a breech baby can be very dangerous because the oxygen supply from the umbilical cord can easily be cut off while the shoulders are being delivered.

I wanted my baby girl, whom we'd decided to name Grace Rebecca, to be born safely, but I'd never spent any time in a hospital room before. I had never broken a bone or even received stitches for a cut. If I opted for the scheduled C-section, my first hospital stay would be a guaranteed four-day ordeal that started with major abdominal surgery—while I was awake—and ended with a newborn baby to care for.

"The doctor said he could try to turn her before my due date if we want," I said. "I don't know, though. It sounds more involved than I originally thought."

"Yeah, I don't know," Jim repeated my words. "I thought it would be simpler, too."

Jim's chair sat directly in front of our first Christmas tree, a bushy fir I'd bought from the grocery store parking lot. Buying a Christmas tree instead of cutting one down ourselves went against all the backwoods values I'd grown up with in northern California's logging country, but I was heavily pregnant and lived way out in the desert. Two strands of colorful lights and homemade fabric bows decorated its limbs. I wished I could go back in time to five days before, when my biggest decision had been picking out which color fabric I should buy for the bows.

There is no easy way to extract a baby from its mother. As Woody Harney told me at the Horseshoe Ranch barn shortly after I became pregnant, "It's not gonna feel nearly as good coming out as it did going in."

Jim gave up on his salad and took a drink of milk from a Mason jar.

"I'm so scared of surgery, but I'm really worried about trying to flip the baby. It's kind of a big deal," I said. "I mean, if I might wind up with an emergency C-section anyway, we might as well just schedule a regular one."

An ECV, or "external cephalic version," was a procedure where a doctor attempted to flip a breech baby by strategically pressing on the mother's stomach. But it wasn't as simple as "push and flip." The way the nurse had explained it, I would check into the hospital and receive an IV port. A Doppler device would be attached to my abdomen to monitor the baby's heartbeat. There was a chance that she might become extremely distressed during the process. If that happened, I'd be rushed to the operating room.

Jim had patiently dealt with my surgical worries during the preceding days. He'd listened to me cry on the phone to my mom and handed me the phone to talk to his mom, whom I still hadn't met but she'd had a C-section to deliver Jim thirty-two years before. He knew I was terrified of going under the knife. He hadn't tried to influence my decision one way or the other. But now, he offered an opinion.

"All I know is that of all the calves I've delivered, there's always a reason why one is breech," Jim said matter-of-factly.

It barely registered that my pregnancy and impending delivery were being compared to a cow's. In ranch country, that's just par for the course.

"I just wish we knew why! Ninety-five percent of babies turn head-down by the end of the third trimester. I'm thirty-seven weeks. Why won't she turn?" I asked helplessly.

"I don't know," replied Jim. "But I do know that I've thought about it, and I've prayed about it, and I don't think we should try to turn her."

I nodded in agreement. I took a bite of salad. I decided to trust my husband and his cowboy instincts. If things went south during an ECV, I could wind up with a C-section anyway, except the emergency kind where they completely knocked me out and my husband wasn't allowed in the operating room. If things really went south, we could end up with an injured—or worse—baby. The risks were just too great to attempt flipping the baby from the outside.

At least I could plan for a scheduled C-section. I could write it on the calendar, notify the soon-to-be grandparents, pack my bags, and drive to the hospital in an orderly fashion. Surgery was scary, but the thought of the doctor trying to physically turn my unborn baby from the outside, when we didn't know why she was stuck in the first place, was scarier.

Two weeks later, the nurses wheeled me into the operating room for my C-section without Jim by my side. This triggered my first wave of tears. He appeared by my head shortly after a large blue curtain was raised toward the ceiling at the top of my abdomen to prevent me from watching the doctor cut my midsection open. Then the nurses placed my arms in an outstretched position on either side of my body and loosely strapped them down. That was the catalyst for my second, bigger wave of sobbing.

I felt like Jesus on the cross. Death was all but certain at this point. I was glad I made Jim promise not to give our newborn daughter away after I died delivering her. She needed to know at least one biological parent. I had no idea how Jim would manage to care for a newborn and hold down a steady job to support her, but that was his problem.

After I'd been stabbed in the spine with a needle the size of a drinking straw and had lost all sensation in the lower half of my body, the doctor looked at me and admonished me to stop crying. Apparently, my chest-heaving sobs would interfere with the precision slicing he was about to do on my bikini line. I was unable to heed his request and continued to cry and gasp for air until he pulled Grace from my uterus, and I could finally see my baby face to face, albeit from across the operating room. She was quiet and red, her brow scrunched together like she was displeased with the change of scenery.

The nurses cleaned her off, weighed her, wrapped her in a blanket like a burrito, and placed her near my left cheek on the operating table. I turned my head to look at her face and tried to hold her but felt too woozy and weak to keep her from rolling off the table.

"Here, take her, I don't feel good," I managed to say before I began to dry heave, a side effect of the anesthesia. I retched into a paper bag while the nurses laid my uterus on top of my body and stitched it up, then tucked the bloody mass neatly back inside my abdominal cavity and secured the whole thing shut with nineteen staples. I didn't actually see any of this because of the big blue curtain. Thank God for the curtain. Across the room, more nurses tended to Grace and took care of her newborn needs, whatever those were.

Then I was out of it, drifting in and out of wakefulness and unconcerned about who was caring for my baby or what they were doing to her. I'd heard of newly delivered moms freaking out when they weren't the first person to hold their baby or becoming angry when the nurses bathed the baby with soap. The soap thing confused me. I thought it was good for people of all ages to take a bath with soap. But apparently it was a source of major stress for some moms to lie on a hospital bed so their own wounds could be tended while their baby was cared for by Not Them, possibly with soap.

Me, I glanced once at Grace and then closed my eyes so I could pass the eff out. She was in a hospital surrounded by trained professionals. She'd be fine.

When I drifted awake again, I was lying on a thin mattress in a hospital bed and tucked under a thick cotton blanket. I put my hands on my midsection and marveled at how my belly, which had been so round and full and firm less than an hour ago, was now half its original size. It also felt soft and squishy, which was weird. I couldn't get over how quickly the belly I'd watched grow little by little every day for nine months had disappeared—in less than an hour.

I couldn't feel my legs and my voice sounded hoarse and cracked when I tried to talk. It was nice to be in a regular hospital room, though, instead of the operating room. That place had been big, bright, cold, and filled with the sound of terrified sobs.

A nurse soon walked into my room carrying a tiny bundle in a white blanket covered with blue and pink footprints.

"Here, Mama," she said as she handed my daughter to me.

I reached up to receive my baby. I cradled her stocking-cap head in my left elbow. Her whole body only took up half an arm's length, and my hand curved around her itty-bitty bottom. Within seconds, I felt the world's tiniest, driest little "toot" on my palm.

I wondered how a newborn infant could even pass gas. I mean, what was she eating in there, refried beans and broccoli? I hadn't eaten a bite since dinner the night before, per standard surgical procedure. But it didn't matter to me if she was flatulent. She was soft, cuddly, warm, round, and mine. She was perfect.

Jim walked into the room.

"Do you want to hold your baby?" I asked.

"Um, yeah," he replied, as if it was the most obvious answer ever.

I handed our small bundle up to him. Jim cradled her with both arms and gazed at her face. He looked so tall, standing straight and proud in his town hat and the blue wool sweater I'd bought him as a surprise during a grocery shopping trip to Elko. Grace looked so small in her daddy's arms, swaddled in a blanky and wearing a beanie with only the middle part of her red face showing.

Later, a nurse told me that Grace had been stuck in the breech position because her umbilical cord was shorter than average and wrapped around her neck three times. Each of these conditions by itself might not have raised concern, but together they would have spelled disaster had we tried to turn her or insisted on a vaginal delivery. The nurse said she used to recommend ECVs to pregnant women, but after seeing Grace's situation, she wasn't going to do that anymore.

I looked down at Grace's sweet face as she slept in the crook of my arm swaddled in flannel. Her tiny, rhythmic breaths and scrunched-up little froggy legs that reflexively kicked in her sleep were worth every bit of the terror of surgery.

Our time together as a newly minted family of three was cut short when Jim got up early the next morning and drove to the ranch for work. He had to "preg check" cows with the crew for two days and would then return to pick up me and Grace.

The blizzard blew into town the morning Jim returned to take us home. It was whiteout conditions, with snow whipping sideways and visibility reduced to nearly zero.

"Should we just get a room and stay in town?" I asked. I was scared to drive into the storm.

"No, we'll be fine," Jim said.

"Are you sure? The roads will be bad."

"We'll be okay. I've driven in the snow before."

And so we headed home from the hospital. Staying at a hotel wouldn't erase all my concerns anyway, since the part that worried me even more than inclement weather was taking care of Grace alone during the night. I didn't know how to take care of a newborn. The thought of being on our own with her in the dark was terrifying, no matter where we were. That night, for the first night since she was born, we would be solely responsible for Grace's feeding, diaper changes, swaddling, soothing, and whatever else an infant might need.

Worst of all, there would be no night nurse to appear at my bedside with the mere press of a button. There would be no friendly, wide-awake, well-trained medical professional coming into my room to administer pain medication and take my baby to the nursery so I could sleep if I so desired. It would be just the two of us clueless new parents and a baby.

Our first stop after leaving the hospital was Walmart. I waited in the pickup with Grace sleeping in her car seat in the back while Jim grocery shopped and filled my pain prescriptions. When you live seventy-six miles from town, you don't pass up a chance to buy fresh produce, milk, and pain pills.

I left the diesel engine running with the heater on and watched the snow blow sideways. Jim was in the store for nearly an hour. Grace didn't wake up while he was gone, so I left her securely strapped in, just like the nurse had shown us before we left. I later learned that most moms insist on riding in the back seat with their new baby on the way home from the hospital. That didn't occur to me even once during our trip home. Besides the car seat, the back seat was packed with my suitcase, a duffel bag full of baby clothes that I didn't use while at the hospital, baby gifts delivered by a local church, and, once Jim returned from the store, two weeks' worth of groceries.

We drove east on I-80 straight into the storm. The whiteout surrounded us and most traffic slowed to forty-five miles per hour. Semi-trucks blew past us on the left. I trusted Jim's driving, but I knew that all it would take was one bad decision from a random stranger to wreck their lives as well as ours. I alternated between staring at the speedometer and glancing in the back seat to check on Grace.

We made it to our exit and turned onto the dirt road leading to the ranch. I insisted Jim drive really slowly because the road was solid washboards.

"You have it all wrong," he argued. "If I go fast enough, the truck tires will only land on the tops of the washboards, and it'll be a smoother ride."

"As the person who had nineteen staples removed from her abdomen this morning, I think we should take it easy and go slow."

He humored me, but I continually strained my incision by turning around to look in the back seat every forty-five seconds. Grace's stocking cap was too big and kept slipping over her eyes. She wore tiny socks on her hands to keep her fingernails from scratching the delicate skin on her face. For some reason, probably in reaction to the bumpy road, she held her hands upright, one on each side of her face. The combination of oversized knit cap and sock hands was so damn cute that I couldn't help but want to look at her constantly.

I kept describing the baby's cuteness to Jim and giggling. "She moved her hand! Oh, now she moved her other hand! Oh my gosh, her hat just slipped down even more!"

Maybe new moms didn't ride in the back seat because they wanted to be near their offspring; their husbands made them ride in the back so they could drive in peace and quiet.

When we finally reached the ranch, Jim got Grace out first, opened the front door of the trailer, and placed the car seat containing our newborn daughter on the carpet in front of the couch. Then he came back to the truck for me. I slowly followed him up the rickety wooden stairs and across the porch, which was covered with uneven lumps of frozen snow and ice. I really didn't want to fall. I pressed one hand against my nine-inch incision, applying pressure to alleviate the pain just like the nurses had shown me.

I stood in the narrow living room of the single-wide trailer and looked down at my tiny infant. Now what? She was still such a little alien creature to me. I had exactly zero experience taking care of a newborn. I'd babysat occasionally in high school and college, but I'd never been responsible for a tiny baby who couldn't hold her head up and sounded more like a kitten than a person. I guessed the first order of business was to unbuckle the five-point harness that held her in the car seat. Beyond that, I had no idea.

Baby Grace jostled awake when I unsnapped the plastic buckles and pulled her resistant arms through the nylon straps. I lifted her to my chest, and she immediately squirmed and started to cry. I knew she was hungry, but I wasn't sure how to feed her. We hadn't formed a solid breastfeeding bond before we were discharged from our four-day stay in the Winnemucca hospital. My attempts to nurse her in the maternity ward were frequent but largely unsuccessful. Breastfeeding was neither automatic nor easy. Since I was the only one who could breastfeed Grace, I felt the pressure to succeed almost immediately.

Shortly after she was born, I'd enthusiastically told one of the nurses that Grace had nursed for five minutes. She'd frowned and said that wasn't good enough. One middle-aged nurse then told me that breastfeeding was the first form of discipline and that babies were like puppies; they'd get spoiled if you let them take advantage of you. She'd held my tiny baby's face to my breast in an unyielding grip while Grace screamed and fought to turn away from the nipple.

This doesn't seem quite right, I'd thought as I watched my newborn daughter's face turn red and felt her cries vibrate my eardrums. *But I'm the rookie in the room, and they're the trained medical experts, so I guess this is what I should do.*

Grace had refused to latch on for any significant length of time during our hospital stay, despite shoving her hand into her mouth several times a day. The girl was born hungry and looking for a snack but didn't seem to want what I had to give.

After reporting more brief breastfeeding sessions and receiving the nurses' frowns of disapproval, I had begun to lie.

"Yes," I'd told the day shift nurse when she came to check on us and asked if Grace had eaten.

"Oh, good! For how long?"

"Ten minutes on either side."

My new response earned the nurses' smiles and satisfied nods, which I craved. I hated feeling like I was failing at caring for my own baby. Even female wombats in Australia could feed their offspring unassisted within minutes of giving birth. Probably while eating their own afterbirth and snarling at a dingo, too.

But the truth of our failure to connect as breastfeeding mother and baby was inescapable once we arrived home. There it was just me, Jim, and baby Grace. Jim was as clueless as I was about caring for a newborn. Grace only knew how to be an infant, which was not helpful. Some women have their mothers to help them during those first few tender yet grueling days at home after giving birth, but my mom and I had chosen to delay her visit and have her meet her first grandchild a month after her birth. Mom had said she could be more helpful when the baby was a little older. I'd agreed, but only because I had no idea how much I would want my own mom once I became one.

"Here, do you want to put her in this?" Jim asked. He set a freshly repainted brown wooden cradle with scalloped edges on the floor in front of the couch. His grandpa had made it when Jim was born, and Jim's mom had shipped it out to us ahead of Grace's birth.

I laid Grace down on the waterproof mat I sewed to fit the bottom of the cradle. She instantly cried more. I quickly scooped her back up to my chest, cradling her head and neck with one hand while supporting her back and bottom with the other.

"It won't work," I said. "The air temperature is way colder down there. I think it's because the sides are solid wood."

A record-breaking cold snap had descended on northern Nevada earlier that day, bringing below-zero nighttime temps and single-digit daytime highs. Since laying her down in the cradle didn't work, Jim and I took turns holding

Grace for the next few hours. She wasn't comforted when we rocked, walked, hummed, or patted her little diapered bottom.

"Why don't you try to get some sleep?" Jim finally said at nine o'clock. "I'll stay up with her a while longer."

I handed Grace to her daddy and gratefully crawled into our queen-sized bed. I pulled the pile of blankets up around my shoulders. They felt thick and luxurious after three nights under thin, scratchy hospital blankets that smelled like bleach. I rolled onto my side and pulled up my knees to ease the strain on my incision. I was tired, sore, confused, and scared. I closed my eyes.

I drifted off to a fitful sleep. When I awoke at half-past twelve in the morning, the first sound I heard was my newborn's cry. I threw back the covers and put my feet on the floor, careful to push myself upright with my arms. I stumbled out of the bedroom in the dark, disoriented and uncertain. All I knew was that I had to get to my baby.

When I reached the living room, I found Jim sitting in his recliner holding Grace. He was lightly dozing and moving the chair back and forth in a barely discernible rocking motion.

"Here, I'll take her," I said as I picked up the baby. "You better go to bed."

"Huh? What? What time is it? Okay," Jim mumbled as he stood up. "I love you."

"Love you, too," I said.

I sat down in Jim's big green corduroy La-Z-Boy and put Grace to my breast. Cool air swirled around my newly bared skin, chasing away the warmth I'd gained while burrowed under the blankets in our bed. Grace wiggled and squirmed, driven by instinct to root her little face around and search for an unseen food source she knew was right there. I wasn't sure if she latched on or not, but she drifted off to sleep within minutes, so I called it a win and closed my eyes. We dozed together under a handmade fleece baby blanket, one of many I'd received in the weeks before her birth.

I placed Grace in her pink Rock 'n Play and found my way to the couch sometime during the night. The rising sun pulled my eyes open a few short hours later when it shone through the single-paned window directly above my head.

I sat up and considered my situation. The night's despair had dissipated in the bright, albeit cold, sunlight, and now I wanted a plan of action. I thought back and counted how many hours it had been since Grace had consumed a confirmed drop of milk.

Eighteen hours. Yikes. I was no baby expert, but that seemed like a dangerously long time. Weren't newborns supposed to eat at least every two to three hours?

I knew I had to figure something out, and quickly. I was afraid for Grace's health if she didn't start eating more frequently. I was afraid the doctor would order me to formula feed if she failed to gain weight by her two-week checkup.

"Honey, Grace hasn't nursed in eighteen hours," I told Jim when he walked into the kitchen from our bedroom.

"Really?" he asked. He filled the coffee pot with water and added four heaping tablespoons of grounds to the filter basket.

"Yeah, I just counted. I really want her to nurse, but I can't get her to. Maybe it's because they didn't let me do skin-to-skin in the hospital."

"Why didn't they let you?" Jim asked.

"They said it was too cold."

"Well, that's ignorant. We paid enough money to that hospital. They could've turned the heat up if it was too cold."

"I know," I said. "And we were inside a building and all. It wasn't like I was sitting in the parking lot during the snowstorm."

"Could you do skin-to-skin now?" Jim asked. "I know colostrum is really important to little guys."

"But do you think it's too cold?" I still half-believed the nurses' warnings, mostly because I had no other wisdom to follow.

"You need to relax. Just turn the heater up, go into the back bedroom, take your shirt off and cuddle with her."

I picked up Grace and headed to the bedroom, determined yet nervous. I really wanted to breastfeed, and I knew this was a last-ditch effort. She had to eat ASAP, whether by breastfeeding or formula. The time for mama's milk was now or never.

I grabbed my breast pump from its box on my way down the short hall. It was a gift from my baby shower that didn't yet feel like mine. Like the car seat base, stroller, baby bathtub, and the baby herself, the pump felt like something I'd borrowed from someone else. I didn't know how to operate any of these things and was only marginally comfortable having them in my home.

At the end of the hall, I pushed the thermostat dial to the far right, maxing out the furnace's capacity at ninety degrees. With all the trailer's drafts and its general lack of insulation, this meant that the actual interior temperature would be about eighty in the tiny back bedroom near the furnace and sixty in the small master bedroom at the other end of the trailer. I shut the bedroom door to hold in the heat and sat down in the glider in the corner. I nestled Grace onto a nursing pillow across my lap and tugged off her little onesie. I attached the pump to my body and hit the power button. I figured I stood a higher chance of success if I waited for a steady stream to flow before I tried nursing Grace again. She seemed pretty much over working hard for no gain.

While I waited for the pump to work its mechanical magic, I examined my baby. I hadn't seen her much in the hospital without a footed sleeper covering her body and tiny mittens over her hands. Her skin was red and wrinkly. Her brow was furrowed, and her fingers clasped at unseen objects. She pulled her scrawny legs up and flexed her toes for unknown reasons. Her face, round and full, strongly resembled her daddy's. She had small ears and dark brown hair, just like I did when I was born.

After barely a minute, Grace started to fuss. Mothers often sing to their babies—at least, they did in movies I'd seen and books I'd read—so I decided to give that a try.

I searched my mental inventory of song lyrics and realized the only ones I knew by heart were Ian Tyson tunes. I figured a newborn wouldn't know the difference between a lullaby and a drunken cowboy song, so I timidly started to sing.

"We were havin' a drink at Stockmen's, listenin' to the guitars ring, Jesse said 'You know, they sold the MC horses…'"

By the time I sang the chorus twice and cussed once because it was part of the song, my milk let down. The sensation was unmistakable even to a rookie mom. The left side of my chest suddenly ached clear up to my shoulder. All at once, a strong spray of milk shot into the plastic bottle attached to the pump. I removed the suction device and quickly held Grace in its place.

Please work, I silently prayed. *Please, please, please let this work.* Whatever happened in the next few minutes was crucial to my ability to nourish my infant.

Grace started to reflexively cry, then tasted a big drop of milk. She quieted down and rooted in earnest. Her efforts were finally rewarded with a big swallow of milk, then another, followed by yet another. Her brow unfurrowed, and her eyes rolled back in her head before gently closing to settle in for the duration of the nursing session.

Jim popped his head through the bedroom door.

"Hey, how's it going?" he asked.

"Great," I smiled. "She's actually nursing."

"Good job," he said and gave me a double thumbs up. "Do you need anything? Maybe a glass of water?"

"Sure, water would be great." Breastfeeding brought on a powerful thirst unlike any I'd ever experienced before.

I leaned back into the glider cushions and smiled. For the first time since her birth, my shoulders felt no tension that I needed to consciously will away. I felt warm, full, and happy as Grace pulled nourishment from my body. For the first time in her five days of life, she fell asleep with the sensation of a full belly.

CHAPTER 8 ✳ **Baby Blues in a Snow-White Winter**

I took one last look at Grace laying in her Rock'n Play before I softly closed the front door. She was still sound asleep. Good. I desperately needed a breath of fresh air, but the outside temperature was too cold for a newborn. Grace was full of milk, swaddled in a flannel blanky, and wearing a knit cap. She would be cozy and safe while her mama walked up and down the lane a couple times.

The frigid January air was brutal and burned the inside of my nostrils every time I inhaled. My nose hairs froze together with each breath, which told me it was less than twenty degrees, a fun fact I'd learned during junior year of college in Bozeman, Montana. I shoved my hands in my coat pockets and headed up the lane. I walked slowly for fear of slipping on the uneven piles of frozen snow and ridges of ice. The incision from my C-section still pulled a bit, but I eased along and looked around. I hadn't seen much of anything besides the inside of the trailer since Grace was born. It was good to know the trees were still there, as were the barbed wire fences and fields beyond. The grass was brown and the trees were bare, but birds still flew from branch to branch. I could hear the engines of ranch pickups and tractors in the distance. There was still life beyond my newly limited existence after all.

I walked to the intersection of the main dirt lane leading from the county road to the manager's house, then turned around to head back and check on Grace. If I poked my head in the door on my way by as I walked the lane, I could check on her roughly every five minutes. She wouldn't have to cry for very long if she woke up during my brief period of escape.

On my second lap up the lane, my thoughts turned to what life was like before I'd had Grace. I thought about dancing at the bar in Texas with Jim, the time I got drunk and wore his ball cap backward. How we stayed out till two in the morning on New Year's Eve, roped calves together all day, and spent all our money on plane tickets and fancy French dinners for Valentine's Day. We did what we wanted whenever we wanted, knowing a new paycheck would show up every two weeks with enough money for beer, food, and gas to get us through till the next one arrived. We didn't have to spend money on diapers, baby wipes, or hospital bills.

But on December nineteenth, everything had changed—Grace was born. Now, I walked the worn linoleum floors in the house around the clock while breastfeeding, changing diapers, finding blankets, and shushing her back to sleep. I couldn't rest until I had convinced a resistant infant to go to sleep, and I was yanked from my slumber every time she stirred and cried, which occurred at irregular intervals of three minutes to four hours.

More than anything, I wanted to return to those carefree days when Jim and I were dating, back when I had a boyfriend and was a girlfriend and he wore his spurs to the dance hall and I drank house wine and we never finished watching *Far and Away* even though we started it a dozen times.

But those days were gone; we would never have them back. Now, we were jointly responsible for a tiny, helpless infant who looked like him and needed me.

I trudged up the lane, looking down to judge the footing and carefully pick my path. At the corner before the cowboss' house, my neighbor opened her door to say hello. I'd hardly seen her, but I knew her name was Samantha. She was around my age and had two little girls. Her husband was Shorty, a longtime Rafter J employee over on the farm crew side.

"Hi," Samantha called from the porch. "I have some baby clothes I've been meaning to give you. My girls outgrew them and we aren't having any more kids, so I thought maybe you could use them." She held up a bulging black garbage bag.

"Thank you," I said. I paused in the cold before walking over to her. "We'll definitely use them."

"No problem. How is everything going?"

I looked at her and didn't answer right away. I turned my gaze back down at the ground because I could feel the tears coming. They were always just behind my eyes these days, and now they were ready to spill over.

"I'm okay," I replied. Then, "Taking care of a baby is really hard."

"I know, it can be a lot to take in," Samantha said with understanding in her eyes.

I spilled my guts right then and there in the ice-covered driveway of my two-doors-down neighbor that I didn't even know.

"I just cry all the time. I don't want to—I mean, I'm happy I have her, but I'm just so tired. And the days are so short and she doesn't sleep worth a darn. I feel so sad and don't know why."

Samantha leaned on the porch railing, seemingly unconcerned with the freezing temperature.

"Yeah, it can be really tough. I had a really hard time with my last baby, too. Honestly, I had thoughts of putting the kids in their car seats and driving my car over the edge of the gravel pit and just ending it all. So I went to therapy and that helped a lot."

Samantha's story made me recall my own dark thoughts. I half-wished I never even had a baby. I wouldn't miss her if I'd never met her. I didn't tell Samantha that I woke up every night pawing at the blankets, convinced that I'd fallen asleep with Grace on my chest and that she'd suffocated. I pulled away blanket after blanket, trying to grab the dead baby I couldn't reach. At some point, I'd either sit up or stand beside the bed, digging through the covers until Jim woke up, when he would point to the Rock 'n Play at the foot of the bed and loudly say, "Look, she's right there." Then I'd look at her doll-like face, snug in her fleece sleep sack and pink knit cap, and crawl back under the covers to snatch as many minutes of slumber as I could manage with the sensation of a dead newborn on my chest until the actual newborn cried and woke me up again.

"Thanks again for the clothes," was all I said. I hefted the black plastic bag by its handle tie.

"You're welcome. I have a baby swing that might still work and some toys I'll have Shorty bring down later."

Samantha went back inside her trailer and I turned back to mine. I didn't cry as I walked home. Samantha seemed content and capable of caring for her two young girls, so maybe there was hope for me yet. She hadn't frowned or scolded me for my sadness. My worst fear was that I would confess my dark thoughts and someone—my doctor, a nurse at the hospital, a friendly neighbor—would declare me an unfit mother and take away my baby. Even though I wasn't sure I was glad I had a baby, I knew I couldn't be separated from her.

Click. Click. I zoomed in and snapped pictures of Grace's chubby cheeks. They looked extra plump squished between the car seat's newborn insert and the top buckle of the harness. I zoomed out to capture the entire car seat in the picture and pressed the shutter of my Canon PowerShot a few more times. *Click click click.*

"Awww, she looks so cute in her little beanie hat," I said to Jim. Behind me in the kitchen, he filled insulated cups with hot coffee as I fawned over our three-week-old in the living room. She looked so snug and cozy tucked beneath her pink-and-blue blanket. I zipped the weatherproof cover over her car seat and stood up.

"Ready?" Jim asked. He handed me an oversized purple go-cup and grabbed the car seat handle.

"Yes," I said with more assurance than I felt. I pulled the hood of my puffy vest over my head and walked toward the front door.

My husband was taking me and our baby daughter on a family trip to a nearby cow pasture, but I wasn't sure I was ready to leave the house. He told me that getting out would be good for me. Deep down I knew he was right. I had cried every day since we brought Grace home from the hospital. I usually cried several times daily. Sundown was guaranteed to bring a wave of sadness that broke into uncontrollable sobbing. I didn't call my doctor and tell him my symptoms, though I'd picked up the phone to dial his office a few times. I always talked myself out of it before I could press a button. I thought it was normal for new moms to feel more sadness than joy. I'd never had a baby before, and the only other mom I'd talked to in person recently, Samantha, had described similar feelings, so I just assumed that resenting your newborn and wishing you'd never had her was part of motherhood.

And underneath it all was that deep fear that if I confessed to feeling completely overwhelmed, someone would take away my baby.

Besides crying to Jim and mechanically going about the tasks of feeding, burping, changing, and bathing baby Grace, I called my mom almost daily. Sometimes I didn't even say hello when she answered the phone. I simply started crying as soon as she picked up.

"It's important that you keep talking about your feelings. That will help you feel better," she said. "I'll be up there in a couple weeks."

I desperately wanted my mom to come to me as quickly as a plane could fly. I needed her to help me learn to be a mom—to show me how to safely hold my soft, limp newborn against my shoulder or give her a sponge bath without her rolling off the counter.

In the meantime, here we were, with Jim stopping by mid-morning on a workday insisting that I bundle up the baby and go for a drive with him. He told me I could just sit in the pickup if I wanted, but I needed to get some fresh air and see something besides the inside of our house.

I smiled as I settled into the passenger seat and watched Jim strap the car seat into the back. The engine had been running for a while and the cab was toasty warm. When I peeked beneath the car seat cover, I saw that Grace was already sound asleep. I looked through the windshield and noticed the bright sunlight sparkling on the snow's crust. A hard frost lingered on the bare tree limbs lining the lane, making it look like our world was covered with tiny crushed diamonds.

"Wow, it's really pretty out here," I said. "Cold, but pretty."

"Yep," said Jim. "Definitely cold. I've had icicles in my beard all morning."

I grinned and glanced over at him, checking for remnants of miniature ice shards. It was good to see him during his workday. I had been so used to riding along with him before my pregnancy.

"So, where are we off to today, Cap'n?" I asked.

"I found a rawhide cow I need to shoot," Jim replied.

Oh.

And here I'd thought we were just going for a leisurely drive around the ranch to admire fuzzy calves and shimmering ice crystals. Now I knew our outing would result in a bovine death, a steaming carcass, and a bloody hide tossed into the bed of the pickup.

It was every new mother's ideal day trip.

"What happened to her?" I willed myself to ask.

"Starved down," Jim said matter-of-factly. "Winter kill."

Like many working cowboys, Jim braided rawhide horse gear for both his own use and to sell for extra income. He knew how to skin a cow and prepare the rawhide for braiding, and he'd noticed the emaciated cow earlier that morning. The cold was too extreme and the feed too scarce for her to recover. She was probably an older cow whose teeth had started to break, hindering her ability to eat. The most humane thing to do was to end her misery.

The pickup bumped over the frozen ruts of the snow-covered dirt road that led through the pasture. We drove past a row of cattle with their heads down, eating from the line of hay Jim had thrown out earlier that morning. I looked out the window, searching for the dying cow but not really sure I wanted to see her.

Jim turned the pickup off the road to the left, and then there she was. The red cow lay flat on her side, unable to lift her head at the sound of the approaching engine. Jim shifted into park, left the engine running so Grace would stay warm, and stepped out of the cab. He loaded six bullets into a .22 pistol.

"You coming?" he asked.

"Sure," I said uncertainly and stepped onto the frozen ground. I didn't look forward to seeing an animal weakened to the point of euthanasia, but I also didn't want to seem like a coward. Ranching was full of life, death, and everything in between, and a person had to learn to take it all in stride.

My breath puffed out in front of my face as we walked the few steps over to the red cow. The sound of the pistol's report cracked through the thin high desert air. For some reason, the .22 shells didn't do their usual job, so Jim wound up unloading all six bullets in the cow's brain before she finally died.

The first part of the job done, now it was onto the skinning. Jim pulled out his razor-sharp pocketknife and began cutting the dead cow's thick hide. I turned away. I knew she had no use for it anymore, but I'd always been squeamish about blood. Looking at a carcass's complex system of muscles, veins, and tendons held no attraction for me.

After several minutes, Jim folded the cow hide into a rough square and threw it in the back of the truck. It was still warm and pliable. The fresh hide would end up in our chest freezer alongside packages of ground beef and ready-made ravioli until he had time to further process it into rawhide.

The car seat cover began to ripple when we got back into the pickup, and I heard Grace start to fuss. I reached around from the front seat and unbuckled her straps.

"Hi there, little sweetie," I cooed. "Did somebody wake up hungry?"

I unzipped my vest as Grace stuffed her fists into her mouth and wailed in frustration. I quickly settled her to my breast, where her cries were replaced with grunts, which soon turned into rhythmic swallowing. I cradled her head in the crook of my arm and stroked her tiny foot through her sleeper with my other hand. Jim pointed the truck toward the house, where I knew I would step through the front door and reenter my new world of diaper changes, baby spit-up, cradle cap, night-wakings, and fatigue. But for the first time in weeks, I didn't dread all these tasks.

"You ready to go back, Mama?" Jim asked.

"Yep," I said. "Take me home."

The ground was still frozen and the air bitterly cold, but I was ready to get back in the saddle for the first time since giving birth. Jim caught and saddled Teaks for me. He'd first let me ride the big sorrel gelding when we were dating, and I immediately fell in love—with the horse. He was gentle and steady, but also fast and beautiful. I'd liked Teaks so much that Jim had told me I could have him—on the condition that if we broke up, ownership reverted back to Jim. Now that we were married, I had no intention of giving up my favorite horse. I'd been looking forward to getting on him again ever since I quit riding in my third trimester.

Jim stood just outside the wooden corral with baby Grace bundled up in the stroller beside him. Another Rafter J cowboy, Dan Gaspar, hung out near the fence with us just for something to do on a cold afternoon.

My body felt good and nothing hurt when I caught the left stirrup with my foot and swung into the saddle. The leather seat was smooth and comfortable, just like I remembered. Almost like I'd never left.

Teaks was still green, but he was good-natured and never bucked, so he was the perfect get-back-in-the-saddle project for me. He needed a little bit of help and support from his rider to lope a balanced circle and stop correctly, but he wasn't a silly, unpredictable colt. I reminded myself to breathe evenly and relax my shoulders. I tended to hold tension in my shoulders when I rode, which made my horse perform poorly and my muscles ache the next day. So I took deep breaths, looked where I wanted to go, and squeezed Teaks into a nice easy jog. I let the rhythm of his long, comfortable stride shift my hips side to side in the saddle with my heels down and lower back relaxed, just like I used to do every day without thinking twice.

I trotted past Grace in her stroller and couldn't help but glance in.

"Don't worry about the baby, she's fine," Jim called.

He was right. I knew he was right. I looked up, sat deep in the saddle, and stopped Teaks in one easy motion. I turned him around to trot the other way. The ground was frozen hard so I kept it slow.

But I looked at Grace again as we passed by. Dan's dog was sniffing around the stroller wheels and it looked like he might lift a leg at any second. I forgot about my relaxed shoulders and perfect stops and imagined the cur peeing all over my baby's portable bed on wheels.

"Hey, can someone call that dog?" I asked the guys as politely as I could manage. I directed the order thinly disguised as a question to no one in particular so as not to assign blame to any one person. But if Dan's dog pissed on my kid's stroller, I was going to kill him.

Dan, being a nice young man who possessed both common sense and common courtesy, immediately called the offending animal to his side. But every time I passed the stroller from then on, I craned my neck to look inside and make sure Grace wasn't fussing or crying. I clearly couldn't trust her father and a family friend to keep an eye on her. If they had the audacity to stand by with their hands in their pockets while a well-mannered dog walked near the stroller, who knew what other acts of child neglect they were capable of committing?

Jim admonished me to focus on my horse and not worry about the baby for the remainder of my ride. I wanted to enjoy the feel of the leather and motion of a horse's stride once more. I wanted to do something I used to do before becoming a mother, feel more like me again, return to my old self.

But as I trotted around and stared at the stroller, I realized I would never again return to my old self. Even if I wanted to ride all day, which I did, and had someone nearby to watch the baby for me, which I didn't, I couldn't saddle up in the dark and ride off with the cowboy crew. Every time I laid Grace down after a nursing session, it was as if someone turned an hourglass over and when all the sand ran out, it was time to nurse again. The longest interval that I could handle between nursing sessions was about four hours. After that, my breasts got rock-hard and started to ache.

I was definitely not like the other cowboys on the crew anymore.

After a few more laps around the corral, I stepped off Teaks and Jim helped me unsaddle at the barn. I patted the gelding's neck under his long red mane, grateful for a chance to hang out with my old buddy and smell sweet horse sweat once again. Then I pushed the stroller to the house to nurse and cry because I knew there was absolutely no way I could physically handle a ten-hour day in the saddle away from my little flannel bundle with the pink knit cap.

CHAPTER 9 ✳ I Can't Live Here

I was cleaning the kitchen after breakfast one cold March morning when Jim came home a few minutes after leaving for work and told me he no longer had a job. Momentarily stunned, I asked him why. He shrugged.

"Chris said he heard I didn't like the way he was doing things, so I should probably leave."

I thought I knew what had happened. We'd gone to a ranch rodeo in Winnemucca over the weekend, where Jim had vented his low opinion of his boss to a friend near the beer garden. Chris's father-in-law, the Rafter J manager, probably overheard the conversation and relayed it to Chris.

Maybe Chris and Jim should have discussed their differences. Jim probably should have kept his loud drunk mouth shut in public. In a regular workplace, somebody would have filed a written complaint and waited out the three-strike policy. But ranches don't have a human resources department and nobody cares if you get your feelings hurt.

Jim made over a dozen phone calls without securing another job. Staying at a ranch where we no longer belonged wasn't encouraged, so we left after about a week without a clear destination in mind. We dropped off our horses at a friend's pasture, shoveled manure out of the horse trailer, stuffed it full of all our worldly possessions, threw a tarp over the whole thing, and parked it at another friend's house. Then we drove to California to visit my dad.

Within a week, Jim found a job at the Panther Creek Ranch, right on the Nevada-Idaho border. We arrived at our new home on a muddy spring morning. Jim carried moving boxes from the horse trailer past where I stood on a cracked sidewalk in the yard.

"I can't live here," I whispered as he walked by.

He paused by my side for a moment, holding a cardboard box marked *"Kitchen—FRAGILE"* in big Sharpie letters. I'd marked most of the boxes *FRAGILE*, even the ones that contained Tupperware and baby diapers. I didn't want my few things to get broken.

"We have to make it work," he said. "We don't have any other options."

I knew Jim was right. We were lucky he'd found a job so quickly since our little family needed both the income and housing it would provide. But I was worried about the house's location. It was at the bottom of a steep canyon with cliffs on three sides. Rimrock crowded in directly behind the kitchen, limiting the view out the north windows to solid rock. The steep cliffs shortened daylight hours by at least an hour. I really liked sunlight and missed it already. Sunlight prevented me from sliding too deep into the seasonal depression that had plagued me for years. Sunrises were glorious and sunsets divine.

I knew I'd never see a sunrise or sunset as long as we lived there.

Jim continued to unload moving boxes. I picked up another one and followed him into our new home. The squat white house had been built in the late 1800s and had walls that were eighteen inches thick. It had been slowly modernized over the years to include an upstairs office with midcentury shag carpet and a bathroom. The original floor plan predated indoor plumbing, and the bathtub was crammed awkwardly under the staircase. Jim would later discover he couldn't stand upright in it. The vanity across from the tub was coated in thick drips of dried blue-and-white toothpaste. (And we'd eventually learn that the previous occupants' little kids had flushed a onesie down the toilet and clogged the pipes leading to the septic system, which created a foul aroma just outside our bedroom window.)

Two bedrooms were downstairs and to the left of the front door. The first one was really small, and the second one was slightly larger but still small by modern standards. It featured a built-in wardrobe in one corner. The wardrobe was about three feet wide and had swinging double doors up top and two drawers down below. People in previous eras didn't require as much storage space as most folks do today, probably because they didn't have as many things. A modern closet with sliding doors and a rod for hanging shirts had been added later along another wall.

The kitchen was open and cavernous, with a washer and dryer wedged awkwardly but prominently between the fridge and counter. An old wood-fired cookstove sat unused in the corner. The stove pipe was missing, but the hole in the ceiling remained gaping to the sky above. A white five-gallon bucket on the roof covered the hole, but it shifted every time the wind blew. Leaves and twigs circled down onto the stovetop.

"Sorry the place is such a mess. I meant to have it cleaned before you guys got here," said Nels Arneson. He managed the Panther Creek Ranch and had met us at the house to show us in. He was an old friend of Jim's, and at six foot five, he was also one of the few people I'd met who was taller than my husband.

"It's okay, we're just gonna track mud in with all these trips in and out of the house anyway," I replied. We were here, it was dirty, and complaining wouldn't help anyway.

I kept my eyes on the sidewalk and walked back to the horse trailer to grab another box. The house was old and cobbled together with an assortment of additions, but at least it had a solid foundation and the ground was not visible through the floor. There was, however, a pile of cat poop in one of the bedrooms. Animal feces on the carpet was becoming a disturbing trend in my as-of-yet limited experience with ranch housing. But no matter—I could scrub it up well enough to suit our needs.

I'd traded a cramped trailer house that should have been condemned and wide-open spaces for a run-down but historical home shoved in the bottom of a box canyon with limited visibility. The situations were very different, but I wasn't yet sure if I'd traded up.

Nels and Jim headed out to camp a few days later for an overnight trip to check fences before turning cattle out for the spring. Nels' wife, Denise, was in California visiting her folks with their toddler son.

I would be alone on the ranch.

"You should be fine," Nels said. "I'm sure nobody will bother you. I mean, there used to be an old Indian who would come over here from the Rez once in a while and just stand there when someone opened the door, but I don't think he ever hurt anybody."

I didn't say anything, because all my internal systems had ceased to function. Was Nels for real? The Duck Valley Paiute-Shoshone Indian Reservation was two hours away by dirt road. An unannounced visit by a resident—or anyone else, for that matter—was plausible. But would some random old guy actually show up and silently stare me down in my own doorway?

I started breathing again and recovered my ability to speak.

"Are you serious?" I asked.

"What? Oh, I mean, there was an old guy who came over from the Rez once or twice."

"Now I'm afraid to stay here by myself." I didn't want to sound like a little kid, but Nels had me spooked.

"Nah, don't worry. I'm sure you'll be fine."

Easy for Nels to say. He stood nearly seven feet tall and had the arm span of a mountain gorilla. He could probably reach around an intruder and tie him up with his own shirtsleeves. I, on the other hand, craned my neck to look up at everyone except school children. I was also responsible for the care and protection of a tiny, helpless infant who would most likely be useless in launching a defensive attack against an armed trespasser.

I didn't want to come across like some paranoid sissy who couldn't handle a night alone in the country, so I kept all further questions to myself and didn't mention it again. I figured I would just be ready to bust an unwelcome visitor's skull with a Maglite, give the baby a switchblade, and hope for the best.

I kissed Jim goodbye and wished him a fun trip. I watched the company truck and trailer disappear over the rim of the canyon and hoped I'd live to see him again.

Later that night, darkness settled in with a completeness known only to wild animals and people who live way off the grid. The creaking of the old house and the rustling of pine tree branches on the roof convinced me that an intruder would be on my doorstep any second. He was probably loading his gun as he walked across the driveway.

The closest "neighbor" was forty-five minutes away in the no-horse town of Jarbidge, a thirteen-mile journey over a dirt road that hugged the river and openly embraced many large potholes. It featured drop-off cliffs and an assortment of boulders. Even if I knew anyone's number in Jarbidge, which I didn't, and the unreliable landline phone actually worked, which it sometimes didn't, help would arrive no sooner than one hour. My calculations included fifteen minutes for the person I didn't know and wasn't going to call to get dressed, use the restroom, put on some shoes, and fill a reusable water bottle for the drive. I'm a considerate hypothetical victim.

I got ready for bed and realized the hundred-year-old front door didn't have a lock. I stared at the brass knob and monitored it for the slightest sign of turning. I sat in Jim's green recliner across the living room and held the baby with a rifle propped in the corner. I probably should have held the .243 and propped the baby in the corner, but fear had addled my brain.

Grace developed a cough during the night and provided her mother with another thing to worry about. I held her to my shoulder, stared at the doorknob, patted her back, stared at the doorknob, shushed her to sleep, held her to my shoulder, and patted her back again, all the while staring at that smooth brass orb.

The wind rattled the door in its frame a few times, but the knob never turned. I was never so glad for the company of the morning sun, late as it arrived to our side of the cliffs.

A few weeks later, we stopped off at Lone Mountain Station on our way home from Elko to visit some friends and celebrate our return to Elko County. I sat around the corner of the bar from Jim's longtime friend and fellow career cowboy, Kris Garzone. We made small talk and he cooed at baby Grace, who sat on my lap and waved her chunky arms spastically. They let babies in bars in northern Nevada because that's the main gathering spot for locals of all ages. Bartenders don't have enough customers to turn away families with young children, so kids grow up knowing to keep walking past the slot machines or Mama will slap their hands. (They might look like video games, but it's a five-thousand-dollar fine if a kid gets caught playing them.)

Garzone was short and squat, built like a brick with olive skin and a big salt and pepper mustache. He stared at the rows of glass bottles behind the bar during a lull in our conversation about the springtime weather, then sat up straighter on his barstool and turned to face me.

"You know what?" he said. "I'm going to give you a horse for your wedding present."

Garzone looked over his shoulder toward Jim. His eyes gleamed with amazement at his own brilliant idea.

"I have a sorrel mare that would be just perfect for you. I'm just going to give her to you, that's what I'm going to do."

I wasn't sure how to respond to this generous gift from a man I had just met. I knew that Jim and Kris were longtime friends, so receiving a wedding gift from him didn't strike me as out of the ordinary. But a horse? That seemed extravagant, especially for a cowboy. Horses could be worth a lot of money. Selling a well-trained, experienced ranch horse was one way a working cowboy could supplement his meager income. I wondered how much this mare was worth, how many much-needed dollars Kris was sacrificing by this display of generosity to his friend's new bride. I couldn't wait to tell Jim.

"Thank you," I said with astonishment. "That's so nice of you!"

"Don't mention it," he said with a wide grin.

Kris turned to order another beer. I stood up from my barstool, baby in arms, and hurried to a nearby table where Jim was drinking beer with other friends and telling stories.

"Jim!" I exclaimed. "Kris just gave me a horse! Can you believe that? He said it's a wedding present. Wasn't that nice of him?"

Jim settled further back in his chair as his eyes turned toward Kris, who was still seated at the long wooden bar. Jim's eyes were glassy from a beer buzz, but they held a glint that was stronger than alcohol.

"Oh, really?" he asked. "Kris gave you a horse, did he?"

"Yeah," I replied, still feeling rich from our new acquisition. "A sorrel mare. He just gave her to me!"

By now all the other cowboys at the table had heard our conversation. They stopped talking and started to smile at Jim, who was not smiling.

"What's the matter?" I asked. "Why aren't you excited?"

"Why do you think he gave us that horse?" he asked. "It probably isn't because she's so nice to ride and he really likes her."

"But it's a free horse," I stammered. "And your friend wouldn't give your wife a bad horse, would he?"

Jim looked down at the wood plank floor and carefully considered his next words. He clearly knew something I didn't.

"I've known Kris for fifteen years. If that mare was any good, he'd be ridin' her himself. She must be an ol' rip if he just injected her into my string."

The pieces of the puzzle slowly fit together in my brain.

"And you can't say no to a wedding gift to your wife?" I asked weakly.

Jim nodded. His words sank in and I began to understand a little more about the ways of men. Jim caught Kris' eye across the room. He shook his head and smiled. Then he mouthed the words *You son of a bitch*, but he wasn't mad. Kris responded with a broad smile and lifted his beer, presumably to Jim's good health and ability to ride his wife's new bronco. The crowd at the table laughed and someone motioned for the bartender to bring another round.

The Rancho Grande crew turned up at the Panther Creek a couple weeks later for two days of branding calves. Kris sent my new mare over in the trailer with them.

Rolly Lisle, manager of the Grande, was a good cowboy and a longtime friend of ours. He offered a few words of advice as the crew unloaded their horses.

"Watch that sorrel mare," he said. "She'll run by and try to kick you when the cavvy comes into the corral. She'll bite you if you're not paying attention. I wouldn't trust her, and I wouldn't turn my back on her."

Rolly typically focused on the good points of every man or beast, so his words filled my stomach with dread. Yep, it looked like Kris really had gotten Jim good in this horse trade prank.

"What's her name?" I asked weakly.

"Garzone calls her Ho O'lena," Rolly said.

Jim looked down and nodded as if to say, *That's about right.* It seemed the mare was named after the well-known Quarter Horse sire Doc O'lena, with the word "ho" tacked on in front because apparently she was one. Or maybe she was named after the song "Hey Ho Alina." Either way, the fact the mare's name included the word "ho" seemed like a bad sign.

I took Jim aside after all the horses were turned loose for the night.

"I don't think we should even keep her. She sounds too dangerous. I don't want you to get hurt," I pleaded.

Jim remained unfazed by Rolly's words of caution. The mare was pretty much just what he'd expected, and she was far from his first bronco.

"Don't worry, I'll be okay," he said. "She's probably not that bad once I get around her a little bit."

Ho O'lena was still treacherous after three months of regular riding. She was prone to kick when being saddled, shod, led, or looked at by a cowboy or other living creature. Jim tied a hind leg up when he shod her. I was afraid to get near her in the corral and kept my distance when I walked through the pasture pushing Grace in her stroller.

Jim had another bronco in his string, a yellow-and-white Paint gelding. He received the gelding by trading a pair of rawhide reins and a Gene Klein bit on an impulse while traveling home from a rodeo, so he named his new mount after the bit maker. Gene was a tall horse with a gentle eye who appeared mellow, even lazy, on the ground, but he bucked hard at inconvenient times throughout the day.

A cowboy can forgive a horse that bucks first thing in the morning, especially if the horse is young or the morning is cold. The horse usually settles down as the workday progresses and he has an opportunity to use his energy in more productive ways. But Gene bucked at random times, usually when Jim was least expecting it. He bucked halfway through the day or just after Jim roped a calf, when he should be focusing on the job at hand instead of pitching around. Gene was good at bucking, too—good enough that Jim tied his stirrups together underneath his saddle using a thin leather strap with a snap on each end. This eliminated most of the movement of his stirrup leathers and gave him a more secure seat. But Gene was smarter than the average bronco. He learned to buck only when Jim unsnapped his feet.

Jim had mentioned Gene's random bucking enough to worry me. He spent the better part of his working hours riding by himself, far from headquarters with no cell phone service. If he got bucked off and was badly hurt, help might not arrive until his saddled horse ran back to the barn and Nels or I somehow backtracked through the sagebrush, trees, rocks, and canyons and found him.

I brought up my concerns one evening in the living room of our weird old ranch house. I sat on the tan microfiber couch with double recliners that I'd bought at the St. Vincent de Paul thrift store in Twin Falls. They'd marked it at five hundred and twenty-five dollars, but I wasn't going to pay half a thousand dollars for a used sofa. I'd negotiated the clerk down to three hundred and twenty-five and hauled it home. Jim gently rocked in his green corduroy La-Z-Boy.

"I love you and don't want you to get hurt," I said. "I know you can ride Ho O'lena and Gene, but should you? It's not just you anymore. Grace and I are depending on you. We'd really be in a jam if something happened to you."

"I'll be fine," Jim said. "I have to ride something to work, and a cowboy just has to ride a bronco once in a while."

I dropped the subject for a couple weeks. Then one day, I overheard Jim on the phone with Anna Severe, a ranch wife and saddlemaker who lived an hour up the road at the Jack Ranch. He was placing an order for a new pair of stirrup leathers.

"One of mine broke when a horse I was riding bucked downhill so hard that it ripped the stirrup leather right out of the saddle," he told Anna.

My eyes narrowed. A horse bucking while running downhill is extra dangerous, because he is more likely to fall or even somersault with his rider still in the saddle.

I sat quietly until Jim hung up the phone.

"I thought you said you rode Gene that day?"

"Yeah, I did," he said.

"But you didn't say anything about him bucking that hard."

"I didn't want you to worry."

"But I am worried. That is, like, really bad, honey."

Jim was quiet for a moment.

"I know," he said.

"Maybe it's time to think about getting rid of them," I suggested again.

I lumped Ho O'Lena in with Gene because the two horses were tied for the top spot on our list of dangerous animals we currently depended on to make a living.

"Selling them to another cowboy would just get someone else hurt. We can't trade them off to someone else and still feel good about ourselves," I continued.

"No," Jim agreed. "We can't do that. I'll call the rodeo team at CSI; maybe they could use Gene as a practice horse."

He called the rodeo coach at the College of Southern Idaho in Twin Falls. The coach said sure, bring your bronco in and we'll see if he bucks. If he bucked, Gene would make a good practice horse for the team to ride.

When the day of his tryout for a second chance arrived, Gene came out of the chute and kicked out his heels in a low-key fashion, then ran straight to the far fence. He didn't bog his head or buck hard enough to mention. The cowboys on the rodeo team tried him again, just to make sure the first trip wasn't a fluke. Gene loped off across the arena. He wasn't going to make the cut for the college rodeo team.

But I'd decided Gene also couldn't keep his spot in Jim's cowboy string. We unloaded him in the horse pasture until we could figure out a solution.

CHAPTER 10 ✳ Showdown at Jarbidge

I knew there would be trouble when Jim and Nels left the house that morning. They were headed to Jarbidge to lay a trap for a couple of mountain lion hunters. Ordinarily, they didn't have anything against hunters, but these two had run over and killed two of Nels' hound dog puppies on purpose. We knew this because the road grader said that he'd seen the guys chase the puppies down the road, where they were following their noses to track new scents, and run them down with their pickup.

One puppy died right away. The other one was suffering and mortally wounded, so the road grader mercifully ended his misery.

The bizarre killings disgusted and infuriated Nels and Jim. They notified a couple friends from North Fork and arranged to meet up at the Jarbidge bar, where they planned to wait for the killers to show up and then confront them.

"You want to come?" Jim asked me.

It was tempting to get out of the box canyon and see people, even if they · were barflies I didn't know and the air reeked like secondhand cigarette smoke, but I knew the whole affair would be fueled by alcohol and rash decisions. It would be nerve-racking to observe as a sober spectator. Plus, Grace had just started crawling. Keeping her from eating toothpicks and cigarette butts off the barroom floor would be a hassle.

"No, thanks, I think I'll stay here," I said.

"I think Brent is bringing Christy," Jim noted.

I wavered. A day of visiting with another woman was a rare opportunity indeed. I liked Christy and she was good company. But I imagined myself prying Grace's chubby arms off a slot machine while she screamed and digging a bottle cap out of her mouth with my index finger while the guys ordered another round. I stuck to my original decision.

"Tell her I said hi. Have fun and let me know how it goes."

Hours passed without a word from Jim. I wrote a first draft of a feature story so I could make my monthly deadline for the *Nevada Rancher*. I read the Associated Press website and scanned the headlines for story ideas. I built a foam block tower with Grace and fed her mashed green beans with a tiny plastic spoon. The pureed veggies were the subject of many jokes about the unappealing nature of baby food, but they were her favorite. She always ate at least one whole container.

I nursed Grace to sleep for her afternoon nap and dozed off for a few minutes while she slept draped over my lap on the couch. Dinnertime rolled around, and I fixed a plate for one. I began to wonder if and when I would hear from my husband.

I put Grace to bed and looked at the clock. It was getting late. Still no word from Jim. I was tired and wanted to turn in for the night, but I wasn't sure if no news was good news when your husband was at a remote bar looking for a fight.

It was almost eleven o'clock when the phone rang in the kitchen. I didn't recognize the number.

"Hello?" I asked.

"It's me," Jim said on the other end of the line. He was calling from the bar phone.

"Are you okay?" I asked. He sounded drunk, tired, and something else I couldn't name.

"Yeah, I'm fine," he said. "There was a gunfight, but the cops just left so we'll be comin' home pretty soon."

"A gunfight?" That didn't sound fine to me. "What happened?"

"We got there and those guys showed up. The big guy looked at Mitch and said, 'You boys lookin' to fight? We can have a fight. I've got guys all over in the bushes.' I put my glasses on the hood of their pickup, stepped past Mitch and said, 'Fuck you, motherfucker.' I bet no one's ever just stepped up to him."

I remained silent, waiting for Jim to continue to narrate the confrontation I was already glad I had missed.

"And then he got his gun. Brent was standing behind me saying, 'Come on, hit that fucker.' I didn't know he had his gun out, too. I turned around to leave. What could I do? I didn't have a gun. I knew I could knock him on his ass, but I wasn't positive I could knock him out.

"Then one of his friends snuck up behind me. I grabbed him by the throat and threw him on the ground, then kicked every bone in his body until all he could do was lie there and groan."

I flinched for the guy. He was on the opposing side, but still.

"Then the other guy pulled a rifle out and went to shooting rounds off," Jim continued. "Me and Brent ducked down in front of the pickup. Brent had his gun cocked and yelled, 'Put that gun down or I'll blow the heads off everyone!' I was punching the window of the pickup, trying to break it and get in."

My eyebrows shot up. I could barely imagine our friend Brent threatening to shoot a bunch of strangers. But I also didn't understand why anyone would deliberately run over a couple of puppies, so I was probably just naive.

"The local lumber mill guy walked by and said, 'You want in that truck?' I said, 'Fuck yeah, I want in that truck,' and he smoked the window out with a handyman jack. I jumped in it and grabbed one guy around the throat and grabbed another guy with my other hand. I was yelling at him with my feet sticking out of the window when they started to drive off, so I let go."

A gunfight in a remote town with one dirt road populated by cowboys and renegades? Was this still the twenty-first century, the one with satellite TV and heart transplants? It appeared my life had taken a detour into the late 1800s.

"Then someone called the cops," Jim went on, "and they had to come all the way from Elko. We had to sit here and wait three hours for them to show up. They just did their reports and left, so we'll be heading home soon."

"Oh," I said, feeling nothing but more tired. "Okay. Well, I'll see you when you get here. Love you."

"Love you, too."

I hung up the phone and tucked into bed. A new-to-us king-sized mattress sat on our old queen-sized bedframe and was covered with twin-sized comforters. I was secretly glad to have it to myself for a few hours. Grace always ended up in our bed at some point during the night and was kind of a bed hog. Jim and I usually fought over the blankets in our sleep since none of them were big enough to completely cover the mattress, so my nights consisted of less sleeping and more kicking and sleepy shouts of, "No, that's mine!"

Sometime during the night, Jim slipped into bed next to me. The next morning, he mentioned that he thought a wife would be a little more concerned when her husband called and said he was the only unarmed man in a gunfight.

"You stomped on the guy's throat and then they all drove off. It sounded like you had it under control, so I went to bed."

Jim shrugged, put his cowboy hat on his head, and walked out the door to catch a horse for the day.

"Love you," I called.

"Love you, too."

CHAPTER 11 ✳ Good Old Days

I loaded Grace up in her car seat, threw the diaper bag on the floorboards, and climbed up behind the steering wheel. My camera bag sat on the passenger seat. The sun was shining, my magazine work was done for the day, and I was taking my Canon PowerShot on an adventure.

I drove a few miles down the dirt road through the Panther Creek Desert to an old homestead that always piqued my interest when I drove past. Grace was asleep by the time I arrived, which worked perfectly into my plan. I left her snoozing in the pickup while I slung my camera around my neck and walked through the dried grass and tall brush surrounding the dwelling ruins.

The buildings were made of logs and in various stages of falling down. The main cabin was mostly intact, so I walked through the door frame. It was a single narrow room about ten feet wide and twenty-five or thirty feet long. An old metal frame and bedspring mattress decayed to the coils in one corner suggested where the former sleeping space was. A low table and wooden cabinet hinted at the kitchen area. A lone shelf was attached to the wall above the table.

I thought about my kitchen with two long countertops and over a dozen cabinets. I had under-sink storage, an attached storeroom, and an attic. The person who lived in this house had a shelf.

I looked out the small window near the shelf. The glass had long since been broken, if it even had glass in the first place. This cabin was of the hand-hewn sort, more likely to feature a piece of greased paper over the window opening. Over a hundred years later, the view through the window was still fantastic. I saw tall sagebrush, remnants of an old log corral, and mountains in the distance. I took a picture from inside the window facing out. The result was a disappointing image with a too-dark interior and a washed-out view of the sagebrush. I took another picture, then checked the little screen on the back of my camera. Another jarring, unequally exposed photo. I wished I knew what setting to adjust on the Canon to capture the scene and how it made me feel. Oh, well—at least I was there. Sometimes we don't get the keepsake picture, just the memory.

I surveyed my surroundings one more time. A small hole in the roof with a piece of flattened tin nailed around it told me where the wood stove used to be. I could imagine a wife lighting a fire, getting the salt down from the shelf, lying down on the bed in the corner at night, looking out the same window I had just looked through.

We probably had a lot in common, this mystery desert resident of centuries gone by and I. She probably enjoyed solitude, the reassurance of knowing you can get by on your own far from town. I bet she probably liked the smell of sagebrush and the sound of a breeze blowing through the trees by the creek before it reached the cabin.

Or maybe she was allergic to sagebrush and hated country life. She might have sneezed all spring and resented every blast of sand the wind kicked up. Maybe she dreamed of Broadway plays and hearing the clang and rattle of "those new-fangled horseless carriages that everyone was talking about." Perhaps she wished for a clean dress and a friend to take tea with on Sunday afternoons.

I certainly had a lot more luxuries than this ghost of the desert. I thought about the insulated walls of my home, lights that flicked on with a wall switch, and my electric clothes dryer. This rancher's wife had nothing but a six-inch-round log between her body and the bitter cold. Winters out here brought nighttime temperatures below zero, and the wind was no joke. I hated when the propane furnace kicked off and I felt a bit chilled for twenty minutes until it kicked on again. Whoever had lived in this cabin was not only tough, but determined.

I stepped back outside and walked to the next building. It was an outhouse that leaned sharply in one direction. Instead of logs, it was made of wooden planks. A scattering of holes on the outside had been repaired with flattened pieces of tin. Back in those days, people didn't do foolish things like throw away the can their beans came in. I snapped a picture of the whole building, then close-ups of the patched holes. The truth is often in the details.

I looked inside the door and saw a long wooden bench with two holes. That confirmed more than one person had lived here. I focused the Canon on the entire bench and took pictures from different angles. Grace was still sleeping peacefully, and I was having fun exercising my trigger finger.

Below the cabin was the barn. It was made of thicker logs than the other buildings and had a stouter roof. It was either built in a brushier spot or the sagebrush had grown up thicker around the ruins since it had been abandoned. Like most old barns, this one had me transfixed. Old homes are neat, but they always seem flimsy next to the sturdiness of old barns—buildings meant to hold cattle and horses, living things that were substantial in size and invaluable to a family's survival way out here. The barn wasn't heated with a stove, so the walls were extra thick to keep out the frigid winter air.

I photographed the barn from various angles. The sunlight slanted through the exposed beams and sagebrush on the southwest end and invited me to play with framing the photo to capture the light just so. But my camera didn't have any dials to adjust the aperture—or if it did, I didn't know how to use them. "Aperture" was a new term I'd learned on the Pioneer Woman blog, back when she wrote haikus about dirty diapers and offered mom-to-mom amateur photography advice. Since I couldn't fine-tune my camera, I just set it on auto and pointed it at things I thought looked pretty. Other scenes didn't look all that pretty but they felt meaningful, so I kept pointing and shooting.

Eventually, I heard wails coming from the pickup.

"It's okay, Grace," I said, even though I knew she couldn't hear me. "Mama's comin'."

I turned off my camera and zipped it into its protective black case. My photography fun was over for the day, but that was okay. I drove back to my little white house and didn't feel so alone anymore. I didn't have real-life friends nearby to hang out with, but I could feel the presence of those who'd lived there before me. If they could hack it out here, so could I.

Two shed hunters showed up at the Panther Creek headquarters while Jim and Nels were out working on the ranch. It wasn't bow or rifle season, but hunters and outdoor enthusiasts liked to prowl around public land in the spring and search for "sheds," the antlers that deer and elk drop when they grow new, bigger replacements each year. Nels' wife Denise had again taken their son Royce to visit her parents in California. She seemed to do that quite a bit. I was jealous she got to leave so often, but I also felt a bit haughty that I stuck it out full-time in the isolated canyon we called home.

So I was the only adult at home on the day the shed hunters pulled up in a small pickup. The driver stepped out and strode toward the house like a man on a mission. I swung baby Grace onto my hip and walked outside to meet them in the driveway. The sound of their engine had broken the stillness of the canyon bottom and announced their arrival well before a knock on the door was necessary.

"Hi, is anyone around?" the first man asked.

He was heavyset, as was his friend. They both wore t-shirts and jeans over big bellies.

"No, everybody else is out working. It's just us here today."

I squeezed Grace a bit higher on my hip and tilted my cheek toward her peach-fuzz head. I hated telling strangers who showed up unannounced to my little home on the edge of the wilderness that I was alone. But I didn't see the point in saying, "Sure, my husband is home. He's inside cleaning his guns and sharpening his throwing hatchet. Did I mention he's six foot two?"

If I did that, we'd all just stand in the yard for a really long time waiting for a gigantic mountain man who wasn't going to show up.

"We found this baby calf abandoned by his mom and thought we'd drop him off," the man said. "His mama was nowhere around. He was just left in the bushes by the side of the road."

His chest puffed out and he pointed toward the black calf in the bed of the pickup like the hero he thought he was.

"Was the calf sleeping in the sagebrush?" I asked.

"Yes, and he was all by himself," the man said. "It's a good thing we found him, or he would've starved to death."

I read the situation differently.

"His mama was around, all right. She just left him in the brush so she could go graze and drink. That's what all these cows do. She would've come back for him."

I answered without a smile and hoped he'd realized what he'd done.

"Oh, no, there wasn't a cow in sight," he insisted. "He was abandoned."

"Cows leave their calves and go quite a ways sometimes. But she didn't abandon him," I replied.

I was growing exasperated with this man's lack of comprehension. Here I was, explaining what had actually happened in plain English backed by a lifetime of experience in the cattle industry, and he wasn't understanding it.

The man turned and walked to his pickup with the calf securely tied down in the back. He'd evidently decided there was no use explaining the situation to a simple housewife wearing denim shorts and flip flops with a baby on her hip.

"Is there a corral we can put him in until your husband gets home?" he asked.

I realized the pair remained undeterred in their mission to somehow aid the little calf. It was also too late to return the calf to the scene of his abduction and reunite him with his mother, if they could even recall and relocate the exact spot. She had likely already searched the sagebrush where she left him and discovered his absence. By now, she had probably moved onto nearby canyons and creeks looking for her missing baby, mooing as she trotted over rocks and anthills.

"Sure," I said. "Just go ahead and put him in that first corral across the creek."

"You should've seen when I grabbed him—man, he really came alive! The little guy almost kicked me. He's stronger than he looks."

The man laughed and shook his head at the recollection.

That's because he's healthy and strong from his mother's milk, I thought.

The hunters pulled into the pipe corral and turned the pickup around so it faced the gate. They let down the tailgate and hefted the newly minted "leppy," or motherless calf, to the ground. He stumbled a bit as he stood and walked around this new, unfamiliar patch of dirt. Blood circulation to his lower extremities was a bit slow to return after being trussed up like a Thanksgiving turkey and joy riding around the desert with Tweedle Dee and Tweedle Dum.

"I wonder why he's not drinking any water. Do you have any hay to give him?" the calfnapper asked.

"Well, he's never had anything but milk, so there probably isn't much point in giving him food and water," I said.

"Just make sure he has some hay to eat. Man, I'm sure glad we found this little guy and were able to get him over here."

It appeared that I could speak or not speak; either response had the same non-effect.

The hunters got in their pickup and started the ascent up the southern road, back the way they had come. I watched them go and listened to the sound of their engine fade once they topped out on the plateau and headed across the first sagebrush flat. They were probably smiling and high-fiving each other all the way to Elko. I just hoped they didn't see any more livestock on their drive home. The ranching community had enough trouble without random strangers delivering baby calves to the wrong ranchers. Because, as it turned out, the calf wasn't even from the Panther Creek's herd. He belonged to the neighbors.

The next day, Jim and I drove the leppy calf two hours to the neighbor's headquarters. No one was around the corrals, so we wrote a note of explanation and stuck the piece of paper to a nail on a board. I felt bad that they now had a calf to bottle-feed twice a day, plus they would lose money because he wouldn't gain as much weight on formula. But it wasn't our doing. Returning the calf and wishing him well was the best we could do at this point.

I unstrapped baby Grace from her car seat on the way home and pulled her up to the front seat with me and Jim. She was usually on my lap but sometimes moved to the floorboards or the console. There were so many buttons, levers, switches, and dials for a baby to explore in the cab of a pickup. Occasionally she'd wiggle her way onto her daddy's lap, where she tried to pull herself up on the steering wheel or stared at the buttons on the door panel with furrowed brows and puckered lips, rolling down the windows and locking-unlocking-locking all the doors.

We were some of the first motorists to traverse the dirt road that season, as it was barely springtime and the road wasn't maintained during the winter. The snow was usually too deep to even attempt driving a vehicle over the many miles of twisting, turning, straight-up-and-switchback-down-again road that linked the Panther Creek to Elko. I would have been nervous to make the drive by myself, but I felt confident with Jim at the wheel. He could handle anything that uncivilized stretch of road threw at us.

Light shone through the windshield and warmed my face with that good, full-strength spring sunshine. It wasn't as strong as midsummer but you could tell it was trying its hardest. Midday had just barely come and gone as we drove back home over the long, rutted road.

There was no cell phone service, which meant our drive was uninterrupted by piercing ringtones or pinging notifications. I tried to find a good FM radio station but turned the volume dial to zero when all I could pick up was static from southern Idaho. So we talked about people we knew, things they did, and how fun it was watching Grace change from a squirmy infant who kicked her feet and didn't know day from night to a mobile baby with distinct facial expressions. The pickup slowly crawled up each hill, down the other side, and puttered along the flats. We were in no hurry and had the entire desert to ourselves. It was a lazy diorama of tan hills, green brush, rushing creeks, hopping cottontails, and unhurried conversation.

"You know, people always talk about the good old days, but these are the good old days," I said to Jim.

"Yes, they are," he agreed. "Hey, don't touch that," he told Grace as she switched on the left turn signal. Grace grasped the steering wheel in her chubby hands and pulled herself up, standing straight on her daddy's lap and looking through the windshield. She wouldn't remember days like this, but her father and I would never forget them.

Horse roping is a big pastime in the Great Basin, and I decided I wanted to try. Roping horses is different from cattle in that the header ropes the horse around the neck, then the partner comes in and ropes the front feet. Unlike regular team roping, there are no field penalties for roping one leg. You either rope two feet and dally, or you slip a leg and don't go to the horn. Dallying on one foot isn't allowed because it runs a high risk of snapping the horse's leg.

Jim showed me how to throw a front-foot loop on a homemade sawhorse set up in the driveway. Grace observed the lessons from her perch in her stroller, usually with a sippy cup and plastic rattle attached to the tray. Front-footing horses was much different than heeling cattle, and you rode your horse to a different position before you threw your loop. You wanted to be perpendicular to the horse's shoulder and deliver a standing loop in front of his front legs. I practiced and practiced until I thought I was ready to try it out on a live animal.

At the McDermitt Fourth of July Ranch Hand Rodeo, we saddled up to enter the horse roping jackpot held after the event's conclusion. You might think that after two days of frying their brains and drowning their livers in the hot sun, the cowboys would be ready to pack it up and head home, but you'd be wrong. If there's a chance to rope horses, Great Basin guys will always stick around.

I left Grace in her playpen near the arena with a family friend while I warmed up Teaks. He was an experienced rope horse, but I was nervous as heck. I'd picked one of the most challenging arenas to make my debut as a front footer. McDermitt didn't have a specialized roping chute for horses, since you need one that's taller than the standard steer roping chute, so they just used the bucking chutes instead. A loose horse was turned out of a bucking chute and the ropers took off in hot pursuit, with the footer hazing the horse into position for the header. This resulted in all three horses careening full tilt around one corner and alongside the arena fence with the header and his horse running wide open to catch the loose one.

Once the horse was necked and brought to a trot or walk, the footer came around the front of their partner to the right-hand side of the horse, then threw a front-foot loop to snag two feet.

The initial burst of speed terrified me. Jim was riding the head horse, not me, but I would be close behind and caught up in the momentum. That was a lot of speed and thousands of pounds of horseflesh racing across the uneven arena dirt. It wasn't uncommon for horses to crash into the fence in the heat of the moment. But all I had to do was haze for Jim from a distance; then he would catch the horse, slow the whole thing down to a reasonable speed, and I could go in there and throw my loop.

We were positioned on our horses in front of the bucking chute when Jim nodded for the chute help to turn our horse loose. The horse took off like a shot and careened around the outside of the arena fence as anticipated. Jim raced his horse into position, threw his rope, and missed. He rebuilt while trailing the loose horse at a lope, threw his loop again, and missed again.

That was it. We were done. The pressure was off before it even started, because I never even got to throw my rope. Each team gets three loops per run. Since we'd burned two loops without securing the horse around the neck, we automatically received a no-time.

I reined Teaks in and coiled up my rope. I jogged to the out gate at the end of the arena, waited for the loose horse to exit into a small panel pen, then rode out of the arena behind Jim. He barely looked at me. His face was tense and his mouth was set in an unfriendly line. He held his reins with one hand and balled his other into a fist that he rested on his thigh. He rode Bob at a quick walk down the racetrack to the other end of the arena.

I glanced at Jim and mumbled an apology for my bad haze. I had no idea if that was the reason he missed, but I felt like I did something wrong. Otherwise, he wouldn't be so mad.

"It's okay, you did great," Jim said to the ground with his head partially turned toward me.

He stopped his horse alongside another cowboy and the two were soon talking and laughing. He gestured wildly with his hands like he always did when telling a story. I looked around at the other ropers waiting their turn. It was a ride-in jackpot, meaning you and your partner rode into the arena, the secretary noted your faces and wrote down your names, and you paid your entries at the end. You could rope with the same partner twice, but you had to switch ends. That meant I wasn't going to rope with Jim anymore, since I wasn't anywhere near experienced enough to try roping one of these big, salty horses around the neck going ninety down the arena.

My baby was still babbling and smiling with her volunteer babysitter under the shade canopies near the arena fence. I really wanted another chance to rope a horse. I surveyed the crowd of cowboys for potential partners and was dismayed by what I saw. Woody Harney, Tub Blanthorn, TJ Thompson, Junior Harney—all handy, experienced ropers who won money more often than not. There was no way little ol' me was going to ride up and ask them if they wanted to rope, since everyone saw my last run and knew it would just be a practice run and a waste of the forty-dollar entry fee.

I rode Teaks over to our horse trailer and dismounted. I loosened my cinch, took off his bridle, and put on a halter. I crouched down to take off his splint boots when a cowboy on a Paint horse trotted up.

"Hey, are you done roping?" It was Jess Lisle, a cousin of Rolly's and a skilled roper. I'd seen him rope at the Panther Creek branding and he rarely missed a calf. He stopped his horse on the other side of Teaks.

"Oh, yeah, I think so. I don't want to ask anyone to rope with me, since I'm just learning."

"I'll rope with you."

I hesitated. I really wanted to rope again. It was tough to find a place to practice horse roping. Paying money at a jackpot was my best chance at getting experience.

"Are you sure?" I asked.

"Yeah, if you want to rope, get back on your horse and come on."

I bridled Teaks, tightened my cinches, and rode back toward the arena. I waited next to Jess with my shoulders back and a loop built. If Jess thought I belonged in the line of ropers, then maybe I did.

When it was our turn to rope a horse, Jess necked it on the first loop and slowed it to a jog.

"Just come around the side there, there ya go, nice and easy," he coached me, while holding his dallies.

I rode Teaks into position and swung my loop. Hands shaky, I threw my loop and missed.

"It's okay, no big deal, just rebuild and try again." Jess seemed so calm, cool, and collected, like someone who had grown up roping horses and could do it with both eyes closed while holding only one bridle rein.

I built another loop and rode back into position. I pointed Teaks' nose at the loose horse's shoulder. I swung and threw, picking up two feet but fumbling my dallies.

"No time," the announcer called over the loudspeaker. I re-coiled my rope and headed toward the catch pen.

"You had him there for a minute, I saw it!" Jess said. He smiled as we rode out of the arena. "Good job. You'll get 'em next time."

My shoulders relaxed and I held my reins loosely as I rode back down toward the crowd of waiting cowboys. I didn't ask anyone else to rope, but I tied Teaks to the trailer and once he was tended to, I headed over to get Grace. I was on my way to being a real horse roper—I had entered the jackpot twice and got to see how it felt to throw my rope at the front feet of a live horse.

Jim later told me that he wasn't mad at me. He was mad at himself for missing a horse—twice—for his wife. He could miss a loop for anyone else and laugh it off, but he really wanted to catch one for me.

*

Jim moved from the huge chunk of meat on the kitchen counter to my laptop balanced on the stove, his hands and arms covered in blood up to his elbows. He watched a few seconds of the YouTube video before picking up the meat cleaver, then quickly walked back to the counter and hacked off another chunk of beef.

"Here, wrap this one," Jim said. He handed me a fresh-cut roast, roughly three pounds in size. It was still bleeding, but at least it wasn't quivering like the horse meat we'd butchered when Brent shot a mare he couldn't shoe and invited us over to share in the bounty. I hadn't been able to eat the horse meat because I couldn't shake the mental picture of the bloody muscle sitting on the kitchen counter and quivering. But Jim and my mom, who was visiting at the time, each ate a horse meat steak for dinner that night.

I took the proffered beef and placed it on a piece of plastic wrap I'd pre-cut and laid on the kitchen table. Before I could wrap the meat, Grace started to screech and flap her arms from her perch in the highchair. My hands were covered in blood, but she was going to keep screaming and Jim was going to keep handing me chunks of flesh no matter what, so I picked up a handful of Cheerios and tossed them onto her highchair tray. They were only a little sticky and red. Blood was natural, so it was probably okay for an infant to eat.

I turned back to the table, then wrapped the cut of beef with plastic wrap. I then rolled it in white butcher paper, secured the ends with masking tape, and wrote, "2013 Roast" on the finished package with a Sharpie. I handed Grace another handful of sticky red Cheerios and reached for the next piece of meat.

We were cutting up the carcass of a nine-year-old range bull that had nearly sliced his foot off during the fall works. The corporation that owned the Panther Creek Ranch didn't supply beef to its cowboy employees. Getting a free box of beef now and then, even if it wasn't choice cuts, was a common perk of working on a cattle ranch. We all felt a bit slighted that the owners didn't follow this custom and so seized an unexpected opportunity that came our way. When Nels and Jim were working bulls through the chute and saw the bull's severely injured hoof, they realized he would be crippled for life and unable to perform his bullish duties. He would be immediately shipped to the slaughterhouse, and so they saved him the trip and shot him on the spot. Cowboys gotta eat, too.

The guys killed the bull and dressed the carcass the same day the injury occurred, before infection could set in and spread to the rest of his body, thereby ruining the meat for human consumption. Once the bull was bled out and skinned, Nels and Jim hoisted him with a front-end loader and hung his body from a hook suspended from the ceiling of the shop for about three weeks. A cloud of diesel exhaust swirled around the bull's carcass every day when Jim warmed up the old Army truck to drive out to the desert and feed cows. It didn't take long for a thick crust to form all over the animal's flesh.

That didn't seem very sanitary. But then again, nothing about my bloody, non-stainless-steel kitchen, complete with a drooling baby and smooshed snacks strewn across the floor, would have been approved by the FDA. I wasn't even wearing latex gloves.

"Are you sure you know what you're doing?" I asked Jim on his next trip to consult the YouTube video with a knife in his hand and a determined look in his eye.

"Yeah, I'm just trying to keep up with how the guy in the video is butchering this quarter."

He rotated the chunk of meat on the counter and sliced off another roast. We'd already cut and wrapped our household's share of backstraps, the sections of loin that are usually the most tender and considered a delicacy in game animals. (We'd learn the backstraps on an aged range bull were neither delicate nor tender. We chewed on pan-fried pieces of backstrap for a while, then gave up and cooked them low and slow like a roast.) Without a meat grinder to make hamburger, roast was basically the only cut of meat we could salvage from the bull's carcass. Jim kept handing me chunks of beef, none of which were shaped like any roast I'd ever seen in a grocery store, and I kept wrapping and labeling until we were out of meat.

"Well, that'll fill the freezer for a while," I said. Then I mentally calculated how many quality cuts of beef we could have bought with the couple hundred bucks we'd spent on butcher paper, tape, and knives, and reminded myself to be a supportive wife and keep my mouth shut.

"Yeah, and it ought to taste okay as long as we cook it on low for at least five or six hours," Jim said. "Maybe ten or twelve on those big chunks."

"Doesn't bother me. I like a good pot roast."

Jim stopped in front of the stove to peer at the laptop one more time.

"Ah, dang it. Looks like I clicked the wrong video. This one is for cutting up a front quarter, and we had a hind."

I looked at him, surprised that he thought using the wrong YouTube tutorial was what was wrong with the scene. Blood splatters dotted my kitchen floor. I'd wrapped meat while feeding our child and never washed my hands. I was certain we'd find at least a few Cheerios when we opened up some of the packages later to cook them.

Grace squealed and raised her hands to be picked up. She was bloody, I was bloody, and the whole place smelled like a slaughterhouse. Time for a breastfeeding break.

Jim burst through the door unexpectedly in the middle of the morning and said he needed my help with a "ranch project." The stock truck had broken down on a steep mountain road and he wanted me to tow it back to headquarters with the company pickup. He would ride in the stock truck and man the steering wheel.

I'd witnessed the DIY towing process plenty of times on rural roads. One rig pulls another down the road with a nylon tow strap or chain while someone sits in the driver's seat of the non-running vehicle to steer and step on the brakes as needed with the gear shift in neutral. But I'd never participated in the event, and I told Jim as much.

"That's okay," he said. "There's a first time for everything."

I packed the diaper bag with extra wipes, a sippy cup of water, and a bag of Cheerios. Jim, baby Grace, and I hopped in the company pickup and drove five miles of two-track dirt road up the mountain to the broke-down stock truck. Jim maneuvered the pickup into position and strapped the chains between the two. He told me that I could drive about fifteen to twenty miles per hour and possibly even shift into second gear on the straight stretches. He added that the brakes weren't very good on the stock truck, so I might have to go a little faster to stay far enough in front so that it didn't come up the chain and rear-end me.

At least, I was pretty sure that was what he said.

Jim climbed into the stock truck, and I buckled myself into the driver's seat of the shiny white Ford. It was a brand-new three-quarter ton with a crew cab that had more buttons than a laptop computer. It was a rare treat to cruise around in a current-year pickup with power everything. The diesel engine sounded much quieter than any other pickup I'd ever driven, including our personal truck. (Especially our personal truck.)

Grace slept peacefully in the back, her car seat strapped in the middle position. We were on a steep hillside and the road was covered with loose rocks, because ranch trucks never break down on a sandy flat. I shifted into first gear and pressed on the gas pedal. I tried not to look down the steep drop-off directly out the driver's window. I crept along until I felt the chain come tight.

Feeling the stock truck resist, I accelerated slightly. As I picked up a little speed, so did the stock truck. Remembering what Jim said about the brakes and needing to stay far enough in front, I accelerated again. So did the stock truck. I accelerated more. So did the stock truck. Worried it was going to rear-end or possibly pass me, I all but floored the pickup.

The stock truck bumped, lurched, and jumped over rocks. It careened toward the mountainside on the right and barely missed going over the ledge on the left. I glanced in the rear-view mirror and saw Jim's hands move rapidly back and forth across the steering wheel, his face barely visible beneath the brim of his cowboy hat. I was glad he was driving the stock truck and not me. It looked very difficult, requiring an advanced level of high-speed dexterity I did not currently possess. I was super impressed. Quite proud of my husband, really.

Jim signaled me to stop when we reached the bottom of the steepest grade. He stepped out of the stock truck and walked up to my window. I rolled it down and turned my head to greet him.

"What is wrong with you?" he asked.

"You told me I could go fifteen miles an hour, so I did."

"When the truck is hitting the end of the chain and bouncing all over the road, you're going too fast." His voice was low. He flexed his jaw several times, like he was trying to hold back additional words.

"Oh. Okay," I said, embarrassed I had screwed up right out of the gate. "Sorry. I've never done this before. I'll slow down."

Jim walked back to the stock truck and got back into the driver's seat. We continued down the mountain, this time at a top cruising speed of three miles per hour. I periodically glanced in the rearview and side mirrors to see if Jim was having trouble, because I was obviously really good at recognizing the signs. Otherwise, I kept my face in the "safe zone" directly in front of the steering wheel where I knew Jim couldn't see my reflection in either of the mirrors. I felt like his mood would not be improved if he saw me laugh. I've always been deeply amused by mishaps, wrecks, and situations where things go as wrong as they possibly can, then a little more wrong. I've noticed that many (most?) people don't share this perspective, so I often try to suppress my ill-timed outbursts of mirth.

But I laughed all the way to the first wire gate. I tried to focus on my tow-truck driving skills but thinking of Jim's hands flying back and forth over the steering wheel made it hard to keep a straight face.

We made it through two wire gates, and then we were on a straight, level part of the road. I accelerated smoothly and steadily, then shifted into second gear just like my dad taught me when I was fifteen. I looked in the rear-view mirror and saw Jim immediately stick his hand out the window and hold up a single index finger. I shifted back down into first.

When we reached the long, slow descent that ended with a drop down the last steep part into the canyon at headquarters, Jim signaled me to stop again. He unhooked the stock truck from the pickup and said he was going to roll down the last hill in neutral.

"Really?" I asked, surprised. "But isn't it better and safer to have a truck towing you?"

"Usually," he said without even looking at me. "But I'll take my chances."

I returned to the company pickup and drove untethered down the final stretch of dirt road. I realized I had just gotten fired from my first unpaid job as a tow-truck driver. I should have felt chagrined, but instead I was impressed with myself. I must have done an exceptionally bad job if Jim thought he'd be better off driving a disabled vehicle without my assistance.

CHAPTER 12 ✳ **Year's End**

We left the Panther Creek Ranch in the darkness before sunrise on an October morning, with baby Grace asleep in the back seat and two horses loaded in the trailer. Jim saddled my horse for me while I cooked fried egg sandwiches so we could eat breakfast on the road. There were no fast-food restaurants or diners on the way to the Owyhee Reservation. There was no civilization, really—only one short stretch of paved road right at the end.

The drive took two and a half hours and covered about sixty miles of mostly dirt road. We were headed to a six-head horse and muley roping jackpot held in the Rez arena. Jim would rope in the main event, and I planned to take another shot at roping horses by entering the mixed horse roping jackpot held at the end. One team member had to be a woman to enter the mixed jackpot, to level the playing field a bit and encourage women to enter up.

Jim warmed up his horse and found his partners at the rodeo arena. I stood beside Teaks and set Grace in my saddle seat, then put my left foot in the stirrup and pulled myself up behind her in a practiced yet awkward motion. Teaks didn't move while I caught my right stirrup and situated myself and my baby in the saddle. We walked around the rodeo grounds and I said hi to friends we only saw at rodeos while Grace clutched the reins and slobbered on my saddle horn. I would have ordered a bigger saddle if I'd known I was going to spend more time packing a kid in front of me than riding solo.

I visited with the other cowboys' wives while Jim roped in the horse and muley roping. "Muleys" are different from standard roping cattle because they have no horns. Each team roped a horse, then a muley, and it became progressive after one head of each. After a while, I dismounted and tied Teaks up to the trailer. I hung out near the bleachers and concession stand that served fresh fry bread and Indian tacos. I took pictures of Jim's runs, timing my shots so that I captured a big, pretty, open loop when he delivered a front foot or neck shot. In between runs, I slowly followed Grace around the concrete pad by the bleachers where she practiced her crawling skills. I did my best not to cringe as she picked up sticks and empty nacho containers, but I bent down and tried to swipe them from her grip before they went into her mouth. Realistically, I knew I couldn't prevent all the foreign objects she found from coming into direct contact with her tongue. I just hoped to raise my percentage.

The mixed horse roping started when the afternoon was more than halfway through. I handed Grace to our friend Laura Gonzalez. She had two young sons and was itching for a daughter, so she was more than happy to hold my chunky girl and watch her blow spit bubbles while I roped. Jim and I rode into the roping boxes to enter as a team. The mixed jackpot was only for horses and didn't include muleys. It was a three-header, progressive after one.

Owhyee was different from McDermitt in that the arena had an actual horse-roping chute. That made the event more similar to regular team roping, where ropers back into boxes adjacent to the chute and all three animals break at roughly the same time. There was no chasing a loose horse at high speeds around the arena to get into position to take your first shot.

Jim backed into the heading box and nodded his head. The horse sprang from the chute with both of us in hot pursuit. We weren't running nearly as fast as we had been in McDermitt, which was a relief. Jim threw his rope and missed. We still had two remaining loops, so he rebuilt and we regrouped as the horse was running down the long fence opposite of the bleachers. Jim threw a "scoop loop," an underhand shot that is classified as fancy but usually his most reliable way of catching a loose animal, and caught the horse. I came around the front, threw a front-foot loop, and missed. We rode out with a no-time once again.

Jess Lisle wasn't at this roping, which was a bummer. I'd roped with him again at a jackpot earlier that summer and gotten my first official time in the horse roping event. We didn't win any money, but I was encouraged to get an actual time. Jim said he going to step back and start paying Jess to rope with me.

Feeling more confident, I entered with another roper after roping with Jim. I don't remember my partner's name, but I know I threw a big, pretty, wide-open loop on the first try that snagged two front feet. I dallied, the flagger called time, and my adrenaline and confidence levels surged simultaneously. I was hooked. I popped my turns and the horse jumped up, unhurt. My loop fell off his front feet and my partner followed the horse to the catch pen, his rope slack as the horse loped out of the arena. I coiled my rope up and walked Teaks back to the crowd of ropers.

I was a little taken aback by how much I liked roping horses. I loved horses and considered the sorrel gelding I rode one of my closest friends. Was it wrong that I enjoyed a sport where horses were on the other end of the rope?

I didn't take much time to ponder the question, because I wanted to get back in the roping box as soon as possible. The number of ropers was small and the number of female ropers even smaller, so I felt more comfortable asking someone to rope with me. Besides, they'd all just seen me throw a good loop. I didn't feel like such a charity case anymore.

I sat on Teaks and contemplated who I should work up my courage and ask to rope when Junior Harney rode up, teeth gleaming white against brown skin beneath his black felt hat.

"You wanna rope?" he asked.

I turned and glanced around. "Me?" I asked. I couldn't believe someone was actually asking me to rope instead of the other way around, especially a handy Indian guy like Junior. As a rule, the Indians up here were almost always better ropers than white guys.

"Yeah, you," he said and reined his horse to a stop beside Teaks.

"Sure." I built a loop and reminded myself I belonged there. Tub Blanthorn had given me a one-on-one lesson after the McDermitt jackpot and showed me how to throw a good loop against the horse's front legs. "Just like layin' a panel against a fence," he said. I'd practiced for hours on the dummy at home and had just caught a live animal in a competitive setting.

All I had to do was ride into the box, take a deep breath like I did when I roped with Jess, and rope.

Junior and I rode into the roping boxes, he nodded, and we all took off. For the second time in a row, I got a time. Then I roped with Junior's dad, Woody, the legendary Nate Kelley, and Nate's son, the ever-smiling Junior Kelley. (The native guys could really rope, but half of them were named Junior, so it got confusing.) I could hardly believe that I got a qualified time in all my runs. Roping horses out of a chute was way easier than running wide-open out of a bucking chute and chasing them down. There was nothin' to it; you just broke from the box with a rope in your hand, waited for your partner to catch 'em around the neck, then, quick, duck back and circle around the front, swing, swing, lay a panel against a fence, and bam, two feet.

I made it back to the "short go," the final round of the competition after the elimination round, where the prize money was won. I'm certain I made it back three or four times, but if you asked Jim, he'd tell you it was seven or eight. He always saw me as better than I saw myself.

My baby-holder, Laura, had to leave before the final round started, and Jim was beers-deep in conversation with his friends, somewhere or other. The secretary announced the short round order, and I only had about two teams to go until it was my turn to rope again. I had to quickly find someone to hold Grace before I was up.

I glanced around and saw that my options were limited. Most people had left, and the few that remained were all in the short go like me. By then, Jim was too drunk to hold our baby and sit on his horse at the same time. I saw a middle-aged woman wearing a tank top and tight jean shorts standing near the arena fence. I'd never seen her or the man she was talking to before.

"Excuse me," I said to the woman. "Would you mind holding my baby? I have to rope, and I don't have anyone to watch her."

The woman's eyes widened and a smile lit up her face. "Oh, sure, I'd love to," she said.

And so I handed my only child to a complete stranger and said thank you. I watched her smile and coo at Grace, who looked at her face and didn't cry. I decided that was good enough and rode into the arena. Junior Kelley headed our first horse right out of the box in the short round, and I threw a front-foot loop so fast we were about to win the whole thing. I saw Junior's eyes get wide and an incredulous smile take over his face when I jerked my slack, and a spike of adrenaline made my hands shake and I fumbled my dallies to miss my first loop. We got a time on my second loop, though. I wound up finishing second overall with a different partner and winning the fast time of the mixed roping with Junior due to our speedy run in the elimination round.

It was late when we loaded up the horses and baby for the long drive home. I couldn't believe that I held two checks with my name on them for winning money in a horse roping jackpot. The second-place check paid almost two hundred bucks, but I was most amazed at the twenty-dollar fast-time check. I'd just roped a horse in under ten seconds. A lot of men couldn't rope a horse in less than ten seconds. There were a lot of handy, experienced horse ropers there, but Junior and I had the single fastest time of the entire mixed roping.

Jim had to get up early for work the next morning, and he'd had a few too many beers, so I volunteered to drive. He fell asleep (passed out) halfway home; I was the only one awake as I drove across the desolate stretch of desert toward home. There were no streetlights, stop signs, or houses, so the blackness was complete. Only the starlight above and our headlights below illuminated the road ahead of us.

I grew nervous as we approached the base of the biggest hill. It routinely made trucks overheat because it was so steep. I knew the engine temperature gauge would most likely redline. I also knew that I absolutely could not stop once I started up the hill. There was no room to turn around on the narrow dirt road, and attempting to back down would quite possibly mean sliding off the edge of the mountain. Even if I stopped straight, I'd never be able to get started going forward again while towing a steel trailer heavy-loaded with horses.

Halfway up the hill, the temperature gauge started to move to the right. I glanced over at Jim. He was sound asleep and half snoring in the passenger seat. I wanted to wake him up, but I knew there was nothing he could do to help me. All the driver could do was mash the pedal on the right and refuse to weaken till they hit the top.

I was grateful Grace slept all the way up the hill. Pulling that steep grade would have been much more difficult with a baby crying in the back seat. On the left was a mountainside and on the right was a drop-off with no guardrail or shoulder. I stared straight ahead and kept both hands on the wheel, sneaking quick glances at the instrument panel as often as I dared.

The gauge was past the red line and into the no man's land of nearly fried engines by the time we reached the summit. I could smell something burning under the hood but breathed a sigh of relief knowing that we'd be on the flat and downhill for a while, hopefully long enough to let the exhaust fan cool down the engine.

It was almost midnight by the time we made it home. I woke Jim up and he put up our horses while I took Grace in the house. She was perky and awake after her long nap in the truck, so I stayed up and played with her in the living room while Jim crashed into bed to catch a few hours of sleep before his alarm clock went off before sunrise. I was bleary-eyed but for once didn't mind staying up until the small hours of the morning. It gave me more time to replay my horse roping runs and relive the accomplishment and relief I felt when the green Dodge topped out on the monstrous hill.

Days grew shorter and nights grew cooler, but neither Gene nor Ho O'lena had turned from their errant ways. It was time to consider our next option.

"Canner prices aren't that bad right now. Maybe we should just take them to the sale yard in Twin Falls," I suggested to Jim one afternoon.

I didn't like it, but I knew we had to have the conversation. We couldn't risk Jim getting killed while riding unfixable horses in the course of his daily job. Those two horses were going to hurt someone at some point. I disliked the thought of slaughtering them or any other horses, but some horses weren't going to be a friend, companion, or work partner, no matter how much their owners tried. Horse slaughter had just been outlawed in America but shipping them to Mexico or Canada for processing outside our borders was still legal. The downside of the ban was that horses sent to Mexico were subject to less regulated methods, and I had no idea if they were humane or not. But if we sold the paint gelding and the sorrel mare into the equine processing channels in Idaho, chances were good that they'd be shipped north to Canada with its more stringent and (presumably) humane regulations.

We hauled Gene and Ho O'lena to the sale yard on a rainy day.

"Hey, at least we got over five hundred for the two of them," I said to Jim. "We finally made a little money on this horse trade."

I was trying to find something to smile about to combat the gloom of canning horses that we'd called by name and earnestly tried to get along with. The check was a pittance and beside the point.

At the sale, Jim and I walked between pens of various livestock species, all with numbered sale stickers affixed to one hip. Dairy cows past their prime milking years, leppy calves that weren't high enough quality to sell with the main calf crop, and the odd sheep or goat filled most of the pens. A handful of horses like ours with collars and numbered tags around their necks stood in a panel lot. Some stood together with a hind foot cocked and heads low, eyes half closed, dozing in the light rain. Others stood alone, farther apart from the group. At least one or two had an obvious swollen knee or an injured hock that wouldn't heal right.

I wondered about each horse's individual story. Were there other untrainable broncos like Gene? Was there another mare with a mean streak? I hoped none of them were gentle kids' horses that had simply outlived their usefulness.

I didn't look too closely at the horses inside that pen as we walked by. The two we had just sold would join them soon, and then they would all be loaded up for one last truck ride.

Fall brought another change to the Panther Creek range, one that also centered around death but in a more celebratory way. Hunting camps appeared overnight up and down the canyons. Suddenly, we had neighbors in the wilderness. They stayed in canvas wall tents and sought the solitude that I so often felt trapped by. Hunting guides set up camps for the season near stands of golden quaky trees and dry creek beds. They hosted a revolving cast of hunters lucky enough to draw a tag and pay for their assistance in bagging a deer or elk to take back to town and mount the antlers on their living room wall if their wives were outdoorsy, or in the garage if they weren't.

One retired couple parked their fifth-wheel camp trailer up the hill from headquarters and stayed two months every fall. Hunting wasn't their priority. They just enjoyed being out in nature. They hung temporary skirting around their camper, did their laundry in Jarbidge once a week, and stopped by the ranch to borrow a cup of sugar or say hi once in a while.

That year, 2013, was Grace's first Halloween. I looked forward to participating in all the holiday traditions for the sake of giving my daughter a fun-filled childhood, but I also realized she was an infant who couldn't read a calendar or carve a pumpkin. She couldn't even tell a pumpkin from a pacifier. I wasn't dedicated enough to drive two hours into Twin Falls to take a ten-month-old baby door to door, begging for candy she couldn't eat. That sounded like a good way to make memories that the child wouldn't remember, but I sure would when she woke up and screamed all the way home in the dark.

But when I stopped by a secondhand children's store in early September, I couldn't resist picking out a costume for her. I was tickled to find an elephant suit in her size, complete with oversized ears and a trunk attached to the hood. Then when I put the costume on her on October thirty-first, it was almost too small. I'd forgotten to account for how quickly a baby grows. Rookie-mom mistake.

Grace looked so cute crawling around the living room floor in her elephant costume. Yes, it was a bit snug, and the plush toenails sewn into the hem of each leg hit her just above the ankles. Jim said she looked like a giant mouse.

I wanted to be social and show my festive baby off to someone, so I decided to reverse trick-or-treat. Mary Ann Fitzgerald, my childhood best friend's mom and one of my "second mamas," had always made Halloween treat platters when

I was a kid. I remembered her taking them around to the neighbors—I tagged along on delivery trips and thought it was such a fun, unexpected gesture.

But what could I make on short notice? I didn't have any Halloween-specific candy in the house. So, I cut out sugar cookies with a mason jar and decorated them with orange frosting. As long as you have an assortment of food coloring on hand, you can make sugar cookies to fit any occasion.

When Jim got home from work, we loaded up our little elephant (or giant mouse) and headed up the canyon to our first stop. The non-hunting party in the fifth-wheel trailer was surprised to see us but welcomed us in for a visit. We crammed around the table that folded down into a bed and traded stories while Grace crawled around and explored the portable propane heater. I kept getting up to gently push her little hands off a cabinet knob or drawer pull, and our hosts kept telling me it was okay; she really couldn't hurt anything in there.

After an hour or so, we stood up to head home.

"Are you sure you can't stay for dinner?" Linda asked. "We have plenty of beef. It's no trouble at all."

"Thank you, but we really better get going. It's been nice visiting with you all. Take care."

I picked up Grace and we drove back down the dirt road. Our hosts seemed disappointed we couldn't stay longer. I was anxious about keeping Grace out of their belongings and hated to overstay my welcome as a rule. Maybe I'd feel more comfortable with a longer visit next time. They were such friendly, welcoming folks and our daughter's grandparents all lived far away. A pair of nice, grandparent-type people would be a nice addition to our lives.

One evening, Jim and I received a dinner invitation from a new hunting party. Nels told us that they camped on the ranch every fall and that food was always lavish and plentiful. I was excited to make a social call, and Jim was excited because he'd heard they'd brought lobster.

I bundled up the baby in her winter coat and we drove half a mile in the dark of early evening to the hunting camp. In the middle of camp was a big wall tent with long folding tables, canvas camp chairs, and a wood stove, crackling away with a belly full of fire. We shook hands with our hosts and could plainly see that they were in vacation mode. Boxes of wine and coolers full of beer were reachable from any position in the camp. The cook's red face and boisterous laugh told me he didn't tolerate an empty cup.

We snacked on crisp grapes and creamy artichoke dip while waiting for the main course of lobster tails, sirloin steak, shrimp, and assorted side dishes. Grace held onto the long table and practiced her newfound trick of standing upright and waving one arm while I fed her pieces of purple grapes and listened to our hosts' stories.

Hunting camps are known for tall tales, and this one was no exception. It was better provisioned than the typical three-man tent stocked with cans of Vienna sausages and greasy potato chips, but the spirit of shooting things with horns and cooking meat over an open fire remained the same. The canvas walls around us were covered with sentiments, short poems, and simple sketches drawn with a permanent marker. That tent had been around for a long time and had seen more victories, disappointments, and harsh weather than most of the hunters seated in it.

A state-of-the-art RV was parked next to the wall tent. It was equipped with air conditioning and satellite TV. Its inhabitant could wear camo pants and shoot a deer with nary a paved road nor power line in sight and still not miss an episode of *Two and a Half Men*. It seemed to me that luxury camping sort of entirely missed the point of camping, but I didn't have enough money for anyone to care about my opinion.

At some point, we migrated over to the huge motorhome with the TV and visited with Zac Dufferena, a cowboy-horseshoer from eastern Oregon who also worked as a seasonal hunting guide. Zac had just found out the second baby he and his wife were expecting was a boy and couldn't stop smiling.

I looked down the mountain in the darkness toward our little white house at the bottom of the canyon. Some people drove hundred-thousand-dollar motorhomes so they could eat lobster and enjoy the desert for two weeks each fall. Some people scraped by on poverty wages so they could live in the desert and enjoy it all year long, come rain, snow, or disruption in their TV service.

As much as I sometimes hated the isolation and felt trapped by the box canyon walls, cut off from town and other women my age by the twisty road that followed the river, I knew I wouldn't be content to only visit the wild places once a year, then park my motor home in a town lot for eleven and a half months. I couldn't speak for the other guys, but I was satisfied with my half of the bargain.

———————

Grace got a cold right after Christmas. First she had a stuffy nose and cough— fairly standard symptoms and not too worrisome. But by nightfall she was running a fever. Still nothing to be too concerned about since I'd been parenting for a full year and knew how to handle basic childhood illnesses. I stripped her down to a diaper at bedtime and plopped her on my chest so she could nestle her head under my chin and drape her arms down my sides to take full advantage of the maternal comfort that was her birthright.

I gave her a dose of infant ibuprofen before she conked out. Her body felt hot to the touch, but that was to be expected with a fever. I took her to our bed and settled in for the night with my back propped up on two pillows so she could sleep partially upright and breathe more easily. I fell asleep to the sound of Jim watching TV with his parents in the living room. They'd driven out from Colorado to spend the holiday with us.

When I woke up it was pitch black. Grace felt like flames on my chest. I stood up and carried her to the kitchen, then turned on the light and reached for the thermometer. I scanned it over her forehead. My eyes shot open and my heart raced when it read one hundred and four. Hands shaking, I passed the scanner over her forehead once again. That time, it read one hundred and three point six. She'd never had a fever that high before, and I knew that internal body temperatures over a certain limit could cause seizures and possible brain damage. I wasn't sure, but it felt like we were approaching that threshold.

I picked up the cordless phone and dialed St. Luke's Hospital in Twin Falls. I punched enough numbers to somehow connect to their nurse hotline and a kindly-sounding middle-aged woman answered my call. I listed my baby's age and symptoms, telling her I was most concerned about the high fever.

"Do you have infant ibuprofen and Tylenol?" she asked.

"Yes."

"Give her one full dose of each. Taken together at the same time, it should bring her fever down. Once it does, give her a dose of just one kind the next time you give her medicine."

I measured and administered the fever reducers while on the phone with the nurse. Grace slurped down the sticky purple and pink liquids with eyes half open. She drifted back to sleep as soon as she'd swallowed the last drop. Her cheeks were bright red and her torso covered with interconnected red splotches.

"I'm worried about her cough, too," I said.

"Does she wheeze when she breathes?"

"Hold on, let me check."

I took the phone away from my ear while I lowered my head next to Grace's chest and listened to her breathe. She didn't seem to have a distinct wheeze. Wait, on that breath I heard it. Yes, she was definitely wheezing. There seemed to be a rattling sound in there, too. Probably some mucus congestion as well.

"She seems to wheeze sometimes," I told the nurse.

"Hold the phone up to her chest and let me hear."

I held the phone in front of Grace's chest for several breaths, then returned it to my ear to hear the diagnosis.

"She sounds okay to me," said the nurse. "Her breathing is fine; she just sounds congested since she's sick."

"Okay."

I didn't feel as relieved as I thought I would. The nurse's words sounded positive, but what if her assessment was wrong? She had a limited amount of information to work with. What if the phone connection wasn't clear enough and she couldn't detect an ominous sound in Grace's breathing?

"I'm just wondering if I should bring her in or let her rest at home. We live two hours from town, so the trip would be stressful for her. But if she needs to be seen, then of course I will get in the truck and go right now."

The nurse considered my words for a moment before answering.

"That's a long way from town and I know it's scary. I think she'll be okay at home with rest and fluids. But if anything about her appearance concerns you, or if you want to bring her in, you're always welcome to do that. We'll be here."

My baby's appearance definitely concerned me. The high numbers on the thermometer concerned me. Being the only adult awake in my house, the darkness blanketing the canyon, the long distance to town, the rutted dirt road with no cell phone service —all of it concerned me.

But the nurse's years of experience and calm voice reassured me that her advice was reasonable and accurate. I knew that if I was worried enough about Grace to insist on an emergency room visit, I could strap her into her car seat and start down the windy dirt road to Twin. The thought of a brightly lit twenty-four-seven ER department with nurses, medicine, and high-tech medical equipment was tempting. I knew my baby would be safe from fever-induced seizures and whatever other alarming symptoms she might develop if I could just get her there.

But the thought of driving two hours with a feverish and crying infant over narrow roads with no cell phone service in the middle of the night was unnerving. The possibility of flat tires, collisions with wildlife, and breaking down was formidable. The nurse had listened to her breathe and said she'd be fine. I decided to trust her and stay home.

"Thank you so much for your help. I really appreciate it."

"You're very welcome. Call back tomorrow if you have any more questions, and of course you can always bring her in anytime and we'll take a look at her."

I hung up the phone and looked down at Grace, sound asleep in my arms. *She will be okay,* I told myself. *This is less stressful for her little body than driving to town. Just let her sleep it off. You gave her two doses of medicine like the nurse said. She will be okay.*

The next morning, I woke early with Grace lying next to me in bed. She was sprawled across the mattress, still clad only in a diaper. I put my hand on her belly. She felt warm, not flaming hot. I picked her up and carried her to the kitchen to take her temperature. The scanner read one hundred and one point two. Technically, she still had a fever, but just a "normal" one. I smoothed the hair on the back of her head and felt my heart rate slow to normal. Daylight chased most of my worries away just like it usually did.

Grace's fever didn't spike again. She was drinking a little and sleeping a lot. I sat in the recliner, watched a Jim Carrey movie, and rocked my sick child while Jim worked on the ranch like always.

I realized this scenario would likely play out again in the future. Who knew what it would be next time—maybe a broken arm or an eye infection. But kids get hurt and we lived a long ol' ways from the nearest medical facility. I figured I should probably put together a more comprehensive first aid kit, and—perhaps more importantly—develop nerves of steel.

CHAPTER 13 ✳ **Changing Ranges**

Two months later, we stopped at a DIY car wash in Jordan Valley, Oregon, on our way to Jim's job interview at the 2 Slash Ranch. Snow, rain, and dirt-road living had coated the Dodge from bumper to bumper with a thick layer of mud. We wanted to make a good first impression, so it seemed smart to hose off our rig before rolling up to a potential new employer.

Jim had gotten laid off from Panther Creek with a month's notice nearly thirty days before. At least he'd had notice. Usually, as we'd already experienced once before, you just got told to pack your stuff and go when things went south on a ranch job.

I sat in the warm cab with Grace while Jim ran the pressure washer. He held it out in front of his body, as far away from his clean jeans as he could, to avoid getting sprayed and splattered with stray chunks of mud. Afterward, we pulled off the concrete wash pad and headed down the highway for one more stretch of paved road before it turned to dirt again. The Dodge wouldn't stay shiny for long, but at least it would look cleaner than if he hadn't washed it at all.

I used the long drive to catch up on my Bible reading. I was using a special version that broke the Bible into daily assignments comprised of one chunk each of the Old Testament, New Testament, Psalms, and Proverbs. If I read each day's assignment on schedule, I'd read the whole Bible in one year.

It was only February, and I was already behind.

I looked up from Proverbs and checked my hair and makeup in the sun visor mirror. Jim was the one interviewing for a paid position, but I knew family members could influence the cowboy's chances. With ranch jobs, you worked and lived next door to your boss. He owned your house, paid your utility bills, signed your paycheck, and heard you argue with your spouse. Close quarters made it all the more important that everyone got along, or at least tolerated each other.

I wasn't worried about Grace making a good impression. At fourteen months old, she had a small collection of teeth, a wispy ponytail on the top of her head, and a bow-legged gait when she walked. She was adorable.

Jim pulled into the 2 Slash Ranch driveway and parked in front of the main house. We walked up to the front door with Grace perched on my hip. We met owners Dave and Paula Harris. They'd inherited the ranch through Dave's family and raised their five kids there. Paula fixed us lunch and then the men discussed the particulars of the job. They walked around the headquarters while we women stayed inside with the baby. When Grace toddled toward her, Paula held her hands out and smiled in the exaggerated way that grandmas do.

On the drive home, Jim told me he'd been offered a job.

"Oh, good," I said. "I've never had an Oregon adventure before."

"I have. I swore I'd never live in Harney County again."

I was silent for a couple minutes.

"But I guess we get to live in the big house with four bedrooms, so that should be good for you," Jim said.

I perked up. A big house did sound nice for a change. I hoped it was clean.

We loaded the last few boxes into the horse trailer, dodging raindrops on the short walk from the house. Two horses stood tied in the front half of the trailer.

The divider gate was shut to separate them from the last few household belongings that hadn't made it to the 2 Slash yet. We crammed in a chest freezer full of tough beef, tossed a handful of halters onto the floor, and slammed the rear door.

I knew the stuff in the back half of the trailer would get pooped on by a horse at some point. I also knew the rain would come in through the top slats on the trailer and soak the cardboard boxes I'd carefully packed. I was past caring, though.

We'd known we were leaving the ranch for a full month plus a week, and it was time to go. The rain made moving more difficult, but it wasn't anything we hadn't done before. It seemed to rain almost every time the Young family moved. If ranchers paid us to move, we could end the drought out West in a year, maybe sooner if we had good tires.

We drove over the road in the windy canyon bottom for the last time and arrived at the 2 Slash just before dark. Jim unloaded the soggy boxes and heavy freezer, then turned the horses loose in a corral. He'd turn them out with the cavvy the next day when it was light. You never turned new horses out with the cavvy in an unfamiliar pasture in the dark, because they might get stirred up and run through a fence they couldn't see.

Paula had a big pot of soup on at the main house and invited us for dinner. After the wet, muddy journey to our new home, I was glad for a hot meal.

A few weeks later, my new neighbor showed up at my front door carrying a white plastic bucket and a wooden spoon.

"Thanks for coming over," I told her when I opened the door.

"No problem, I'm happy to help."

I'd asked Kim to teach me to make bread because I was tired of running out of bread. Our new home was two hours from the nearest grocery store. The first thirty-mile stretch was a dirt road, so about the same as our last home. I sensed this was to be my new normal, so I thought I better be proactive about making my own food. Kim was married to the 2 Slash Ranch's longtime mechanic and lived across the driveway from me. She baked bread, canned apricots, and butchered chickens from the flock she raised in the backyard. If anybody could teach me how to turn yeast and flour into something fluffy I could use to make a sandwich, it was Kim.

"Now, do you know how to measure flour?" she asked.

"I think so. Don't you just put it in a measuring cup?"

"Most people think so, but no, not if you want your bread to turn out right. First, you fluff up the flour in the bag. It's best if you can weigh it on a kitchen scale, but most people don't have one. You'll be fine as long as you don't pack the flour down into the cup."

Kim demonstrated how to fluff the loose flour, then scoop out a cup in one smooth motion. She leveled the flour with the side of her hand without shaking it further down into the cup.

"You need your water to be a hundred degrees. I can show you how to measure that without a thermometer, though, because the human body is just barely under that at about ninety-eight degrees."

Kim turned the tap water on in the sink. She let the hot water run, then turned the cold tap on halfway.

"Put your wrist in the water. If you can barely tell the difference between the water and your wrist, then you're close to a hundred degrees."

We left the tap running at the perfect temperature while we measured three cups of water into the bucket. Then we added one tablespoon of yeast, one tablespoon of salt, and six and a half cups of flour. Kim used the master recipe from the book *Artisan Bread in 5 Minutes a Day* for our lesson. It was simple, easy, required no kneading, and she promised it would turn out light and fluffy.

I remained skeptical yet optimistic. I'd been trying to bake bread since I was a teenager but could never get it to rise more than three inches tall.

Kim went back to her house while the bread dough rested on the counter for the first rise. She came back a few hours later and showed me how to divide the dough into two balls and place it on parchment paper in a cast iron skillet. Thirty minutes later, I popped the free-form loaves into the oven. Thirty minutes after that, I set my golden, cracked, aromatic, yeasty creations on the counter.

And that is how Kim the Mechanic's Wife changed my life. I'm not even kidding. I later learned to make cinnamon-raisin bread, brioche sweet rolls, and pizza dough. When we were flat broke or snowed in, I discovered I could elevate the spirits of my entire family if I baked a loaf or two of bread. The ingredients were cheap and simple, but the finished loaf, rolls, or pizza pie filled the house with a warm aroma that made our worries melt away—like butter soaking into a thick-cut piece of crusty buttermilk bread.

The weather was warm and the green grass grew strong. It was early summer and finally t-shirt weather in southeastern Oregon. I'd finished writing for the magazine early, so I shoved Grace's chubby feet into a little pair of hot pink cowboy boots and headed for the barn. I slung my Canon around my neck just in case.

Jim and his cowboy helper for the day, Dave's twenty-year-old daughter Elizabeth, were just heading back out to the barn to catch horses for the afternoon's projects. Elizabeth was getting ready to wrangle in the cavvy on the four-wheeler when I told her that Grace and I would take the job if she didn't mind.

"Sure, go for it," Elizabeth said.

Wrangling is a chore that's usually assigned to each member of the cowboy crew on a rotational basis. On some outfits, a person can earn extra wrangling duties for having a messy stall, being late to work, or other infractions of the ranch's unwritten rules. But as someone who rarely got horseback anymore and looked for any excuse to do any type of cowboy job, wrangling on a "Japanese Quarter Horse" sounded pretty good.

I lifted Grace onto the seat of the Honda and climbed on behind her. I stopped at the first gate in the lane to snap a picture.

I imagined the caption I'd later write for a blog post. *This is what the lane looks like without any horses in it. Keep reading to see what it looks like when horses are in it. Spoiler alert: It's the same thing, only with horses.*

I chuckled to myself and shifted into second gear. Grace leaned forward to grab the handlebars, her short arms straining from the reach. She gazed straight ahead with confidence.

I eased off the throttle just before the first dry creek bed crossing. A doe stood on the smooth rocks, framed by wild roses and Russian olive trees on either side. She picked her head up and stood stock still at the sound of the approaching engine. I lifted my camera to my eye and snapped a picture before she bounded out of sight.

We drove through the creek bed and headed for the back of the horse pasture, scanning left and right for signs of the cavvy. This wasn't a few acres of flat, irrigated grassland. It was three square miles of trees, creeks, brush, and rocks. But it was still easier than wrangling at the Van Norman Ranch, where the horse pasture was six square miles of rocky hills and draws too steep to drive a quad.

Grace and I spotted the horses off to our right at the same time. She held a pointed index finger above her ear and bent it up and down, pointing with her other hand. At seventeen months, she had yet to utter an intelligible word, so we were learning infant sign language with her as a means of temporary communication until her words came in. She didn't know very many signs yet, but our little cowgirl dang sure knew the sign for horse.

I steered off the rutted dirt track and headed cross country. The horses saw me coming, picked up their heads, and turned for the corral. They knew the drill. The usual leaders went to the front and trotted, and the habitual stragglers fell to the back and poked along at a walk, their ears switching toward me as they waited for the expected reprimand. I hollered and shook the flag stick I carried to urge them to pick up the pace.

We drove toward each straggler in turn, hollering and waving the flag until they picked up at least a slow trot and joined the rest of the cavvy. I made sure to glance all around so we didn't leave any horses behind. That was a major no-no, whether you were a hired man or a cowboy's wife wrangling for fun. Horses quickly learn to evade capture if they can. It was a bad habit to get started.

Grace and I drove into the corral behind the dust of the cavvy trotting through the lane. She squinted her eyes and ducked her head, her hands still clutching the handlebars. I eased off the throttle and let the horses get ahead of us once they were between the fences of the lane so we didn't have to eat so much dust. We drove into the corral after the last straggler and Elizabeth shut the gate behind us.

"Thanks," I said.

"No problem. Thanks for wrangling for me."

"Any time. It was fun."

I parked the four-wheeler outside the corral, turned off the key, and lifted Grace off the seat. I wasn't roping yearlings alongside the highway on a horse that might buck, but it sure felt good to get outside and do an actual cowboy job again. Taking my daughter along for the ride was an unexpected perk.

I planned an overnight trip to Winnemucca for June sixth so I could drive the two and a half hours to town without falling asleep behind the wheel. It was the closest town with a Walmart and a branch of our bank, so there was no avoiding the drive when we needed to stock up on groceries and run errands. I usually did the five-hour round trip, plus approximately seven hours to shop, bank, eat lunch, swing by the feed store, and do whatever else popped up, in one day. But I was exhausted from being eight weeks pregnant.

I'd only known our second baby was on the way for two weeks. We told our parents, other ranch employees, and everyone at the Jordan Valley Big Loop Rodeo that I was pregnant again. There were no conflicted feelings or a crushing desire for secrecy this time around. I was married and already chasing one kid. Adding a second was the next natural step.

The two weeks since the positive pregnancy test had been marked by few symptoms other than an irresistible urge to fall asleep during the middle of the day. I usually conducted phone interviews, researched articles, and typed stories during Grace's naptime, but those powerful first-trimester hormones left me no choice but to fall into a deep slumber whenever she did.

When I woke up the morning of our mother-daughter overnight trip, I felt different. No limb-dragging fatigue, no foggy head. *Great!* I thought. Maybe I could make the drive without any issues.

Then I hesitated. Wasn't it a bad sign to have your pregnancy symptoms mysteriously vanish? I'd read something to that effect somewhere in a pregnancy book or one of the countless websites that modern moms-to-be are obligated to pore over so they know what size of fruit their baby is at all times. I was bright-eyed and cheerful on the long drive through the desert to town, grateful to catch some relief from the all-day tiredness, but I bought a pregnancy test at Walmart just to double check.

I peed on the stick in the bathroom up front—the one between the customer service desk and the nail salon that was never busy. Two pink lines showed up immediately, the ink dark and confidence-inspiring. The baby was still there. He or she was just giving me a temporary respite from the havoc that a tiny pinpoint of cells with a heartbeat can wreak on an expectant mother in the early weeks. I needed to enjoy feeling good instead of worrying so much all the time.

After our quick Walmart trip, I checked into Scott Shady Court. It was an old motor court founded in 1928 that had been rebranded as "retro" at some point, probably because it looked like it hadn't been updated since the sixties. The lounge featured an old couch and deer heads mounted on the faux wood paneling behind the front desk. Receipts were handwritten on actual carbon paper, which I hadn't seen since I was a little kid in the early nineties. Rooms were furnished with a boxy TV, and you couldn't adjust the thermostat yourself—the front office turned it on for you. You had to wait an agonizingly long time for the heat to reach your room if you were staying at the far end of the last building. But it only cost forty-five dollars to rent a room with a double bed and cash was welcome. For that reason alone it was a favorite with the local buckaroo population when they came to town on a ranch rodeo weekend.

Once I dropped our bags in the room, I trailed behind Grace as she explored the parking lot and outdoor swimming pool area. The plastic chairs, raised curbs, and cracks in the old asphalt were all new objects for a toddler to look at, touch, stand on, and jump over. Traffic rolled by on the interstate to the west, just beyond the motel grounds. The overpass that allowed cars, trucks, and big rigs to zip past Winnemucca, and every other small town in America, without even slowing down told the story of the end of the motor court era with each honk of the horn and whoosh of an exhaust brake.

I turned and stopped when Grace did, and we slowly meandered between a row of parked cars and a line of single-story cinder block rooms. We ventured left, right, and in circles as the toddler's curiosity shifted. The afternoon sun was getting hot, but I didn't want to cut her exploring short.

A sudden rush of warmth changed all that.

"Grace, honey, come quick," I said as I snatched my little daughter to my hip and walked toward our room as fast as I could. "Hurry, hurry, before Mama makes a mess."

The situation between my legs developed quickly, in a hurry, all at once. I didn't stop to check my underwear in the parking lot. I didn't look around to see if anyone was nearby to notice the red stain that must surely be growing on the back of my shorts. I simply clutched my child to my body and sped to the privacy of our motel room without looking left or right as I passed by the office.

Once inside our room, I set Grace down and went into the bathroom without bothering to close the door. The inside of my underwear and shorts were filled with blood. There was so much bright red blood, and more kept flowing unabated. I needed something to soak up what was coming out of me. I grabbed a washcloth, thin and coarse from countless bleach treatments, and folded it to fit inside my panties.

I felt guilty about ruining the motel's washcloth. I'd paid cash for the room, so they couldn't even recoup the damage I was doing to their property by charging an exorbitant fee to my credit card. I considered asking at the front desk if I could use the washcloth, saying, *Sorry...I'm desperate and have no other options*. But I couldn't bear the thought of walking across the parking lot and verbalizing that request out loud. I couldn't tell a random stranger what was going on.

I grabbed my cell phone and called Tami and Brogan Kendall. They were friends of Jim's and became friends of mine when we started dating. They lived on a ranch near town and had a daughter, Morgan, who was Grace's age.

"Hi, Tami? This is Jolyn. I need to go to the doctor. Can you come pick up Grace for a couple hours? I think I'm having a miscarriage."

I broke down sobbing as I said the last words. Of course that's what this was. There was nothing else it could be.

I called my best friend, Casey, while I waited for Tami and Brogan to load up their toddler and make the half-hour drive into town. Casey worked in a hospital as an ultrasound technician and had an array of personal experience with pregnancy, including one miscarriage of her own, one healthy son, and a new daughter on the way.

"I'm so sorry, Jo. I know how hard this is. You can go to the doctor just to confirm, but there's nothing they can do at this point. You'll bleed for about two weeks, but it's generally pretty safe to go home and just watch for signs of infection."

I cried some more, then called Tami and told her never mind, I didn't need to go to the doctor after all. Once again, we were still in the waiting period of a new job and didn't have health insurance yet. I didn't feel like dragging my crying self plus a rowdy toddler to the ER, only to have them restate Casey's diagnosis and charge me hundreds of dollars or more for the bad news. Getting the situation verified by a board-certified professional would not change the outcome.

"We're already on our way," Tami said. "We'll just come by and say hi, let the girls run around for a while."

I was sitting on the low concrete steps in front of my room when Tami and Brogan pulled up in an older blue sedan. The crying had stopped but the bleeding had not. She gave me a big hug and told me she was sorry. Brogan expressed his condolences and said that at least it happened sooner rather than later. I was too numb with shock to be offended. I figured he was just a guy trying to say something comforting and almost getting it right.

After the girls had played for a while and we parents had caught up on enough sagebrush gossip to temporarily distract my mind from my current situation, Tami and Brogan gathered up their daughter. I said I had to go to the store for supplies and Tami offered to make the run for me.

"No, it's okay. I can make it," I said. I probably even smiled to demonstrate how okay I was.

They drove off and I called Jim one more time. He usually worked beyond cell service all day, and I hadn't been able to reach him earlier. I held the phone to my ear and stared straight ahead at the gray cinder block wall as I told him I was having a miscarriage. None of it seemed real. Not losing the baby, not experiencing it alone in a cheap room far away from my husband, not the fact that I was no longer pregnant.

"Okay," he said. "Are you all right?"

"Yeah, I'm fine. I'm not going to go to the doctor. There's nothing they can do and it will just cost money."

"Okay," Jim said again. "Well, I'm sad, and I'm sure you're sad. I'm sorry."

"Me, too. Tami and Brogan were just here to visit, so that was really nice of them. They just sat with me on the steps. They're good people."

"Yes, they are."

"I still have to go to the store and get Grace ready for bed. I'll call you later."

"Okay. I love you."

"Love you, too."

I strapped Grace into her car seat and drove a mile to the grocery store. I pushed a metal cart and walked the aisles of Raley's gathering snacks, a small bottle of milk, and giant sanitary napkins, all the while talking to Grace and vaguely wondering if the blood had leaked through the washcloth yet, and if so, had any strangers noticed.

The dark-haired cashier at the checkout counter looked barely old enough to be out of high school. Maybe he was still in high school. I always tried to get in line at a register with a female cashier when I bought menstrual products because I blush easily. But that night he was the only option—he and the equally young and male bag boy. I gritted my teeth and put my items on the conveyor belt. I absolutely needed those huge fluffy absorbent underwear liners with the peel-off adhesive on the back, and I was numb to who noticed anything now.

I paid for my purchases while they talked and laughed, completely unaware that they were ringing up a customer who was currently in the process of losing a baby.

When we returned to our room with my supplies, I stuck Grace in front of a cartoon with a bag of goldfish crackers and a sippy cup of milk while I took a shower. I stood under the hot water and watched the red run down the drain. There was so much red. It seemed like it would never stop.

After I'd dried off and put on my pajamas, I climbed into bed next to Grace. I wrapped my arms around her small, warm body and she instinctively nestled closer to me. Then I sobbed again, crying and bleeding and hugging all night.

Jim couldn't drive into Winnemucca to be with me the next day because we only had one vehicle and I was driving it. But I still had to grocery shop and run errands. The logistics of remote ranch life yield for no one, and we still needed flour, sugar, milk, eggs, and diapers.

I stocked up on household supplies at Walmart and took Grace to the park as planned. She was unaware of Mommy's troubles, and I saw no reason to skip the fun outing. But I kept to myself instead of exchanging friendly small talk with the other parents. I watched Grace go down the slide and pushed her while she giggled and screamed with delight on the swing. I made myself smile and say, "Wheeee!" when she swung toward me, grinning and throwing her head back in the summer sunshine.

Back at the ranch, I told Jim I planned to keep to myself until the bleeding stopped. I allowed myself that time frame, the one with the constant physical reminder of what had happened, to wallow and dwell on the couch. I would venture outside and resume normal activity once it was over. In the meantime, I asked him to tell everyone he saw what had happened, to reduce the number of people who would ask me about it as much as possible.

It felt like we had already told everyone we knew plus a bunch of people we didn't know that I was pregnant. It seemed so easy, breezy, and simple: Two pregnancies equaled two babies. We'd be a family of four by the following January. There was nothing to this whole "building a family" thing.

I realized that creating other people from scratch could be much more complicated, messy, and sad than I'd previously thought. I sat on the couch in the sunken living room and watched cartoons with Grace most of each day, swallowing ibuprofen tablets every four hours for the intense cramps and holding my toddler as much as she would allow.

The physical contact of her body on mine brought more comfort than all the painkillers and parenting websites that said miscarriages were common and usually caused by nothing more than simple chromosomal abnormalities. I let Grace sit on my lap, rub my arm, and lay her head on my chest as much as she wanted. She was alive, and she was mine.

Jim had been looking forward to the Rope for Hope for weeks. It was an annual team roping held each summer to benefit local ranching families affected by cancer. It had grown since its inception in 2009 to become a fun family day complete with a burger stand, games for the kids, a silent auction, and Basque dinner with a live band in the evening. I knew my husband liked to team rope and knew he'd overspend whatever budget we agreed on for entry fees, but win, lose, or draw, it was all for a good cause. It was mid-July and enough time had passed since the miscarriage that I actually looked forward to seeing people and socializing.

The night before the roping, Jim learned that it wasn't a ride-in format like we'd previously thought. Instead, the rules called for each roper to enter with one partner they picked beforehand, and then they would be drawn two additional partners. We knew he wouldn't be able to find a partner on such short notice. I hated to see him miss out on a day of team roping, so I volunteered to rope with him. Or maybe he asked me. I want to think I was noble enough to step up to the plate when the stakes were high and the chips were down and there was no other relief hitter and all those other metaphors that I only vaguely understood, but I distinctly remember my heart dropping and the tension rising through my chest at the thought of team roping the next day.

I'd only ever team roped once before. It had been the previous year at a benefit roping for a cowboy friend of ours who'd wrecked his truck and wound up in a wheelchair. I'd ridden Teaks and caught two feet, but my favorite horse didn't stop in time for me to get my dallies and we got a no-time. I'd never once team roped in the practice pen where everything was slow and there was no money on the line.

But I didn't want Jim to miss out. Besides, I'd roped calves and yearlings in pastures and branding traps plenty of times. Roping in an arena was just faster and more pressurized than anything I'd done so far, but what the hell. We decided I'd heel and ride Bob, Jim's number one heel horse. I loved Teaks, but he really was more of a head horse. I needed a mount that would stop when I threw my rope, since I was a rookie and might not be able to handle delivering my loop and signaling my horse to stop at the same time. Bob used to buck every day when Jim first bought him out of the kill pen for cheap because he was a blown-up barrel horse, but he hadn't bucked in a couple years. Not hard, anyway. Also, I'd never ridden him before.

But I would probably be fine.

The next day, we loaded up and drove to the Dufferena Ranch where the Rope for Hope was held. It was already hot before the roping started. Jim watched Grace while I warmed up Bob in a pasture full of gopher holes that doubled as a parking lot for the event. I reminded myself to breathe evenly and relax my body as I cautiously asked the big sorrel gelding to trot and lope both directions. He didn't want to take his right lead and I didn't try to make him. I didn't want to pick a fight with a horse I'd never ridden before that was previously condemned to die because he bucked people off on a regular basis. Besides, we were team roping. He didn't need the right lead.

I tied Bob up to the trailer when he felt relaxed and retrieved my toddler from her dad. Jim was settling into his standard procedure of drinking beer and swapping stories with the other guys while he waited his turn to rope. I wandered around the silent auction and checked out the kid games, but Grace was a little too young to participate. One of the moms running the games asked if she could have an Otter Pop, and I said yes. I was surprised by the offer, since I was usually isolated from other families with small children and hadn't realized she was old enough to eat popsicles.

After entries closed, the event organizers generated a list of teams randomly by a computer program. They announced each set of six teams but never posted the draw. I stuck close to the arena once the roping started, because I couldn't hear the announcer over the loudspeaker from the concession area.

I left Grace strapped in her stroller near the arena and roped with Jim first, since he was the partner I picked. He rode in the box calm and steady like the experienced competitor he was. My heart fluttered but I backed into the heeling box and held a loop out to the side. I looked at Jim, ready to squeeze Bob with my legs and break with the steer so I could haze him away from the fence. I'd seen the process enough times to know what I needed to do.

Jim nodded and was swinging before he left the box. He caught the steer and turned left. I rode the corner, tracked the steer a few jumps, and missed my heel shot. I missed my second loop and loped down to the catch pen with Jim and the steer.

My first randomly drawn partner was Marshall Smith, a good local roper.

"You drew one of the best partners here," Jim said. "That's really lucky. You'll do great."

I smiled a hello, shook hands with Marshall when Jim introduced us, and rode into the heeling box for my next run. Marshall nodded and we broke fast. Then Marshall necked the steer and went left like it was the tenth round of the National Finals Rodeo and a gold buckle was on the line. Me and Bob were left so far behind that I had time to be surprised. I timidly kicked him up and threw my rope in an unorganized wad at the steer's hind end as soon as my partner realized I was slow and reined his horse up.

"Wow, that guy was fast," I told Jim afterward when we were both outside the arena. I was impressed with my header's abilities, but also a little confused why he was trying to outrun me. After all, we were on the same team.

"He'll go slower next time," Jim reassured me. "He must have thought you were a higher numbered roper. Don't worry, he'll rate down."

That made sense. My husband had a reputation as a good roper, so my partner must have seen that I was Jim Young's wife and assumed I could keep up with the big boys. But it also made sense that he would forget about the clock and slow down for me next time. It was a benefit roping and we were all there to have fun.

I loosened Bob's cinch, stuffed my roping glove in the gullet of my saddle, and grabbed the stroller handles again. Two runs down, at least four more to go. Maybe more if I advanced to the final round with one of my partners, but even I knew that was highly unlikely.

Grace was hungry around lunchtime, so I took her to the burger stand in between runs. I had no idea when I was up next since the announcer only read the next six teams to compete, and the loudspeaker only broadcast a garbled collection of sounds into the concession area. I broke off small pieces of hamburger to feed Grace and watched the roping from across the driveway.

After I fed my daughter, I headed back to see if I was up in the next six teams.

"Jolyn Young and Justin Thompson, ride into the box. Jolyn Young, you're up. This is your last call or your steer will be turned out."

The announcer sounded irritated and impatient. Apparently she had been calling my name for a while, but I couldn't hear from across the way where I was taking care of my child.

"It's okay, just take your time, it's not a big deal," Jim told me. He stood by Bob's neck while I tightened my cinch and put on my roping glove. My hands shook and made it hard to put on my glove. I hated being late. I hated being in trouble. I hated being publicly called out for being late and in trouble. Jim assumed stroller duty and I rode into the arena, shaking out a loop and trying to control my breathing.

"Don't let them rush you." Justin looked me in the eye as he spoke to me. "It's no biggie. Don't let it get to your head. Just ride in there like you own the place."

I nodded and took a deep breath. Jim and Justin were right. I walked Bob into the heel box. Justin nodded, we all ran down the arena, and he turned the steer nice and slow after he caught. I kicked Bob into position, swung my rope and threw just like I did in the branding trap, caught two feet and went to the horn. I might have slipped a leg and taken a five-second penalty, but I felt like I'd won the round. My goal was to get a time at least once during the Rope for Hope, and I did.

I stuck closer to the arena gate for the rest of the roping and didn't get publicly chastised for being tardy again. I didn't make the short round but didn't mind at all. I'd gotten a time in a team roping—and a "slick horn" team roping, no less. In regular team roping, the ropers wrap their saddle horns with rubber, making their rope stop quicker since rubber is sticky. The Rope for Hope kept to buckaroo tradition and the rules stated everyone had to wrap their horns with a slick piece of leather. Plus, I'd had a successful run for the second time I'd ever team roped with a partner I'd never met before while riding an unfamiliar horse.

I counted that as a win and headed over to the silent auction. We'd saved money on entry fees, so for once we had a little cash in the wallet for shopping. I bid on a beautiful red and green hand-stitched quilt, a hand-carved kid's rocking chair shaped like a bear, a leather bracelet and pocketknife set, and more. I won most of the items I bid on and we headed home before dark with the wallet a little lighter but my horsemanship confidence a bit higher.

CHAPTER 14 ✳ To Bail or Not to Bail

I knew Jim would get arrested and hauled off to jail as soon as the police car's lights flashed red and blue behind us. It was stupid. I should have driven, but I was mad because I always had to drive. I'd already driven two and a half hours from Elko, so I made him take his turn at driving the remaining two and a half hours home to the ranch like he'd promised earlier that day. That promise was made before he drank beer all day at the horse sale, but still. A deal's a deal.

"Can I see your license and registration?" the officer asked as he stood at the driver's side window.

Jim pulled his license out of his wallet while I dug through the glove box for proof of registration.

"Don't worry, it'll be fine," Jim said. "I can pass the field sobriety tests, no problem."

I wasn't so sure. His eyes were bloodshot and bleary. He smelled like the inside of a beer can. I shoved something around on the floorboard with my foot and heard a distinctive hiss. Then the cab of the pickup smelled even more like beer.

"Oh, shit," I said. "I just poked a hole in a can of beer."

Jim looked over at me but didn't have time to help figure out a solution (besides to drink it, as would be his first choice) before the officer came back.

"I'm gonna need you to step out of the vehicle, please," he said.

Yep, I thought, this is it. He's going to jail.

I tried to sop up the mess from the beer I'd accidentally shot-gunned at the worst possible time while the officer instructed my husband in the field sobriety tests. I was not sure exactly what they were doing back there, and I didn't look. I was too nervous. I knew he was drunk. It would take a pretty dumb cop to not catch on at this point.

After a while, the officer returned alone.

"Is there someone else who can drive this vehicle home?" he asked.

"Yes, I can."

"And have you been drinking today?"

"No, I haven't had a single drop of alcohol, and if you're suspicious, just give me a Breathalyzer and let's get this over with," I said.

My husband was being arrested, it was late, and I had a cranky toddler in the back seat who was starting to fuss and strain at her car seat straps.

"Okay," the cop replied. "Would you like to say anything to your husband before you leave?"

I climbed down from the pickup and walked to the rear of the police car behind me. Jim sat in the back seat. I looked at him then looked away, forcing back angry tears.

"I'll call you in the morning," Jim said.

I nodded.

"What's the matter? Are you mad?"

A chopped-off laugh escaped from my mouth. For once, I had the ultimate trump card to end a marital dispute. Of the two of us, I was the only one not handcuffed in a police cruiser. I turned away and strode back to our pickup. It was after ten-thirty at night, and I still had to find a motel, check in, and get my small daughter settled in for an unexpected stay without even a change of clothes or a toothbrush. Then in the morning, I had to figure out how the hell to bail someone out of jail.

Grace was throwing a full-blown tantrum by the time I drove to Scott Shady Court. I carried her into the one-story brick building and put her to sleep in the double bed. Then I sat in the desk chair and assessed my current life situation.

It wasn't good. My husband was in jail for drunk driving. It was official: he was a drunk, and now everyone would know. I'd suppressed the truth to myself and everyone else for years, but now the facts would be in the newspaper within a few days. The notice would run in the paper printed by the company I worked for. My boss would see my husband's name in the police record. Our friends would soon hear of it through the "sagebrush telegraph."

I called my mom, but she didn't answer. It was late, though, and she was probably asleep. I called my best friend, and she picked up after two rings.

"Hey, Jo," Casey said. "What's up?"

Between sobs, I told her Jim was in jail and certain to get a DUI.

"Oh, no, I'm so sorry," she said.

I was embarrassed but relieved to have shared the news out loud with someone. I cried it out for half an hour, then we hung up the phone and I sagged into bed. I was exhausted.

The next morning, I took Grace to The Griddle, my favorite restaurant in Winnemucca. I was halfway through my favorite breakfast, fruit-filled crepes and a cappuccino, when an unknown number showed up on my caller ID.

"Hi, it's me," Jim said when I answered the phone.

"Hi." I forced out the word. I knew he'd call, but I still wasn't happy to hear from him.

"I only have a few minutes, but go to the bail bond place on Bridge Street. Just show up and the lady there will tell you what to do."

"Okay."

"All right, thank you, honey. It'll be okay. Love you," Jim said.

"I just want you to know that I'm going to do this, but I am not fucking happy about it."

Then I hung up the phone. I was done talking to him, plus I realized I'd just said the f-word fairly loudly in the middle of a crowded family restaurant on a Sunday morning.

After I finished my cup of fancy coffee and paid the bill, I loaded my toddler into the truck and drove to the bail bond place to see about springing her daddy out of the slammer. I walked into the small office and saw a middle-aged, overweight, red-headed lady sitting behind the desk. She looked far less intimidating than the muscle-bound bouncer type I'd imagined.

"I guess I need to bail my husband out of jail," I said. "And I have no clue how to do that."

The red-headed lady looked up at me over her glasses and kindly explained that bond rates were based on a percentage of the bail set by the jail. It was basically paying a fee to get a person out as long as they promised to return for their court date. If I bailed Jim out, I was technically on the hook for the remainder of his bail if he failed to show up for his court date for his arraignment. Whenever that was and whatever it was for. Or something like that.

"So, your husband's bail is $237.64," she said.

I silently stood on my side of the desk and pondered that figure. Paying it wouldn't represent a financial hardship, but I wasn't sure I wanted to pay any amount of money for jail-related fees. I made no reach for my purse and instead silently pondered my other life decisions, like why I'd married a man who would get a DUI with his own baby in the back seat.

After a couple long minutes, the red-headed lady spoke up.

"You don't have to bail him out."

"What happens if I don't?"

"Then he just stays in jail until his arraignment."

I had no idea what an arraignment was and didn't ask for a definition. Time was all that currently mattered.

"And how long until that?"

"Usually about six days."

I immediately knew I had to bail him out for two reasons. First, the money in our bank account was equally his, and second, if he stayed in jail for six days he'd get fired for sure. And since we lived in company housing, we'd all have to move, change our address at the post office, tell our friends and family our new house phone number, notify the bank of our new zip code for credit card purchases, make new friends, and find a new grocery store. If we made it back to the ranch later that day, he might get fired, or he might not. But I knew I had to at least flip the coin. I gritted my teeth and paid his bail.

I chewed Jim's ass up one side and down the other the entire drive back to the 2 Slash. The ranch was two and a half hours north of Winnemucca, so I had plenty of time to tell him what I really thought. I made it abundantly clear that I was not impressed with his behavior and that I would never bail him out of jail again. He stared straight ahead, listened quietly and said, "Yes, ma'am," a couple dozen times.

When we reached the ranch, I parked under the towering shade tree behind our big white house by the meadow. I took Grace inside and Jim headed to the barn to find his boss and see if he still had a job. He was supposed to work on Sunday, since he'd taken Saturday off to go to the horse sale. The ranch had a strict policy of four days off per employee per month. If your mom died and you wanted to drive three days to attend her distant funeral, you better cry quickly and show up at the barn with your boots on and a rope in your hand for each of the remaining twenty-six workdays.

I was in the living room with Grace and her toys when I looked out the picture window and saw Jim walking back toward the house. He'd only been gone ten minutes. He looked down at the ground while he walked.

I knew what he'd say as soon as he opened the front door.

"Well, I got fired."

I wanted to be on his side and say, *What? Just for no-showing one day of work? You weren't even that late getting back!*

But then again, he got a DUI and blew off a workday without even a phone call to his boss. So instead of saying anything, I just stacked another Mega Block onto Grace's tower. It didn't matter whose side I was on or how mad I was—either way, we had to move again.

"We're not moving until at least next week," I said. "My magazine deadline is Friday, and I really don't see myself polishing up six articles, packing up the house, and taking care of a toddler before then."

To his credit, Jim packed a lot of boxes while I wrote stories about sage grouse and cattle prices. He used an excessive amount of tape and packing paper, but I didn't complain. He also called everyone he could think of that ran a cow outfit in the Great Basin looking for a job. He called ranch managers in northern Nevada, cowbosses in southern Idaho, and friends of friends from Tonopah to North Fork.

For the first week, he struck out.

When I filed all my stories by deadline and he still didn't have a job, I felt a little bit more like complaining. We were homeless and jobless for the second time in our eighteen months of marriage. Was this what my future looked like—unpacking boxes only to repack them and throw them in a horse trailer just a few months later? Would I constantly say goodbye to just-started friendships and introduce myself to new acquaintances I knew I most likely wouldn't be seeing within six to twelve months?

Worst of all, would my husband always be a drunk? He'd been a big drinker when we dated, so it wasn't like I had no clue. But I was eternally optimistic and thought he might age out of drinking so much. The DUI with a blood alcohol content reading of 0.123 made his drinking problem too much to ignore. The legal limit was 0.08. Like my dad said, he was "drunk and a half."

I hardly ate and my stomach constantly churned for several days. I barely looked at Jim and avoided talking to him. He must have known something was up. He was chronically drunk, not dumb.

I sat in the office chair behind the rolltop desk that wasn't ours. Both belonged to the ranch. They were in our house because the owner's wife had invited me to choose any furniture item I wanted from her personal storage unit to use while we lived there. She was also the source of most of my curtains.

I called the only person I could think of to help me reason my way through the situation. I didn't know her well, just from visiting at rodeos and horse sales.

Her husband was a local legend, a buckaroo who'd been a fearless bronco rider, a county jail inmate more than once, and a falling-down drunk until he got sober after a drunk driver killed one of his kids. Or maybe he'd wrecked a pickup while he was drunk and killed all the horses in the trailer. It was hard to keep all the stories straight. At any rate, Missy was still married to Travis. I needed to know how she did it.

"Hi, this is Jolyn," I began. "I know this is out of the blue, but I just needed to talk to you. Jim got a DUI and I'm really struggling with it."

"Oh, I'm sorry to hear," Missy replied. Her voice was sympathetic but sensible. She shared stories from her past as the wife of an alcoholic and one line made me sit up a little straighter and stop crying.

"But you know why we stay with them? Because they are good men."

Missy was right. Jim was a good man. He always remembered my birthday, held his baby daughter in the evenings after work, and was one of the hardest-working cowboys I knew. He wore his shirts until they were threadbare so Grace and I could buy new clothes and only got grumpy if he ran out of Copenhagen or coffee.

Secretly, I was glad Jim got a DUI. Maybe a fine and some jail time would change his attitude toward drinking all day and half the night until he passed out in his recliner. Maybe that Winnemucca cop and the Nevada justice system would sober him up for good, even though the four DUIs he'd gotten over the past fifteen years hadn't.

As I said, I was eternally optimistic.

Jim and I drove two hundred miles south to the Circle 4 Ranch in central Nevada so he could interview for a job. We hauled a horse down and planned to stay the night because it was a riding interview. His potential boss, John Young (no relation), wanted Jim to rope a few calves in the corral with him at headquarters so he could assess his abilities. A riding interview was unusual, but maybe John had hired enough dinks that he wasn't taking any chances on the new guy being a dud.

The ranch was far from town and visible from miles away because of the huge, old trees that surrounded the houses at headquarters. That was pretty much how all the ranches in Nevada were marked. Most of them weren't locatable by consumer-grade GPS systems, but we all knew to turn at the trees.

We unloaded Bob and put him in a corral for the night with hay and water. The Circle 4 headquarters featured all pipe corrals, a spendy upgrade not commonly seen on desert cow outfits. It made sense after we learned the place was owned by a big pharmaceutical company that provided funding beyond profits the cattle brought in.

John showed us to an empty single-wide trailer for the night. I opened the door with a duffel bag on one shoulder and a toddler on the other hip, surveyed the interior, and said, "Nope."

The trailer was at least as run down as the one we'd moved into on the Rafter J. I used the hall bathroom and noticed the toilet bowl didn't refill with water after I flushed. I discovered it was because the water to the toilet was shut off. Apparently, it was necessary to do so between flushes because otherwise, it would leak out the bottom and onto the floor. The carpet looked like it hadn't been cleaned in months, maybe years. (I didn't rule out the possibility of decades.) I didn't even bother to inspect the kitchen because it was just a temporary situation. Or was it? Maybe this would be our home if Jim took a job at the Circle 4.

"If you want to work here, go for it. But I'm renting a room in Elko. Grace and I will come visit you on the weekends," I announced before we turned in for the night.

I had a salaried job that I could do while staying at home with our child. If Jim wanted to live in another shithole and rope for his wages, good for him. At that particular juncture in my life, I did not have the fire in my belly to deep clean another trailer that should be condemned while working full-time, caring for a toddler, and chauffeuring Jim around because he'd lost his driver's license. I was no longer a newlywed ranch wife with stars in my eyes when I looked at these decrepit houses hours away from town.

The next morning, I played with Grace just outside the big pipe corral while Jim, John, and another Circle 4 cowboy roped a set of cattle. They roped ranch style—no chute, just setting up shots and taking them while all the cattle were loose. John used a sixty-foot-long "riata," or rope made from rawhide, and lost his rope twice. Jim scoop-looped a calf running down the fence and never missed a shot.

After the second time John lost his rope and Jim kicked up his horse to fix his mistake, I wondered why John had bothered to set up this "interview." It was shaping up to be more like a roping clinic with Jim as the instructor. I figured Jim would either slam-dunk get the job or not stand a chance on account of showing up the boss.

"If you want a job, we'd dang sure like to have ya," John said at the conclusion of the morning's roping activities.

So that was the way this was going to go. I kind of had a feeling, since John smiled and laughed the whole time, even though he was having heck with his rope. I wanted to ask which house we'd have, but I held my tongue and decided to prod Jim about it later.

Jim and John agreed on a start date and how many head of horses he could bring. We said our goodbyes, and then I drove us north toward our former home to finish packing.

By the time we hit the interstate, Jim's chin was bouncing off his chest in the passenger seat. Grace slept in the back seat. She hadn't slept much the night before, which meant I hadn't, either. I watched Jim's eyes close and his shoulders slump. I was not having it.

Why should he get to nap in the truck while I did all the work? I leaned over and shook his shoulder.

"Huh? What?" Jim's eyelids fluttered, then his chin landed on his chest again.

With one hand on the wheel, I reached across the front seat and shook his arm, a little rougher this time.

"Wake up," I said. "I'm not going to do all the work while you take a nap. I would love a nap, but I don't get one."

"Don't get mad at me. It's not my fault the baby didn't sleep."

That time, his eyes didn't even open. His head rolled with the rhythm of the truck tires on the road.

I leaned over and punched him hard on the shoulder.

"You either wake up or I will push you out of the truck."

He woke up enough to say, "And how are you going to do that while you're driving?"

"I will stop on the side of the road, reach over and open your door, and push your ass out."

Jim stayed awake the rest of the trip home, but he wasn't happy about it. I wasn't happy about being an enraged woman who fantasized about shoving her husband out the door of a moving pickup, but there we were.

I was just glad our daughter slept through it all.

CHAPTER 15 ✳ One Box Per Month

I stood up from the bedroll and shoved my feet into a pair of tennis shoes.

"Where are you going?" Jim asked. He stood fully dressed in the doorway of our new bedroom. It was six in the morning and he'd just stepped back into the house to tell me goodbye because he was going to camp for a few days and could I please get up because he needed to take the bedroll I was sleeping in.

I stormed down the hallway and out into the gravel driveway, still in my pajamas. "I'm going to find whoever runs this place and tell them my husband needs to stay here long enough to unload the boxes from the horse trailer," I said. The ranch office was just across the driveway. I'd check there first for the manager.

Jim followed close behind.

"Wait," he said. "I'll find John and tell him I need to unload your stuff before I leave. I'm sure it won't take long. Just go back inside. I'll be right back."

I turned around and walked back into the trailer house. It was a double-wide this time, with four bedrooms and a big orange water stain on the ceiling below the swamp cooler. There was carpet in the main bathroom that smelled wet even when it wasn't and a sofa in the living room that smelled like cat pee even though we didn't have a cat. A group of single cowboys had been the last residents, and they'd left a trash can stuffed full of pizza boxes in the kitchen and streams of urine on and around the toilets. But I'd relented on my declaration to not move into another run-down house when I'd learned we were moving into the larger trailer. I thought maybe once I got it cleaned up, it would (hopefully) be vaguely livable.

Grace woke up shortly after I returned to the house. I gave her a breakfast of instant oatmeal and milk, then set upon the task of cleaning our newest house with a fervor and enthusiasm usually only seen in generals heading to war. I scrubbed, washed, swept, vacuumed, shampooed, and bleached till I was too tired to lift a sponge. It was not my favorite part of moving, but I had accepted it as part of the cowboy lifestyle. At least we were in a double-wide with four bedrooms and not the single-wide with the broken toilet we'd stayed in during the interview.

Jim came home at lunchtime and told me that Shawn, a cowboy from another division of the ranch, would come over later to help unload the horse trailer full of boxes.

"Good," I said, partly mollified because the house was now cleaner. "Because I can't cook dinner unless you unbury my kitchen boxes from behind the couch and the roping dummy."

Jim departed for camp later that day, leaving me with a toddler with a runny nose and several towers of cardboard boxes stacked through the rooms like a 3D maze. I shoved most of them into one of the spare bedrooms. I also decided to leave most of our things packed to streamline the next move. The cowboss at this place had already stood on the roof of the vet shed and shot a rifle in the direction of the cowboy crew. I had no idea why. The cowboys seemed confused on this point as well. Nobody was hit, thank God. Plus, the house was filthy and sparing two hours for a new hire to unload moving boxes apparently required written permission and approval from a third party. This place was nuts. I figured we'd be gone within six months. If we stayed longer than that, I'd unpack one box per month.

I stood in the dining room and looked out the sliding glass doors. Semi-trucks and passenger cars glinted in the sunlight as they passed by on Highway 50, a mile and a half across the sagebrush flat. The rolling metal and glass specks never stopped. There was no reason for them to stop. The nearest community with a post office was twenty miles away. The nearest town with a bank was another fifty miles past that.

Behind me, two-year-old Grace chattered to herself and played at the kitchen table. Outside, the wind picked up and banged the loose skirting against the side of the trailer house. A forceful gust rattled the framed Charlie Russell print on the wall. It was one of my favorites, a painting of a mountain man wearing snow boots with a rifle slung in the crook of his arm. He stood at the edge of a cliff and looked down at the bighorn sheep he'd shot on the ledge below while his pack horses waited behind him in the snow. Titled "Meat's Not Meat Till It's In The Pan," a larger reproduction of the same print had hung on the wall of my childhood home.

What was I doing out here? Other moms my age lived in actual neighborhoods. They had friends within a ten-minute driving distance and ordered lattes at drive-through coffee shops five days a week. I was alone in the barren desert with only a toddler for company. I hadn't talked to my best friend in weeks. Casey had settled with her own husband and family in California, and she was usually too busy with a job and her own young children to talk on the phone much. I figured she spent a lot of time taking her kids to visit friends and play at the park, having fun and enjoying her life. It seemed unfair, but that's just because I was jealous.

I could have married Jesse Eichhorn. He'd landed a good job straight out of college and was a "keeper"—everyone told me so when we were dating. I didn't keep him, though. But I bet if I had, he wouldn't have made me live this far from town. He probably would've bought us a house with a few acres and a horse if I wanted one.

But then I would never have followed my dreams to Nevada, gotten a cowboy job, lived on several historic ranches that most people never even got to visit, and felt the sagebrush flats and desert wind expand all around me to the mountains until I became a natural part of the landscape.

I reminded myself that I chose this lifestyle. When I married a cowboy, I chose this—the dirt, the frequent moves, the lawlessness, the rough edges that either drew blood or left calluses. I looked through the glass again at the cars silently zipping by in the distance, then turned to the kitchen to see about getting dinner ready for my husband and daughter.

Jim and I learned we had another baby on the way a few months later. I'd sworn I would never get pregnant again after the miscarriage, but we both knew I would change my mind once the grief subsided. We'd always imagined a family with children, not just child. I knew that early-term miscarriages were common and that I shouldn't be afraid of another one. To create life, you have to be willing to risk seeing it slip away without your permission.

We were excited but cautious in telling friends until I reached the twelve-week mark, which would supposedly bring some level of reassurance. We shared the big news with our parents but for the most part kept it under wraps. When depression set in within the first six weeks, Jim put Teaks in the corral by the vet shed so I could ride him. I enjoyed a few short rides around the corral on my favorite horse with the smell of his mane on the wind before I felt too nauseated to saddle up.

Within days I was puking every morning when I changed Grace's diaper. I developed a system where I laid her down on the floor in front of the hall bathroom, held my breath while I wiped her bottom, then rolled the used diaper and pushed it aside while I lunged for the bathroom, making it just in time to vomit into the sink. I retched into the plastic basin until I dry-heaved and beads of sweat popped up on my upper lip, but it was okay because I'd read that strong symptoms meant a lower chance of miscarriage. I'd puke all day if it meant I could keep this baby.

This went on for weeks. Then one day, the puking was replaced by just a strong sense of feeling like I had to puke. When the cowboy crew made plans to brand calves at the Home Ranch, a sister ranch to the Circle 4, my mile-away neighbor offered to keep an eye on Grace for a bit if I wanted to rope.

"No, thanks," I said with regret. "I'd just have to get off my horse to pee every ten minutes."

It was tempting to clamber up in the saddle and swing a rope like old times, but the bladder situation was real. If I tried to be tough and muscle through the urge, there was a good chance I'd end up wetting myself. That's never fun, especially with a crowd of mostly male onlookers.

But I also knew the limitations were temporary. It was just one branding season. Besides, I'd be looking over my shoulder at Grace the whole time anyway. I could hand my baby to a friend—or a complete stranger, even—and rope at a jackpot in town, but I didn't trust anyone else to care for her in a branding situation. There were needles, knives, ear tag guns, and other sharp tools lying around that could injure a toddler.

Nah, I was better off staying on the ground, where I could keep an eye on my child and make it to the nearest bush in time.

In the dark of night just after closing time at the bars, I stormed through the bedroom doorway in my gray plaid pajamas, the flannel ones my mom had given me for Christmas. My pregnant belly pushed against the fabric and made a small mound under my shirt. I was barefoot, braless, and didn't care.

"Where have you been?" I asked.

"I can eshplain—" Jim started to say as he stood just outside the sliding glass door. Jeremy stood on one side with Jim's arm slung across his shoulders. Hezzie held him up from the other side.

"I don't want to hear it." I cut Jim off mid-sentence. "You are beyond drunk, I can tell that much."

Jim had gone to the horse barn after work to drink beer with the guys, then they'd migrated to the only bar within twenty miles. I knew he was down there. I wished he was up at the house with me and Grace but didn't try to make him come home. I also knew that with his old friend Hezzie day-working at the Circle 4 for a few days, Jim was liable to drink more than usual, which was already a lot.

"Now, Jolyn, there's no reason to be mad at Jim. It's all my fault." Hezzie stepped forward and spoke in a low, soothing voice.

"Don't you dare try and cover for him. You didn't pour the drinks down his throat. This was all him." I stepped forward as well, but I did not speak in a low, soothing voice. I hoped my shouting wouldn't wake Grace up.

As soon as I raised my voice, Jeremy dropped Jim's arm and shot off the porch like his boot soles were greased. Hezzie didn't even flinch. He was an experienced drinker and a longtime friend.

"No, I mean it," he continued in that same level tone. "He wanted to come home sooner, but I made him stay out. Don't be mad at him. Be mad at me if you gotta be mad at somebody."

I was beyond mad. I was done.

"You know what? Just take him with you, because I sure as hell don't want him like this."

I could feel my face growing red. My whole body felt hot. All I could think about was how pissed I was that Jim had gotten falling-down drunk at some crappy bar with his buddies while I was at home putting our toddler to sleep, wondering if he was safe, and growing our next baby in my belly.

Hezzie somehow persuaded me to let Jim come into the house. Jim couldn't even speak by then. He stumbled through the dining room, leaning on Hezzie as his friend guided him around the table and chairs. His eyes barely opened. It looked like he was starting to pass out as he walked.

Hezzie helped Jim lie down in the bed and walked into the dining room.

"Now again, Jolyn, I'm sorry for tonight. It's all my fault. Now I'm going to go, but I'll see you guys in the morning." His voice never rose above the volume that you'd use to persuade a scared horse to get out of a stock trailer.

I closed the sliding glass door behind Hezzie and crawled under the covers beside Jim. I was glad he was home safe. I truly didn't want him to die in an alcohol-related car crash, even though the odds were good that it would happen one of these nights.

Within minutes, Jim was snoring like a rusty chainsaw. I knew that elbowing him would be futile. He'd just resume snoring as soon as he was fully passed out again. I made my way to Grace's room at the other end of the house. I was glad for an excuse to take myself out of my husband's bed. I walked down the hall and crawled in with our little girl, wrapping my arms around her body and snuggling my chin on top of her head. There, with Jim's loud snores steady but fainter from a distance, I was able to fall asleep.

Jim and I had bickered all day before the tension escalated into a full-blown fight. I woke up cranky because I had slept in a bedroll on the floor of a grimy motel room in McDermitt again. I was seven months pregnant and tasked with taking care of our two-year-old daughter while Jim roped with his buddies and drank himself into a stupor for three days at the Fourth of July rodeo. The truck and trailer were loaded with suitcases and horses on the afternoon of the last day when we stopped by the Say When so Jim could say goodbye to his buddies at the bar. I stayed in the truck with Grace, who was strapped into her car seat and ready for the five-hour drive home. I kept the engine running and the A/C going full blast because we would only be a minute.

Fifteen minutes later, I stepped inside the casino and found Jim seated on a barstool.

"Are you almost ready to go, honey?" I asked with a smile.

"Sure, sure, just lemme finish this beer."

I returned to the truck and thought he might actually finish the beer in his hand and join me. Twenty minutes after that, I walked back into the Say When.

"Jim, can we get going soon? Grace is already asleep, and I want to get most of the drive done before she wakes up."

"Just one more beer," Jim said. His words ran together and his eyelids were at half-mast.

I turned around and walked back to the parking lot without replying. His butt was stuck to that barstool, and he didn't seem to realize that a smoky bar on a bright weekday afternoon was no place for his pregnant wife and young daughter. We were stuck outside in the parking lot by ourselves, and he didn't care as long as he had a beer in his hand and someone to swap stories with.

An hour later, I walked in and was definitely not smiling. I told Jim I didn't care who he was talking to or how full his beer was, it was time to go home.

He started to say, "Just one more round," and I punched him in the shoulder. I tried to hit him hard, but I'm sure it didn't hurt. The pain on impact wasn't the point, though. That was the first time one of our fights had gotten physical. In public, no less. And it was I who had crossed the line. I didn't like that.

I somehow poured Jim into the passenger seat, loaded his friend and fellow Circle 4 cowboy Taylor Hoatson into the back seat next to Grace, and drove two hours to the Maverik gas station in Battle Mountain.

I parked at the diesel pump, the one on the north side that the truckers used. I watched Jim walk into the convenience store and hoped there wouldn't be trouble. He was mad because the gas pump had declined our debit card. That doesn't put a guy in a good mood when he's coming off a runner and his wife nagged him until he left the company of good friends.

I stayed in the pickup with Grace still strapped in her car seat. Taylor was passed out drunk next to her, tipped over in a pile of empty potato chip bags. They crinkled when he twitched and shifted in his sleep.

I didn't want Jim to go into the store. I wished he would have tried our credit card at the pump like I'd suggested instead of looking for the manager and demanding to know why the card reader didn't work. My reassurances that we had money in the account and it was simply a mechanical error did nothing to cool his anger. He was mad, drunk, tired, and most likely had a thumping headache. He needed someone to take out his anger on.

Jim walked into the building and came out a few minutes later with an employee in a red shirt and a name tag.

"Are you the manager?" I heard Jim ask him.

"Me? No. Is there a problem?" The guy looked young. And maybe a little scared of the big cowboy with a hard look in his eye.

"Yes, there is a problem. My card won't work, and it's fucking bullshit. Get me your manager."

"I'm sorry you're having a problem. Just a minute and I'll get him."

The young employee went back into the gas station and the manager came out and faced Jim. They went through the "Is there a problem?" routine until both were yelling and standing nearly chest to chest in the middle of the parking lot. I unbuckled Grace, put her on my hip, and speed-walked over to the developing situation with my hands trembling.

They looked seconds away from throwing the first punch. I placed myself between my husband and the gas station manager, knowing Jim wouldn't do anything to cause me physical harm. I then realized then that I was carrying our toddler daughter into the middle of a potential fistfight.

I looked straight up into Jim's face. His face was red, his eyes were blood-shot, and his jaw was tense.

"Jim, do not hit this guy and start a fight right here. You're on probation. If the cops get called, you'll go to jail."

I spoke low and steady. I didn't say the other part of my argument: that if he was arrested and charged with assault and violating the terms of the two-year probation he received at his DUI sentencing, he'd lose his job. Then his family would be out of a place to live. And we were about to have another child, so I'd have to work to pay all the bills and take care of two small kids by myself.

Jim and the manager exchanged insults over my head while I remained rooted to the pavement between them. Neither backed down, but they didn't advance, either. By then a growing crowd of onlookers had gathered around us. I heard someone say something about calling the sheriff. With law enforcement on the way to run checks on the involved parties' IDs, I was extra motivated to prevent fists from flying.

"Jim, don't do this," I pleaded. "It's not worth it."

I adjusted Grace's leg to fit more comfortably under my belly. At seven months along, the evidence that I was expecting was obvious. I realized what the growing number of spectators saw: A heavily pregnant woman wearing a stretchy dress and flip-flops clutching a small child to her hip, standing between two angry men yelling fightin' words at each other in a parking lot in broad daylight. It was definitely one of my trashier moments.

The cops showed up soon after that and got Jim and the manager to step apart. Taylor had woken up by then and the cops asked to see the IDs of the two cowboys and the manager. After running checks on everyone and asking questions to find out the full story, they let us all go with a warning.

I climbed into the truck to drive us to the Circle 4 after finally getting the tank of gas we'd stopped for in the first place. I stared straight ahead at the blacktop and held my breath to hold back my tears, but they spilled over before we passed our turnoff.

"What's wrong?" Jim asked when he glanced my way and saw me crying. He and Taylor had been rehashing the almost-altercation ever since we'd left Battle Mountain. Jim laughed and joked as he relived the parking lot scene.

"Nothing," I replied. I didn't want to cry in front of Taylor, but I couldn't help it. I couldn't believe that what had just happened was my actual life. My husband had put himself in a position to get arrested, jailed, and fired for absolutely no reason whatsoever. And afterward, he didn't seem remorseful. In fact, he seemed jovial about the whole incident.

Jim and Taylor resumed talking back and forth over the seat backs. I continued looking straight ahead and tried once again to contain my tears. I was not successful. I cried and drove, turned and braked, and tried to ignore my hungover husband and the tagalong cowboy who'd witnessed my blubbering.

<hr />

I left Jim for the first time the next day. I packed clothes, toys, and road snacks, then loaded Grace into the Dodge. I left a note on the kitchen counter that said, "You need to decide if you want to be a drunken cowboy or a married man." I peeled out of the driveway before Jim got home from work.

I drove straight to Allie Bear's in Elko, my home away from home. Allie was one of the wisest people I knew, and I always crashed at her place when going through town. Coincidentally, I had an assignment from *American Cowboy* to write an article about the Flying V. The ranch was an hour north of Elko so it would be a good way to kill two birds with one stone. I could teach my husband a lesson and make a little money. How practical and efficient of me.

I stayed at Allie's for two nights and spilled my guts to her. She listened while I cried. She also told me stories about a middle-aged cowboy who was always in the bottle and one day walked unsteadily along a highway overpass in Reno with traffic flying past mere inches away while his wife desperately tried to convince him to get back into the truck. I realized I was on the path to being that wife. That didn't sound like a future I wanted.

Allie took me and Grace to a rodeo in Elko and never once told me what I should do. She did tell me that I could hide my truck in her garage if needed, though.

I drove to the Flying V one afternoon during my trip to take pictures. Back at Allie's, I hashed things out with Jim through text messages while Grace played on the swing set. He said he'd cut back on his drinking but said I had to make some changes too. He probably meant have sex more often, since that is a frequent point of contention between married people with small children. I agreed to what he wanted. I figured I probably had some culpability in his drinking habit. Maybe he wouldn't drink so much if I didn't nag him so much or said yes every time he initiated sex. All I knew for sure was that he said he'd reduce his alcohol consumption, which meant I could go back home, stay married, and not break up my family. I had come from a broken home and desperately wanted my kids to grow up with two parents under one roof.

Besides, he said he wouldn't drink as much. He probably meant it this time, too.

CHAPTER 16 * And Baby Makes Four

I stood on the flatbed parked in the long driveway and delivered instructions to Jim.

"If you could just lope through the sagebrush next to the road, that'd be great. I want to get the mountain in the background, and the light is flattering from this angle."

I held the Canon to my eye and practiced framing the shot before adding the moving horse and rider while Grace played at my feet. I leaned back slightly to compensate for my big belly. Baby Number Two was due in two months and was a challenging one to carry. My stomach stuck straight out like a horizontal watermelon. Walking or standing for any length of time hurt, but I pushed myself to stand on the flatbed long enough to get the shot I needed.

The photo was for another assignment for *American Cowboy* that immediately followed my story on the Flying V. They wanted a picture of a Great Basin cowboy to print alongside individual images of his gear and explanations of how and why he used each piece.

"Okay," Jim said and reined Teaks toward the mountain range. "I feel kinda dumb just loping my horse along for no reason."

"Hey, two hundred bucks is two hundred bucks. Ride up there and lope back. Please and thank you."

I concentrated on framing the photo just right and preparing to press the button at the exact split second when Teaks' ears were forward, at least two of his feet were on the ground, and Jim's face had a pleasant expression. I knew I'd get only one shot at capturing the right image, maybe two if I was lucky. The Canon had such a slow shutter speed that I had to press the shutter release button about 1.5 seconds before I actually wanted to take the picture, accounting for where Teaks' body, legs, and ears would be during that time. I had to wait until Jim was fairly close to take a picture because the lens didn't zoom very far out. If I waited one second too long, he would be too close or too far past me and we'd have to start the whole process over again.

I held the camera steady and focused on my timing. This would be my first full-page photo for a national magazine. My camera was chintzy and under-powered, but I knew exactly where a horse's legs would be at each point in his stride. I could nail this shot in two takes or less.

Jim gathered Teaks up, asked him to lope, and headed toward the pickup. I snapped a few pictures and reviewed them on the screen. One was blurry and Jim had a weird look on his face in the other.

"I missed it on that try. Could you do it again?"

Jim tightened his jaw and looked down at the ground.

"Sure." He rode back down the driveway.

Another Circle 4 cowboy, Jake Powers, was on hand to view the proceedings and heckle Jim as he saw fit. I doubled down my concentration and held the camera steady. Well, as steady as I could with a toddler tugging on my arm and a horizontal watermelon under my shirt.

"Just a few more minutes, honey," I told Grace. "Watch Daddy run toward us! Daddy's going to run his horse! Quick, watch!"

Grace's interest was piqued long enough to let go of my arm and look down the driveway. She'd only be distracted for about five seconds, but that was all the time I needed to pull this off.

I pressed the shutter release button halfway to focus the camera. I waited one, two, three strides until Jim was positioned in the right-hand third of the frame. His rope and chaps were in full view, just like I wanted. I pressed the button once, waited two seconds for it to take the picture and reset itself, then pressed it again for a second shot just in case.

"Alright, I bet one of those will work." I didn't want to tax my model too much and wear out his patience. If my photography skills improved and I continued selling pictures, I wanted him to let me point my camera at him again sometime.

Of the handful of pictures I snapped that afternoon, one was high enough quality to run in the magazine. I was relieved, proud, and intrigued. It was the quickest $200 I'd ever made. I was interested in exploring other ways to make money with my photography. But I'd need a bigger, better camera before I could step up my skills and increase profitability.

I had to figure out how to buy a new camera later, though. In two months, I'd be a mom times two with a whole lot of sleeplessness and crying on my hands. I just hoped I wouldn't be the source of most of the crying this time.

I was late getting to the hospital for the birth of our second baby on the twenty-eighth of September, 2015. I wasn't in labor or anything; it was another scheduled C-section since we lived too far away from the hospital to try a VBAC (vaginal birth after Cesarean). I shouldn't have worried so much about being late. It wasn't like they could start without me. But I sobbed as we walked into the hospital because that is my child-birthing MO.

We were late because we got up at half past four in the morning and drove four hours to the hospital with a toddler who was in the middle of potty training. For some reason I thought we'd get more sleep if we stayed at our own home the night before the birth rather than sleeping on an air mattress at my mom's house twenty minutes from the hospital. Not sure why I didn't entertain the idea of getting a motel room close to the hospital. Probably just trying to save money, since we had a baby on the way and all.

The whole way to Reno, Grace kept making the sign for "potty." We'd find a side road and pull off the highway, unbuckle her car seat straps, hold her in a crouched position in the gravel, wait five minutes until she stood up and shrugged, then climb back into the truck only to repeat the process in twenty minutes. After a half dozen such stops, I told her to just go in her pull-up. Like my friend Theo once said, "Sometimes, you just don't have time for patience."

When we hit Reno, a wreck on the interstate slowed all four lanes of traffic to a near-standstill. I kept my eyes glued to the clock as we crept along. My mom was meeting us at the hospital to pick up Grace. I hoped she'd snap our last picture as a family of three in the parking lot. Instead, we arrived at the hospital entrance thirty minutes late and I shoved my crying kid into her grandma's arms in front of the automatic sliding glass doors.

Grace was still wearing her pajamas and clung to my arm as my mom reached for her. Grace cried and screamed, "Mommy! Mommy!" as Grandma buckled her into the back seat. Jim threw the diaper bag and sippy cup into my mom's car and steered his crying wife toward Labor and Delivery, where he would welcome an additional family member who would undoubtedly also cry a lot.

The C-section was easier to handle the second time around. I focused on my happy thought: finding out the gender of our new baby. I'd decided I didn't want to learn if we were having a boy or a girl during the pregnancy, since I knew I'd need something positive to focus on during the surgery.

Plus, I already had one girl and I felt societal pressure to produce a male child. If we knew we were having another daughter, people might say, "Was Jim hoping for a boy?" or "Better keep trying till you get a boy!" I didn't want to listen to that for several months. Once the baby was born and cute and healthy, maternal hormones would take over and I'd growl at people if they so much as frowned in my baby's general direction. Then I wouldn't care what anyone thought about his or her genital arrangement.

I lay on the cold steel table in the operating room with the blue drape in front of my face and my arms outstretched beside me while the doctor tugged and pulled at my insides, then said, "Come on, Dad, take a look and tell her what it is."

Jim stood up from his post at the left side of my head, peeked over the blue curtain, and said, "It's a boy."

I smiled. A boy. I couldn't wait to see him. I loved him already.

Later, Jim told me that he saw my guts sitting on the table beside me with the doctor elbow-deep in my abdominal cavity. He said it was bloodier and gorier than any calf-pulling or cow-skinning he'd ever participated in. I was glad he was the one who had looked and not me.

We also were ninety-nine percent sure the baby was a boy before we entered the hospital that day. At my thirty-four-week checkup, the doctor had absentmindedly looked at my chart and told me that "his heartbeat sounded great." I pretended not to hear him say "his," then went home and cried to my closest mom friend on the ranch that now we knew the baby's gender and everything was ruined. I told Jim about the doctor's slip-up because I can't keep a secret to save my life. He said he didn't mind knowing. He said having babies was stressful enough without adding extra things to be surprised about.

We named the baby Milo James Young, and he started nursing like a champ in the recovery room. Grandma and his big sister came to meet him, and the next day my dad drove out to see his newest grandchild. Neither of my older sisters showed any inclination to become mothers, so it looked like I was going to be his sole source of grandchildren. It's rare to claim the title of First and Only when you're the third daughter, and I'd be lying if I said I didn't enjoy it.

At some point during our hospital stay, Jim walked to the gas station down the road and bought me a bottle of cheap wine.

"I thought you might want to drink this and celebrate," he said.

"No, thanks. I'm on a lot of pain meds right now. Plus, I just had major surgery and a baby."

Prior to the actual delivery, I thought a glass of wine would be a nice way to celebrate adding another branch to our family tree. But after being gutted like a fish and doped up on Percocet, I changed my mind. Jim drank the entire bottle and passed out on the boxy armchair that pulled out into a very uncomfortable bed. I wondered if he really needed to drain a bottle of wine while staying overnight in the hospital after his wife just gave birth, especially since I knew he hated the taste of wine.

We left Reno four days after Milo's birth. The doctors circumcised him before we left rather than waiting until the customary one-week mark since they knew we lived far away and that an extra trip to the hospital would be a hardship. Neither one of us attended the surgery. We intuitively sensed that having a parent stand on the other side of the glass and look horrified would not benefit the baby, who would not recall the experience anyway. Instead, we waited in my hospital room and fretted until the doctors brought our son back safe and sound.

On discharge day, Jim carried Milo in his car seat while I walked down the long hallway, across the parking garage, rode the elevator, and walked across the pavement to where Jim parked the truck. I wondered why no one offered me a wheelchair. I also wondered why there was a bruise the size of my fist on the left side of my incision. I figured I should ask the doctor about that, after we picked up Grace and I got settled in at home with the new baby.

We had a four-hour drive from the hospital. I realize this is an exceptionally long drive home for most parents of newborns, but it was what all my distant neighbors of childbearing age endured at the time. No one we knew thought twice about transporting a four-day-old baby and a sore, still-bleeding, newly delivered mother more than two hundred miles in a Dodge pickup.

We stopped at Big R in Fallon so that I could use the bathroom. The parking lot was smaller than Walmart's, so I thought it would be easier to make the walk. Every customer and store employee tried not to let me see their stares as I slowly hobbled past stacks of salt blocks and bags of chicken scratch, looking six months pregnant with my soft belly and hunched shoulders. I gently pressed my left hand over the big bruise. It was starting to turn green and purple.

We made one more stop at Walmart before heading down the long highway for home. Jim took Grace into the store to grocery shop, and I stayed in the truck with Milo. I unstrapped him from his car seat, nursed him, changed his diaper, changed his clothes because he'd peed all over them, and looked at him. His little face was so red. His tiny hands opened and shut like soft, adorable crab claws. He scrunched his scrawny legs up when I draped him over my shoulder to burp him. I'd never held his big sister up to my shoulder to burp her when she was tiny, because it felt too unsteady and like a major drop risk. But I slung my second-born up to my shoulder and patted his little back with confidence.

By the time Jim and Grace returned, my incision started to hurt. I rummaged through the bag with the hospital paperwork but couldn't find the pain meds. I hadn't taken anything stronger than ibuprofen after I'd had Grace. I figured I'd be fine without the Percocet the nurses gave me on a schedule at the hospital.

Rain was pouring down by the time we reached Austin, a tiny town at the top of a mountain sixty miles from the ranch. We stopped at a gas station and Jim ran in to buy a Dr. Pepper and a Reese's Fast Break while I checked on Milo. His clothes were wet, soaked through with his own urine once again. That seemed to happen every time he peed. He had drenched his last dry sleeper for the ride home, so I changed his diaper and strapped him back in, wet jammies and all. We still had an hour to drive, but he'd lived surrounded by fluid for the previous nine months. He'd be fine.

Thirty miles from the ranch, it rained so hard that one of the windshield wipers came apart. We wouldn't have thought twice about it, but it was on the driver's side, and Jim couldn't see the road without it. Jim pulled over on the shoulder of the deserted highway, zipped up his jacket, and stepped out to replace the wiper. I felt like this was more adventure than the average American family had when they brought a new baby home from the hospital.

We finally made it just before dark. Grace ran up the porch steps in her rainbow tutu dress, her favorite one that she took off only under protest. Jim lifted Milo's car seat out of the truck while I bent over in pain. I tried to walk up the steps, but I could barely stand up straight. My incision burned. It must be coming apart, something I really did not want it to do. I glanced inside the waistband of my sweatpants and saw that the nine-inch incision was still closed. Whew. There was no bleeding, but the bruise had swelled and turned dark shades of green and purple.

Jim dropped all our luggage in a heap on the dining room floor. I didn't have the strength to unpack clothes and diapers, so I dressed the kids for bed on the floor beside the suitcase. Jim dumped a handful of ice cubes in a mason jar and poured Early Times whiskey until it was two-thirds full.

He topped the drink off with a splash of water and settled into his recliner in the living room.

Thirty minutes later, Jim made his second drink. I bathed Grace and nursed Milo. After drying her with a hoodie towel and threading her arms and legs into footie pajamas, she raced into the living room and jumped into the recliner with Jim. She snuggled under one arm, and I placed tiny Milo, curled up in his blue beanie hat and jersey knit mittens, in the crook of Jim's other arm.

Jim's drink sat on the floor beside his chair while he held his two children. He looked first at his daughter, then his son.

"Yep," he said. "I've got two good kids."

I smiled at the scene from my perch on the couch.

"I don't know what the one's good for, and the other one's good for nothin'," he finished the joke.

I shook my head and rolled my eyes. But the punchline came too late. I'd seen the way my husband cradled and looked at his children. It was no joke—he truly loved being a dad.

Jim passed out in our bed after drinking five or six whiskeys with just enough water to call them a highball. I had hoped he would help me put Grace to sleep since I now had a newborn to care for as well, but he was snoring on his back with his mouth open when her bedtime rolled around. I tucked her pink and zebra-striped comforter under her chin and sat on the edge of her mattress to hold her hand until she fell asleep.

Minutes after I sat down, Milo wailed from the other room.

"Hold on, baby," I told Grace. "Mommy will be right back."

I picked up Milo from his Rock'n Play in the living room and carried him back to Grace's room. My incision burned and I wanted nothing more than to collapse into bed, or a clutter-free patch of carpet, and close my eyes. But I couldn't go to sleep until I'd convinced two tiny people to go to sleep.

I resumed my perch on the edge of Grace's bed. She rubbed my forearm with one hand, her go-to comfort move, and I held Milo to my breast with my other arm. I hunched over and pressed the newborn into my abdomen. The nurses said to hold a pillow against my incision to dull the pain, but a seven-pound infant seemed to work just as well.

I listened to Jim's snoring and sat in Grace's bedroom willing her to go to sleep for about twenty minutes. I knew she finally conked out when her hand dropped off my arm. Milo had fallen asleep while nursing, so I carefully stood up and tugged my shirt back down. I carried him past the pile of suitcases, diaper packages, and outerwear that Jim had dropped in the dining room. Then I tucked my infant son into his Rock'n Play and positioned it near the couch where I slept so I could awaken at his first stirrings.

Jim went back to work the next day. I wondered how I would get through the day alone taking care of a toddler and a newborn while recovering from major surgery.

Grace watched Disney Junior for six hours straight and Milo mostly slept in his Rock'n Play. When Grace was hungry, I made her instant macaroni and cheese in the microwave and left the disposable container on the table after she was done with her meal. I kept a constant eye on the clock so I wouldn't be late for my next dose of Percocet. I'd learned my lesson about the importance of not skipping doses on the drive home. Knowing that magic pill would dull the pain every four hours gave me hope to get through the hour-and-a-half time period of each dosage cycle when the burning sensation in my abdomen grew hotter by the minute.

My neighbor and fellow ranch wife Martie Powers stopped by in the afternoon to pick up Grace so I could rest. She had four kids of her own, so she knew what the first few days of motherhood were like. She also probably took one look at me slouched on the couch surrounded by cracker crumbs with a pile of dirty dishes in the sink and an open suitcase on the floor and could tell that I needed a hand.

Grace played with Martie's kids while Milo napped and I dozed. After a morning of changing two sets of diapers and trying to convince an active toddler that sitting on the couch was more fun than running through the hallway and coloring on the walls, it was heavenly to just close my eyes and fully relax my body.

Jim heated up a frozen lasagna for dinner when he came home from work, then drank himself to sleep. This time, he passed out in his recliner.

I put Grace to bed and pondered how I could take a shower. It seemed like Milo inevitably woke up crying to nurse every time I put him down so I could get cleaned up. I saw that Jim's elbow rested on the arm of his chair and his forearm fell on his leg. It formed a perfect baby resting spot. I snuggled a sleeping Milo into the crook of Jim's arm and stepped back. The baby looked snug and secure. He wouldn't roll onto the floor unless Jim moved his arm in his sleep. That might happen. But I really wanted to shower, and this was my best chance. I hurried to the bathroom and returned less than ten minutes later with my hair wrapped in a towel to discover Jim and Milo exactly as I'd left them.

I picked up my infant son and wondered how the average American mom managed to take a shower. I imagined dads in other homes stayed awake to hold their babies, maybe even played with them while their wives tended to their own basic hygiene needs. I wondered if maybe things would change as time went on and I would get to experience that one day.

A longtime family friend arrived to help the next evening. Laurie Robustellini drove eight hours from northern California to stay a week and help with the newborn, the toddler, the housework, the cooking—all the things that were suddenly so much harder because my body hurt and I only slept for two hours at a time.

By then, I'd called the nurse and learned the ugly bruise on my incision was called a hematoma. It happened when the doctor was cauterizing the wound after surgery and would go away on its own. Until then, there wasn't much I could do about it except not weaken on the Percocet.

Laurie tackled the pile of dirty dishes that stretched across the kitchen counter on both sides of the sink. She took Grace for walks in the afternoons so I could catch a cat nap. She vacuumed muffin crumbs off the living room carpet at least twice a day and scrubbed the bathtub because I couldn't lean over that far.

In the evenings, we sat on the couch and talked about horse training. Laurie was masterful at starting colts and working with mules, probably because of her limitless patience and problem-solving abilities. I'd worked for her off and on as my school schedule allowed since I was sixteen. We'd gone to horse-manship clinics together and she introduced me to the joys of experiencing the wilderness via horseback. Muleback was almost better, though, because those critters were so sure-footed when going downhill that it's not even funny.

Sometimes Jim joined our evening conversations, and then Laurie hurried to the guest bedroom at the end of the hall and returned with a little notebook to jot down notes as Jim talked. She had dozens of notebooks filled with notes from horse training clinics, conversations with trainers, and other sources of information that could further her horse training knowledge.

Watching Laurie sit on the couch and cradle my newborn in her arms, ex-amining his tiny features and smiling at the marvel of life's new creation, I was so grateful she'd driven all day to help me. I'd been meeting new people and changing scenery every few months for so long, it was comforting to enjoy the company of an older woman who'd known me almost my whole life.

Laurie drove me four hours back to Reno for Milo's newborn checkup on her way home. As a thank-you gift, I handed her an unwrapped kitchen towel and potholder set I'd originally made for my mother-in-law but then didn't give to her because she'd made me mad. I wondered if I should give Laurie something bigger—not money because that would be crass, but maybe a nice painting or something. But how do you calculate the dollar value of someone's time, effort, and compassion when you really need it? I hoped the newborn cuddles and a sincere thank you were enough.

"There's no replacement for this time together," Laurie told me before she hugged me goodbye. "This was something I wouldn't miss for anything."

CHAPTER 17 ✳ **The Flying V**

pulled into the Flying V headquarters in the gray light of late afternoon in February. I'd left the brown mud of central Nevada earlier that morning and arrived at a northern Nevada ranch yard filled with small hills of unevenly frozen snow and puddles of smashed ice. Nothing was fully thawed, only half frozen and on its way to a hard freeze once again during the night.

I pulled the horse trailer with all our horses in it behind me. Grace rode in her car seat behind the passenger seat and Milo was strapped in the middle. I'd planned the arrangement so I could reach him easily to give him a pacifier or otherwise soothe him on the drive north, but it hadn't worked. He'd pretty much cried for five hours straight.

Our recently acquired house cat had started the drive in a cat carrier beside me on the front seat of the Dodge. She'd peed within the first five miles and was immediately banished to the flatbed, where the carrier was held in place with a ratchet strap for the rest of the drive. I'm pretty sure both kids peed more than once during the drive, but I didn't kick them out of the truck.

Jim drove ahead of us in a U-Haul that the Circle 4 cowboys had helped us load the night before. We'd left only a handful of things to pack the day of our departure, which of course we underestimated in size and scope and thus ran around all morning grabbing random household items and shoving them into the nearest open box—which is why I found a coffee cup and a cloth diaper shoved inside a boot bag.

But we eventually made it to our new home at the Flying V. Jim had worked there a few times before as a young single man, and I'd written an article about it a few months before. He hadn't been too keen on my idea of us moving there, but he finally relented when he decided the Circle 4 wasn't where he wanted to be anymore. It was fun to leave a job on purpose for the first time in our young marriage.

I was excited because I had learned the Flying V not only provided health insurance but also groceries, an unusual perk of any job. They still ran a cookhouse where the crew ate three times a day and furnished the same food to the married men's wives for use in their own households.

Jim had already parked the U-Haul in front of a white single-wide trailer directly across the driveway from the cookhouse. I pulled up beside him and stepped out to check out my new home. The trailer was small, but the exterior paint wasn't too flaky. It had a big yard, a swamp cooler on the roof, and a decent-sized shed out back. It was certainly in better shape than our first trailer house at the Rafter J.

Tired from the long drive with a toddler and a baby, I opened the front door. All I saw was an outdated living room with factory-installed turquoise valances over the windows and a maroon carpet. All I smelled was cat pee.

The ammonia smell overpowered my olfactory senses as I walked from room to room exploring our new abode. It irritated my eyes. I felt like I could taste it. I wandered from one tiny bedroom to another, down the narrow hallway and through the living room, past the miniscule dining room off the kitchen and into the small master bedroom at the far end of the trailer. Jim was already carrying boxes inside. I hurried past him so he wouldn't see me cry. Again.

I couldn't believe Jim had quit his job and we'd moved across the state to live in a house that reeked of cat urine. I was no expert, but it probably wasn't healthy for young children to constantly breathe the noxious odor. As for myself, I was a work-from-home-mom who spent most of her waking hours indoors. That was a lot of time to spend inhaling animal piss.

But this time, there was no one to blame but myself—Jim had quit his job and we'd moved five hours north at my urging. Maybe I needed to just start expecting our house to be filthy at the start, and then I wouldn't be so shocked each time we went to a new ranch.

Whether I was disappointed, angry at ranch life, or mad at myself, it didn't change the fact that we were committed to making this place work so we could have a place to live and a paycheck. Here we were, a family of four with a fully loaded U-Haul and stock trailer full of horses out front, waiting to be turned loose with the cavvy. Like it or not, this was our new home.

I looped the strap of my new Nikon camera around my neck. It smelled like brand-new plastic and chemicals and felt weighty like progress in my hands. I had no idea how all the buttons, dials, switches, and settings worked, but I couldn't wait to find out.

Jim and I had an agreement that the paychecks from our regular jobs went straight to our joint bank account and paid the family's expenses, but earnings from any side jobs we worked were considered "fun money" and ours to spend as we chose. I'd saved the money I earned from writing blog posts for a horse enthusiast website to purchase my new camera. My last fun money purchase had been a .45 Glock. I'd chosen a big handgun because I only wanted to have to shoot once.

My new camera was a big step up from the little Canon PowerShot. It came with a big fancy bag and two interchangeable lenses. They were technically called something with numbers and millimeters—maybe a decimal point— but I immediately named them "the big one" and "the little one," terms that I continue to use to this day. If I could figure out where the decimal point goes, I'd probably switch to using the technical terms.

With my fancy new camera around my neck, I slung the camera bag over one shoulder and picked up baby Milo with my other arm.

"Come on, Grace, let's go for a walk." I herded my toddler daughter out the door of the single-wide. The barely-spring air was chilly and damp, but I wanted to see what five hundred dollars' worth of Nikon products could do in outdoor light.

The fresh air smelled good, but thankfully, the air inside the trailer had also drastically improved since the maintenance crew scattered a bag of lime underneath the structure. The white, powdery substance worked like magic to absorb most of the foul smell, and now only certain rooms had a lingering odor when the heater was running. Every now and then we heard a terrific ruckus come from underneath our feet—angry snarls and yowls followed by metallic clanging, as feral cats fought and banged their bodies against the forced air ventilation ducts that crisscrossed the underside of the trailer. I figured the lime would hold up against the smell for a while, but we'd need to scatter another bag eventually. Feral cat populations might do a lot of things, but decrease generally isn't one of them.

I strapped Milo into the stroller and pulled his hood over the beanie cap on his little peach-fuzz head. Grace wore her rainbow tutu dress over leggings with pink cowboy boots and a pink Carhartt jacket. We headed for the ranch's playground, an outdoor structure consisting of a slide, plastic rock-climbing wall, ladder, swing set, and monkey bars donated by the manager after his own kids outgrew it. It was set on a large patch of native grass and just across the driveway from our house.

I crouched down on the grass and aimed the camera at Grace as she pumped back and forth on the swing set. The steel gray clouds behind her contrasted sharply with the pink, purple, yellow, and blue tulle of her dress. Each strand of her fine blonde hair was separately visible on the screen on the back of the camera. *Click...click...click click click click.*

I could press the shutter and take a picture with just a split second in between shots if I wanted. It made me want to take my old Canon and beat it with a rock. But at one time it had been my big splurge and had served its purpose of getting me started in photography, so I didn't. Also, I was busy snapping pictures in rapid succession and didn't want to stop shooting.

I took pictures of Grace on the swings, on the slide, and running across the grass. I turned around and photographed Milo sitting in the stroller, his brow furrowed as he smacked the cup holder with a mittened hand. He stuck his tongue out and fell back against his stroller seat, then pulled himself up straight again and squawked. I wondered what the heck he was thinking, then lay down on the grass to take a picture looking up at his face from the perspective of his feet. He probably wondered what the heck I was thinking.

"Come on, Grace, let's go see the horses," I called. Her cheeks were rosy and her steps up the ladder were slowing. I figured we better move on before she ran out of steam and Mama's camera walk was over.

Grace ran ahead while I pushed the stroller. I'd switched my camera to "off" and replaced the lens cap so it wouldn't get scratched. The Nikon bounced heavily against my chest with each step. I unzipped my coat and stuck it inside for protection.

We walked over to the pipe corrals near the horse barn. A couple of the cowboys' horses were there for various reasons. One was a mare, and mares weren't turned out with the Flying V cavvy. Keeping them separate helped prevent squabbling and potential injuries. Grace climbed up the nearest corral fence and I removed the lens cap. I switched the camera to "on" and twisted the lens until the focus was clear, then rotated it back and forth until I had the picture framed how I wanted and in focus.

At least, I thought it was in focus. I actually had no idea—I was too thrilled to be holding a camera with a twistable lens to think about yet another photography concept. I aimed it at the nearest horse's head and pressed the button. I checked the instant image on the back, held the viewfinder up to my eye, twisted the lens some more, and took another picture. This went on for twenty or thirty frames. I'd look at those pictures later, and none were worth keeping. But twisting that lens and pressing the button in rapid succession was rewarding all the same on my first day with my new toy.

On our walk across headquarters back to the house, I stopped to photograph an old rusty horseshoe nailed to a fence. The wood of the fence was weathered gray and old. I zoomed in close with the little lens and captured all its grainy, splintery goodness in sharp relief.

In the following weeks, I photographed approaching storm clouds, wild-flowers, all kinds of barns, my baby's fat cheeks, my toddler's chubby hands, my husband shoeing his horse, and more. If it happened on the ranch, I doc-umented it with my camera. I'd found a new way of telling stories, and to me, everything looked like a story to tell.

In early spring (or, as we liked to call it, "second winter"), a storm dropped a foot of new snow on the Flying V. The night was dark and the air was cold and instantly turned my cheeks red when I stepped outside to warm up the pickup before we drove home. Jim and I had gone to Tom and Chandra's for dinner after work, and it was time to leave.

I decided it was time to go because it was eleven o'clock at night, past when I usually went to sleep and way past the kids' bedtime. Baby Milo was sound asleep in a corner of the living room, wrapped snug in a blanket and cozy warm. Grace was still playing with Todd and Colt, but her eyelids were starting to droop, and she was on the verge of a tantrum. Jim sat at the kitchen counter on a stool next to Tom. His eyes were bloodshot, and his words slurred as he told cowboy stories.

Tom was the cowboss at the Flying V and therefore Jim's boss, but they were approximately the same age and had known each other for years. They both liked to ride, rope, and drink beer, so let the good times roll. Tom's wife Chandra liked to drink beer and hang out with cowboys who drank beer. I was the odd one out, being a breastfeeding mother and never much of a beer drinker even when not lactating.

"Come on, Jim, it's time to go," I said to my husband for the fifth time. The truck was warmed up, sippy cups and baby wipes rounded up and returned to the diaper bag, and I held Milo in my arms. He was still sound asleep. I really needed Jim to stand up and help me get his daughter away from her friends, out the door, and into the truck.

"Alright, alright, I'm comin," Jim said. He stood up, swayed on his feet, and tipped back his can to down the last swallow of Keystone Light. "Tom, Chandra, thank you for the wonderful dinner and good company."

Jim remained rooted to one spot while I started walking toward the door.

"Yes, thank you, it was fun." I commanded my mouth to form a smile instead of a yawn. I hoped that if I just kept walking, Jim would eventually follow. I made it to the mud room, then turned around to make sure Jim was coming. He was, but not steadily. His legs with their forty-inch inseam made his swaying steps even more noticeable. I kept going and waited at the door while he shoved his cowboy hat onto his head and put on his coat.

"Could you carry Grace, please?" I asked. "Grace, go to Daddy."

We each carried one of our children to the Dodge. Jim set Grace in the back seat and I held Milo on my lap, still wrapped in his warm blanket. Jim climbed behind the steering wheel and shut the door. I had a feeling I should drive since I was pretty sure Jim was drunk, but Jim was the default driver in our relationship. I didn't want to challenge his authority in Tom and Chandra's front yard. I reasoned that we were just going a few miles down a remote road and were unlikely to encounter any travelers other than maybe an antelope or a jack rabbit. Besides, Jim was such an experienced driver while under the influence that I figured he knew what he was doing.

That was my mindset at the time, but I couldn't fool myself forever.

Jim slowly drove down the driveway, the headlights shining on the frozen snow drifts and puddles crusted with ice in the ruts of the tire tracks. He always drove slowly, especially in bad weather. I was glad he was driving and not me.

Jim turned right at the end of the driveway, and then we were on the paved road. Snow began to fall through the beams of the headlights, cutting vertical white lines through the night. Jim hunched toward the steering wheel and the truck veered toward the right shoulder of the road.

"Jim!" I said sharply. "You're about to drive off the road."

He jerked the wheel back to the left and sat up straight for a few seconds. I looked closely and realized his eyes were only half open. He was much drunker than I'd originally thought. It looked like he was about to pass out behind the wheel.

If he completely drove off a country road going fifteen miles per hour, it would just be an inconvenience, not a wreck with injuries. But I'd thought that having his wife and kids in the truck with him would motivate him to drive better, to be more sober and responsible.

What if he had farther to go with his babies in the truck? Would he get behind the wheel again when he was that trashed? I thought about this after we parked and while I carried Milo up the steps to the trailer house. Jim lifted Grace out of the truck, set her on the snowy ground, then staggered across the porch. He took off his boots and passed out cold on his side of the bed. I helped Grace put on her pajamas and pulled the blankets up around her, then sat on the edge of her mattress and nursed Milo back to sleep like I always did, while Jim snored loudly down the hall.

I began to notice that we spent more evenings at our neighbors' house than we did our own. After living so far from neighbors for so many years, it was nice to have friends. But I wanted to eat a dinner I cooked once in a while, unwind in my own living room with just my husband and our kids, maybe go to bed before midnight.

I also noticed that Jim was drunk nearly all the time. Before, there was a noticeable pattern of being drunk after he got home from work, passing out at night, waking up hungover in the morning, then looking almost sober in the afternoon until he found another beer and the cycle continued. Tom drank from morning till late into night all day every day, and so did his cowboy crew. Jim took full advantage of a free pass to drink beer through all his working hours.

His eyes were permanently bloodshot, and he got flabby. He was the heaviest I'd ever seen him, puffy in the face and bloated in the belly. His gut strained the snaps on his shirts when he sat down. I found him less physically attractive, but I told myself to bite my tongue until it bled before I said anything to him. If the roles were reversed and the wife fluffed up, I would think her husband was a jerk if he told her she was fat and should lose some weight.

Besides, Jim's weight was hardly the issue. Thirty or forty extra pounds were just a symptom of the real problem, which was looking like my husband might be an alcoholic. The thought had first crept into my mind the night he was arrested for driving under the influence in Winnemucca. I'd pushed it aside when he said he would cut back on his drinking. He had since increased his drinking, though, and the thought came back.

An alcoholic. Could he really be one? I didn't want Jim to be an actual alcoholic, someone who was addicted to alcohol. He probably wasn't. His drinking caused problems in our marriage and got him arrested. But almost everybody in our circle was a heavy drinker. You had to drink to fit in, and Jim was friends with everyone.

Most of the women in the cowboy world were like me: drank a little when we were single, then quit drinking when we got married and had a couple babies so we could take care of our kids and husbands. We kept beer and whiskey at the house at all times and drove our passed-out husbands home from every rodeo/horse sale/bar/neighbor's house. That was just what a cowboy's wife did.

But it was starting to seem like a bum deal to me. So, I was expected—encouraged, even—to change diapers and chase a toddler while my husband stood next to the beer stand for an entire ranch rodeo and got completely wasted? And then I coaxed him into the pickup after five or six "one more beers," strapped the kids into their car seats, and drove us home through God knows how many hours and miles of pitch-black desert to a crummy trailer house we didn't even own, only so he could get up and leave before dawn, then come home and immediately start drinking to kill the headache?

Plenty of ranch women stayed married to drunks for fifty or sixty years. They smiled and handed their husbands another beer until it was time to go home, then they let them lean on their shoulders while walking to the pickup. All the while smiling and calling, "Bye, drive safe!" with their smooth white faces next to the husbands' ruddy red noses.

I didn't want to do that for another few decades, though. I wasn't even sure I wanted to do it for another month.

I looked out the living room window and searched the driveway as far as I could see once again. There was still no sign of Jim's truck and trailer. I strained my ears for the sound of a diesel engine and heard only tractors driving around headquarters and the occasional shout of a Mexican farm worker.

I turned away from the window and looked at the clock on the wall. Jim should've been back from Jordan Valley three hours ago. He'd called when he left the rodeo, but I knew he wouldn't drive straight home. He'd stop at a friend's ranch on the way home, and then he and the friend would drink a few beers that turned into the better part of a case, then he'd come home later than expected and completely plastered.

I looked out the window again. Still no sign of my husband. It was now late afternoon, almost evening. Jim had taken Teaks, my favorite horse, to enter the big loop horse roping and muley team roping events.

I watched the driveway and prayed. *God, please have Jim wreck the truck and trailer on the way home. Taylor Canyon is windy and narrow; I know lots of people wreck there. Please let him crash and live but kill Teaks.*

I'd heard of other cowboys who'd gotten sober because they'd gotten drunk, wrecked their pickups, and killed a horse or two. Maybe that could happen to us. Maybe Jim would choose of his own free will to quit drinking cold turkey and I wouldn't have to draw a hard line, then back up what I said and break up our family if he continued to drink.

It was a cowardly prayer. I know it now and I knew it then.

"Are you sure you can't go, even just for a couple hours?" Chandra stood on my front porch with her kids in the truck and a thermos full of boxed wine in her hand.

"I wish I could, but no, I have a deadline on Friday," I said.

"Does writing for the *Nevada Rancher* really take up that much time?" Chandra asked.

"Well, no, but it takes me all day to find two hours to write," I said.

Grace slipped out past my legs in search of Todd and Colt; I held Milo on my hip and hoped the conversation wouldn't take too long. I had dishes to wash, the table to wipe down, news sources to skim for story ideas, a first draft to write, and at least three other things to do that I couldn't think of at the moment.

Chandra was headed off to the desert in search of the cowboy crew. She liked to do that quite a bit—take her young sons while her older daughter was at school and drive around looking for Tom so she could say hi. She always brought beer for him and the crew.

I appreciated the invitation and half wished I could take her up on it. Chandra was fun and friendly and I enjoyed her company. But the monthly deadline cycle at the magazine kept me tethered to my computer, and I didn't see anyone offering to watch the kids while I researched stories, typed articles, and conducted phone interviews, so I pretty much devoted myself to staying in the house and stealing minutes here and there to do my job.

Plus, I suspected I might be on my own with my kids one day. And I knew I'd need a paycheck to make it work.

CHAPTER 18 ✳ **Gone for Good**

I wanted my first marriage to be my only marriage. I wanted my kids to grow up in a house with both Mom and Dad. But I also wanted a husband who could walk past his drinking buddies and come home every day after work. I wanted a partner I could trust to stay sober when he drove the kids to town without me. I wanted a man who could get a dang driver's license so that I was no longer the only legal driver in the house. The kids and I deserved to outrank a bottle of bottom-shelf whiskey.

I thought about other families in our situation, real-life case studies I could briefly examine before telling Jim how it was going to be. A friend and fellow ranch wife I knew had recently packed suitcases for her and her four kids, then her alcoholic husband quit drinking and saved their marriage the day she intended to leave. Another ranch wife in our circle had told her husband to choose between her or the booze, and she now lived by herself in an apartment in town with their daughter. It could go either way.

For a full week, I suggested daily that Jim seek help.

"Maybe you have a drinking problem," I texted while he was at work. "If you want to go to AA, I'll drive you." His driver's license was still revoked because of the DUI. He drove on backroads and remote highways anyway, but I thought offering to take him would show my support.

"I don't need AA," he texted back. "Those are for drug addicts and perverts."

"Maybe you could come home and play with your kids after work instead of sitting in the barn and drinking a case of beer with the cowboy crew," I said over the phone another day.

"I work my ass off all my day long to provide for my family," he said, much louder than necessary. "I don't know what more you want from me. All I do is work. I work for you and the kids all day every day."

"I know, honey, you've always been a hard worker," I said in a quiet voice that I hoped would have a calming effect. "But we just want to spend time with you. You spend all day with those guys. Can't you just come home in the afternoons?"

"Fine, I will come straight home the minute work is done every single fucking day. It doesn't matter if a guy is shoeing a colt and needs help—I will just hurry home so you can be happy," he said.

And that is usually when I stopped trying to talk to him about the constant juggle between drinking time and family time. Unless I was frustrated with trying to potty train a belligerent three-year-old while meeting a magazine deadline and exhausted from staying up all night with a teething baby. Then the screaming match commenced in earnest, complete with cuss words hurled from both sides and a little blonde girl hiding behind my legs.

I half-lay, half-sat in bed, propped up by pillows behind my back and the covers over my legs. It was late and I knew I should sleep when the baby slept, but I had research to do.

I Googled "low-income housing." If Jim and I divorced, I'd need to find affordable housing for me and the kids. The two grand I brought home each month writing articles for the *Nevada Rancher* was a decent income if I had free housing and a spouse's paycheck to match, but it would fall pitifully short of paying all my bills as a single parent. Sure, Jim would pay child support, but I had no idea how much that would be.

The housing images that popped up on my laptop screen weren't as shabby as I'd expected. They were new, white apartment buildings in Elko. Looked like some were near the golf course, which was also near the freeway, but at least it was green and had some open space. Living in town would be a big adjustment after years of living on the desert ranges.

The apartments looked clean and fresh. They were nothing like the image I'd concocted in my mind of a narrow, first-floor duplex next to the train tracks with mildew on the walls and stains on the carpet. My worst fear was that the only dwelling I could afford on my own would smell like moldy cheese and sweaty socks.

If I left Jim, I would have to live in a small apartment in town. But it would be okay. The housing options I saw online were clean and bright, which would be a major improvement over all the ranch houses we'd lived in so far. Best of all—no one would be drunk all the time.

Jim's snoring hit an extra loud note, then paused for a few seconds before resuming its usual steady rhythm. He was passed out in his recliner for the remainder of the night. I Googled "signs of an alcoholic."

Do you or your loved one drink in the morning? If you run out of alcohol, will you or your loved one become anxious until you can go buy more alcohol? Do you drink alone? Does your loved one cancel plans to stay home and drink?

The wording was a bit clinical and stilted. The articles always ended with "consult a licensed professional." But what really caught my attention was the comment section where real-life people, mostly women, wrote lengthy posts about their spouses.

He isn't drunk all the time. He'll stay sober for several days or even weeks at a time. But when he drinks, he is the drunkest person at the party. This has been going on for years now. He keeps saying he'll stop or cut back and I be-lieve him. I want to believe him and help him. I will give him as many chances as he needs, but will he ever stop drinking? Is he actually an alcoholic, since he can go several days without a drink? I just don't know what to do anymore.

Same, sister. Same.

I called Missy after I passed the bottom of Adobe Summit, right when the cell service got good enough to make a call.

"Hello?" she answered after a few rings.

"Hi, this is Jolyn."

We exchanged hi-how-are-you and the-weather-sure-is-nice before I got to the real reason for my call.

"I think Jim definitely has a drinking problem. I just don't know how much more of this I can take."

Saying the words out loud made the tears come without stopping. I bawled as I drove and the road and other vehicles blurred in front of my eyes.

"Pull over. You need to stop driving. Find a good spot and pull off to the side of the road." Missy was twelve years my senior and spoke with the authority of an experienced mom.

I pulled up next to the sidewalk alongside The Star, a historic Basque restaurant in downtown Elko. I left the diesel engine running so the A/C would stay on and Milo would stay asleep in the back seat. I'd left Grace at home with her dad even though she'd cried when I left. I needed some time to think.

"Do you buy beer for Jim?" Missy asked.

"I do the grocery shopping, so yes, I pick up beer for him when I come to town." It seemed like a weird question. I purchased our family's food, and beer was at the food store, so therefore I purchased it as well.

"Then you need to stop. You're enabling him."

Missy's words hit me like a gentle but firm slap to the forehead. I'd never refused to buy alcohol for Jim, but it made perfect sense. If someone is abusing a substance and I provide that substance for them, I am part of the problem.

"Okay," I said cautiously. "I can tell him I won't buy beer anymore. He's not going to like it, but it makes sense."

I was starting to visualize and verbalize a life in which I didn't hand beer directly to my husband, who was most likely an alcoholic. I still wasn't sure yet, but I knew his drinking was a big problem that wasn't going away on its own.

"And another thing is that nothing will work, as far as him quitting drinking, until he decides he wants to quit. He has to make that choice for himself."

I stopped crying and listened. Missy knew a thing or two about these things. She wasn't sugarcoating the facts. Facts were what I needed. I was tired of telling myself Jim's drinking wasn't that bad, or at least he didn't hit me, or that he was a hard worker. The justifications weren't enough anymore. I wanted an honest, upright life I was proud to call mine.

"But I'm afraid to throw down an ultimatum. What if he doesn't choose to stop drinking?"

"I know Jim is a good man and I know he loves you. But kids grow up and they do what they saw their parents do. You have to look at your son and decide what kind of an example you want for him."

I knew that Missy's words were true. I felt the anguish that had previously twisted my decision this way and that quietly and completely leave my mind. There was no way I was going to watch my infant son, so perfect and innocent at eight months old, grow up to follow in his dad's drunken footsteps while I stood by the wayside with a case of beer in my hand and a smile on my face.

I went to Grace Baptist Church after hanging up the phone with Missy. Attending the Sunday evening service was the reason I'd given Jim for going to town. I'd insisted that he stay home with Grace and said I needed some alone time. Well, alone time with a baby, but that was as close as a nursing mom could get.

I sat with Milo in the cry room for most of the service. Attendance was sparse like usual for a Sunday evening. Another mother-and-baby pair sat near us. I half-listened to the pastor's message through speakers above the soundproof glass while Milo sat on the floor and chewed on the handles of the diaper bag. I picked him up when he squawked, settled him under my shirt when he cried, and patted his back while he burped.

Church had been my sanctuary since I was a kid, both before and after my parents divorced. I'd always talked to God, learned about Him, and strained to hear His whispers in my heart. Divorce was strongly discouraged in Christian circles. I knew many women who stayed with their husbands regardless of their unsavory behavior because they believed the New Testament explicitly says to not divorce your husband under any circumstances except infidelity. He's distant from the kids? Love him through it. He drinks too much? Stay by his side. He doesn't love the Lord like you do? Bring him into the fold with your warm smile and forgiving nature.

But surely God wouldn't want me to sacrifice my own happiness and raise my kids with an example of how not to be just so I could stay married for the sake of not getting divorced. Surely the Lord of Love and King of Kings wanted better for His children during their time on Earth.

I didn't scour Paul's letters to pinpoint an answer. I decided to do what I was going to do and explain myself on Judgment Day along with everything else I would be held accountable for.

I was going to get myself and my kids a better future. I just didn't know yet if it would be with or without Jim.

"Thank you." I smiled and waved to Margarita on my way out of the cookhouse. Margarita looked up from browning ground beef in an enormous skillet on the stove behind the serving counter and smiled a goodbye in return. She was shaped like a potato, had short black hair, and didn't speak English, but her cooking was amazing. I was extra grateful that day for the ever-present sheet cake that sat at the far end of the counter. This one was yellow cake with a simple powdered sugar glaze frosting.

I grabbed a piece on my way by and nibbled a corner. The sweetness of the glaze and airiness of the cake made my mouth water and spiked my blood sugar with a quick, much-needed hit. I had barely eaten anything for the past week. Nerves killed my appetite and I was way too distracted trying to guess what Jim would choose to think about food.

But food cooked by someone else always tastes better, and I had a sweet tooth. So I looked for a daily excuse to step into the cookhouse, swipe a piece of cake, smell the hamburger grease cooking in a skillet, and trade hello and goodbye smiles with Margarita.

I hitched Milo up on my hip with one hand and ate my cake with the other before I reached the single-wide on the other side of the driveway and felt too anxious to eat again.

The next day, Jim confronted me by the yard fence. He was drunk, not dumb, and he knew something beyond wifely nagging was going on.

Grace ran and played on the thick grass behind me with the cowboss' three kids. It was lunchtime, and the cowboy crew had come into headquarters to eat at the cookhouse. I stood nearby with baby Milo in his stroller, both of us bundled up in winter coats even though it was officially spring. The warm season was characteristically late in coming to northern Nevada.

Jim broke away from the rest of the crew as they walked to the barn after lunch. He strode toward me. He looked me straight in the eye and asked what I wanted from him. I could tell by his unwavering gaze that he would no longer accept an ambiguous platitude as a reply.

"I'm going to take the kids to my dad's for thirty days," I said evenly. "You have that long to decide if you want to continue to drink, or if you want to live with me and the kids. If you quit drinking, we will come back. If you don't, I'm going to look for a place in Elko."

Jim turned without saying a word and headed to the barn. I hated that I'd had to say my piece in the cold, open air, with other people nearby, but I was relieved to have said it. I hollered for Grace and pushed the stroller across the gravel driveway to our home. I had some packing to do. I had finally found the strength to put our suitcases in the pickup.

I packed enough clothes, diapers, toys, and board books to last a few weeks. I hoped we would return to our home at the Flying V at the end of one month, but I made myself face the fact that I might only be coming back to collect the rest of my belongings. I threw the suitcases onto the flatbed pickup, then added my daughter's pink bike with training wheels as an afterthought. I secured the whole load with ratchet straps. The green Dodge was our only vehicle, but Jim wouldn't need it for a while anyway. The cowboy crew would be camped out in the desert, branding calves most of the time I was gone. I needed wheels more badly than Jim did just then.

I glanced toward the bunkhouse as I slowly drove through the complex of buildings that made up the ranch headquarters. The bunkhouse was a cinderblock building with few windows and cramped accommodations for single cowboys. It was legendary for being filthy, but its occupants were usually too drunk to care. The only time they weren't drunk was when they were hungover, which was basically just a post-drunk waiting period until the next runner. I figured Jim would spend every evening in that bunkhouse from then on.

But even if he was drunk for a month straight, I would still bring the kids and move back if he called and said he quit drinking once the month was up. I viewed the terms of my ultimatum like a test run. I was giving Jim the chance to hang with the drunk single guys and see if he wanted to rejoin their ranks. If he did, I would let him go. I couldn't make Jim be something he didn't want to be. If he gave the drunken single lifestyle a shot and it cured him of wanting to continue that lifestyle in the long run, then he could be a family man again.

Because I knew Jim had it in him to make us his top priority. He always had a job. He bought me thoughtful birthday gifts and was thrilled with the births of both our children. He told me I looked pretty even when I had greasy hair and undereye circles; he saddled my horse for me so I could set down the baby and lope a few circles in the evening; and he wore patched jeans every day so we could afford good tires for our pickup. He didn't want to worry about me changing a flat tire every time I drove sixty-five miles to town with the kids.

But all of that added together didn't equal more than his drinking took away.

As I drove the diesel pickup down the long lane leading to the highway, I looked at the hay meadows that lined the dirt road. The grass was green and tall. Yellow and purple wildflowers bloomed along the fence line. A handful of black cattle gathered around a dirt stock tank, taking long drinks and calling to each other in the early afternoon. Graceful white egrets circled overhead, their long orange legs sticking straight out behind their feathered bodies. The air was cold and damp, with great big gray rain clouds blowing in from the north.

I knew this might be the last time I enjoyed this scene as a ranch resident. Divorce papers would render my invitation to live on a historic cattle ranch null and void. If Jim chose the alcohol over us, I would no longer have a horse pasture out my back door. I couldn't drive up to the old wooden corrals and take pictures with my Nikon while the cowboy crew doctored yearlings and my daughter played with the other kids in an empty chute. I wouldn't fall asleep to the constant bawling of fresh-weaned calves in the fall or stop to point out a newborn calf to my daughter in the spring. I forced myself to acknowledge all that, just like I forced myself to keep my foot on the accelerator and steer the pickup down the lane.

I reached Elko in just over an hour. My first stop was the Burger King drive-through. A cheeseburger and milkshake sounded delicious. I ordered a small vanilla cone for Grace and realized that the lady who took my money at the window had no idea that I was a woman who had just left her husband. She didn't know that my future had been flung up into the air and I didn't know yet if it would land right side up or shatter into a million sharp pieces.

She smiled and commented on my daughter's bike strapped to the flat bed. For all she knew, I was just a fun mom taking her small kids out for an afternoon adventure.

Paper bags of greasy comfort food in hand, I drove east on Interstate 80. My second stop was my mom's house near Reno. I hit rush hour and was instantly overwhelmed by four crowded lanes of speeding interstate traffic. My cell phone kept ringing, but I stuffed it into the cup holder and ignored it. I was definitely not town-savvy enough to attempt answering my phone while navigating lane changes in a flatbed pickup with two kids in the back seat.

I checked my phone when the traffic cleared and saw that Jim had tried to call me six times. When I called him back, he told me I needed to answer my phone because we needed to communicate.

"That's what I have been trying to tell you," I said, almost laughing in frustration at his delayed realization.

"Don't do this. Come back. You know you still love me," Jim said.

"You're right, I do still love you. I will always love you and will probably never get over you. But I won't do another year like the last three," I said. "Love isn't enough anymore."

I told Jim that I had to go and hung up the phone. Somewhere on the interstate, I took off my wedding ring and placed it in the ashtray under the dash. I slid the drawer closed. He would have to earn that diamond ring back onto my left hand.

———————✦———————

The rusty metal chairs and huge old juniper tree were familiar sights. So was the weed-filled dirt yard that surrounded us. I'd been coming to Don Brown's place since I was in middle school, usually riding my horse one mile through the subdivision between his and my dad's place.

But the depth of understanding I saw in the eighty-year-old cowboy's eyes was new. I'm sure it was there all along; I'd just never had a reason to tap into this side of his character. Our previous conversations had been limited to the best type of bit to use for a particular colt, how to teach a horse to turn around, or how to braid rawhide.

I sat in my rusty chair and spilled my guts. I told Don that I'd left Jim and why. His eyes softened into the distance and his brows furrowed together. I knew I'd been foolish to ever think I needed to keep up a happy front and conceal the truth from my old friend.

"No, that's not a good way for him to be," Don said when I told him about the extent of Jim's drinking and how I'd told him to choose between alcohol or his family.

Don's wife, Chrissy, sat quietly beside me. Grace played in the weeds, and I held Milo on my lap to keep him from crawling on the ground and eating puncture vines. Every time Grace wandered a little too close to one of Don's hound dogs on a chain, loud baying filled the dry desert air. It was hot in northern California, even for May.

"Quiet!" Don turned in his creaky metal seat to yell at a dog, then turned back to me. He spoke while continuing to look off in the distance. "Yeah, some guys—and cowboys are the worst—they get to drinkin' and partyin' and pretty soon they can't stop drinkin' and partyin' and that's all they care about."

We sat and I stared at the weeds.

"Yep, that drinkin' is just no good. And don't let him tell you that O'Doul's are okay. They have alcohol in 'em, too, and if he drinks enough of them, that's enough to keep an alcoholic going. Just that little bit is all it takes."

I nodded and looked at the ground. Don knew what he was talking about. A lifelong cowboy and professional bareback rider in his younger days, drinking had cost him his first marriage. His ex-wife had taken their twins and left him because he wouldn't stay sober. To rub salt in the wound, she'd burned all his old rodeo pictures. Don hadn't put the bottle down for many years after that and alcohol had cost him watching his kids grow up. He was still estranged from his daughter and had only reconnected with his grown son just a few months before his son unexpectedly died. If there ever was a cowboy who knew about drinking and its effects on a man and his family, it was Don.

"I'm sure glad you came over, kid," Don told me. "I hate to see you struggle like this. But it sounds like he's doin' the right thing. I sure hope he sticks with it. You deserve all the happiness in the world."

Don smiled wide beneath his gray mustache and looked straight at me. The faraway look was gone from his eyes and the familiar sparkle was back where it should be.

"Thank you," I said. I held Milo under his arms while he practiced jumping on my lap and waved to no one in particular. "I should've told you guys sooner. I've been covering for Jim and trying to hide how bad his drinking was. I didn't want to admit it to myself, you know?"

"I know. Oh, boy, do I know," Don said. "But you don't have to hide anything from us."

Chrissy seconded her husband with an emphatic "no" and shake of her head.

"No, you don't ever have to hide anything from us," he repeated. "We just want to see you happy, and the kids happy, and help you any way we can. Because, oh, boy, you sure made some cute kids."

Don grinned as his eyes twinkled. He watched Grace play near the giant trunk of the juniper tree we sat beneath. He examined Milo's round face and laughed when the baby screeched at who knows what. Looking at Don that afternoon, over thirty years sober and sitting beside the woman who stuck with him through the end of his bad drinking days, gave me hope that Jim could make it, too.

I also realized that even if he didn't, I had people who loved me and wanted only good things for me, regardless of whether I chose to end my marriage or not.

I sat beside Milo on the living room floor at my dad's house. Grace played with plastic toys that Susan, my dad's girlfriend, kept for when her toddler grandson came to visit. I sat cross-legged on the carpet beside Milo and guided his little fingers away from uncovered electrical outlets and splinter-filled chunks of kindling from the box by the wood stove. Grandpa hadn't done much babyproofing, which made sense because we only visited about every six months.

"When do you think you're going to head back?" Dad asked me. "I mean, you're welcome to stay here as long as you want. I was just wondering."

I wasn't sure when to head back. What was the protocol for returning home after you said that you'd be gone for thirty days, then your husband surprised you by putting down the bottle the day you left? I had a month-long trip scheduled and wasn't sure how or if I should change my plans.

"I don't know," I replied. "I guess I could stay a few more days and then maybe head back this weekend."

Dad nodded.

"You wanted him to quit drinking, and he did. What are you waiting for? You might as well go back."

He made an excellent point. My trip had accomplished what I'd hoped it would, so there wasn't much of a reason for prolonging my stay in California. Besides, I was eager to see the new, sober version of my husband.

CHAPTER 19 ✳ **Marriage, Act II**

I drove east on Interstate 80 through the warm afternoon of a late-spring high-desert day. Both kids were buckled into their car seats in the back of the cab and peacefully sleeping. They had no idea what Mommy had done.

But I knew what had just happened. I could scarcely allow myself to believe my husband had chosen us over alcohol. I considered the possibility that maybe Hallmark had it right all along and some things worked out at the last possible second. Maybe my story could have a happy ending after all.

But what if he started drinking again in six weeks, six months, or a few years? I realized that having a long marriage was not the ultimate goal that I had previously thought it was. I was giving my marriage and my family the best possible shot I could at staying intact and celebrating a fiftieth anniversary with my first and only husband. But if he chose to start drinking again, it would not devalue me. It would be his choice and I could walk away knowing I had done all I could.

I looked at the small band of diamonds on my pawn shop ring, reinstated to its place on my left hand and shining in the sunlight on top of the steering wheel.

I kept my foot heavy on the accelerator all the way home.

A few hours later, I stood in the driveway in my secondhand blue plaid dress that poofed out over my belly and made me look a little bit pregnant even though I wasn't. The dress was cotton and cheap, my two main requirements in a piece of clothing. I also liked the way it swirled around my legs when the wind blew.

Jim stepped out of the trailer house and walked across the driveway. He stopped in front of me and we kissed hello. That part was familiar. He didn't taste like booze, which was new.

"I thought you'd be at the wagon camp when I got home," I said.

"I rode in with Tom," Jim said. "He had to come back to headquarters, and he said I better come in and see you since you came back and all."

I smiled and hugged him.

"It's good to see you," I said.

Jim helped me unload the kids and carry our bags into the house. I was exhausted from driving all day with a toddler and a baby. Jim had to leave before daylight to catch a ride back to camp with Tom, so we only had a few hours together until life picked up like I'd never left.

"So, Tom knows why I left?" I asked. I wasn't sure if this new stage of our relationship permitted us to talk about it out loud, but I was curious what our friends and Jim's co-workers knew about the situation.

"Yeah, I told him."

"Okay. We can tell other people whatever you want. We can say I just took a last-minute trip to see my dad. It doesn't matter to me. What happened is just between us and nobody else's business as far as I'm concerned. I only told three people, and they won't say anything."

I made myself stop talking and wait for Jim to reply.

"No, it's fine," he said. "I told the truth."

We didn't bring up the subject again that night. I changed Grace and Milo into their pajamas and they fell asleep on our laps while we watched TV in the living room. I carried them to the small room they shared at the end of the hallway and laid them on the mattress on the floor. Milo scrunched up his face and squirmed at the motion, but he drooled a little milk out the side of his mouth and stayed asleep.

Later that night, Jim and I reunited in a more private way. For the first time, his eyes weren't bloodshot when they looked into mine mere inches away in the darkness of our bedroom. Our faces were so close that our noses touched, but I could no longer smell the stench of whiskey on his breath.

We were heading back to the Flying V from Elko late one afternoon when I said my final piece about drinking to Jim. He drove up Adobe Summit with me in the passenger seat and both kids buckled up in the back seat.

"I'm not going to follow you around and call your friends to check up on you and see if you've been drinking," I told him. "You're a grown man and you're going to be driving by yourself with easy access to grocery stores and gas stations. If you want to drink, you're going to get a drink. I either trust you or I don't. Right now I'm choosing to trust you."

Jim nodded. I could tell by his expression that my short speech made him extremely happy, but I wasn't entirely sure why. I was just too darn tired from working full time, cleaning the house, and taking care of the kids to manage my husband's sobriety as well. That one was going to be up to him.

Looking back, I realize this was one of the best decisions I could have made. A man wants his wife's full trust and will often exceed her highest hopes once she gives it to him.

Baby Milo slept in his stroller at the edge of the pavement where asphalt met grass. Grace ran and played on the big grassy area near the Indian taco truck and a tent selling necklaces. Her short legs and shaggy blonde hair darted and bobbed around the grass, and she shrieked with laughter as she tagged another kid and he turned to chase after her.

I stood near the stroller and kept watch over my sleeping infant. The night was dark and the rodeo was over, but the party crowd was just getting revved up. Tall light posts illuminated the crowds that gathered at either end of the long grandstands. They clustered around the Cowboy Bar's plywood structure and the portable, shiny beer trailer with Coors on tap at the other end. In the shadows beneath the bleachers, kids swung on the metal supports and teenagers made out beyond the watchful eye of their parents. It was Friday night at the Silver State Stampede, Elko's annual professional rodeo.

Without warning, Jim walked up and took my hand. He pulled me to the middle of the paved area between the grass and the grandstands, which served as the designated dancing area that night. He pulled me close and stepped in time with the music. His shoulders were tall and his feet sure of every step. We were the only couple on the dance floor. Sometimes his movements argued with the timing of the music, but I spun when his hand directed me to and generally tried to move in the direction of his confident albeit occasionally off tempo lead. The musical timing truly didn't matter, anyway.

It felt like our first dance as a married couple, the one a bride and groom traditionally do at a wedding reception to a favorite slow song with all eyes on them—the one we hadn't had. The song was a fast one and later I couldn't remember the name of it, but that didn't matter, either.

What mattered was that he chose to dance with me.

⬦———————⬦

I grabbed Milo and pulled him back to me, re-snuggling him under the blankets. I'd repeated this process every forty-five minutes to two hours all night. It was cold, so I switched on the portable propane heater in the corner of Jim's teepee. Then it was too hot, so Milo kicked off the covers and the little hairs on the back of his neck felt sweaty to my touch. We repeated this process until Jim quietly slipped out of bed, got dressed, and snuck out the heavy zippered door to catch a horse and gather cattle for the day's branding.

We were camped at Summers, a longtime campsite for the Flying V wagon. It was July, but nights were so cool on the high desert that we woke up to ice in our water bottles one morning. Our family of four slept in the ten-by-ten canvas range teepee that Jim bought when he was nineteen. The rest of the cowboy crew set up their teepees nearby, with the cook wagon on the middle of one side.

There was no running water, electricity, or clean patch of ground to let Milo practice his newfound crawling skills. But I packed up the kids and joined Jim for a few days of dry camping for two reasons.

One, I wanted to spend time with him. Since he was camped on the desert for weeks at a time until all the calves were branded, joining him in the dust and sagebrush was my best chance at seeing my husband in the flesh until the spring works were done.

Two, I'd been assigned a big article for a national magazine. I was to write fifteen hundred words about branding calves on the Flying V wagon and provide all the photos. It was a great opportunity to expose my work to a larger audience and receive a bigger paycheck than I usually earned by freelance writing.

I was awake when Jim zipped the canvas door shut and decided to give up trying to go back to sleep. Besides, it would soon be time to get up, feed and dress the kids, and drive the short distance to the branding trap. I lay on my bedroll mattress and burrowed down in the blankets next to my children in a little white world that smelled like canvas and dirt, and listened as the cowboy crew got ready for the day.

They saddled horses at the corral a fair distance from camp and then passed by our teepee on their way to start the gather. Their voices grew from incoherent murmurs to distinct words as they rode a few feet from camp. Intermittent thuds and snorts told me someone's horse was bucking.

"I remember when I used to like this stuff," I heard Tom say in between his horse's jumps. The crew laughed and trotted on.

I mentally stored that line away. It would make a snappy quote for my article. I couldn't write it down, because getting up to find a pen and paper would wake up Milo. He'd finally drifted back to sleep with his head on my shoulder. I knew a well-rested baby was more likely to be a happy baby, and I needed him and his sister to be happy and cooperative for the day ahead.

I loaded the diaper bag and kids into my Jeep after the cowboy crew was long gone and the sun hung high in the sky. We'd bought a 1995 Jeep Cherokee about a month before to have a more economical vehicle to get groceries and run errands, and it was proving to be exceptionally useful for driving over the rough roads to the wagon camp, too.

The day ahead looked like it was going to be a scorcher. Most ranches were done with branding calves by this time of year, but the spring works at the Flying V usually dragged out into summer. This was partly because the ranch was so big and partly because the crew was usually drunk.

The cattle were in the wire trap and the dust rose thick in the air by the time I parked and helped Grace hop out of the back seat. I strapped Milo to my back using a long, wide piece of red muslin cloth I'd bought on sale. Backpack-style baby carriers made my shoulders ache almost immediately, but I still wanted to be a hands-free mama. I'd watched online tutorials and learned how to tie an infant to my back, using an elaborate system of wraps, loops, and tucks while leaning forward at the waist, almost parallel to the ground, so the baby didn't fall. It was as hard as it sounds.

But when I stood upright and smoothed the wide fabric straps over my shoulders, I could carry my infant securely for up to four hours. I could walk, stop, turn, and shoot pictures with ease. Well, with as much ease as allowed by doing all this with a twenty-pound squirming ball of baby strapped to my back, but at least I could zoom and click.

I stood on the flatbed of a pickup parked near the fence with Grace. She played with empty vaccine bottles and pieces of baling twine while I snapped pictures and tried to keep her away from the sixteen-gauge needles used to administer vaccinations to the young calves.

The corral was bone dry and thick dust surrounded the cowboys and cows. The morning sun shone through the dust cloud, surrounding everything with a golden haze that deepened the farther the cowboys rode into the herd. From my vantage point at the far side of the corral, the horses' heads were the clearest image. Their hooves and legs swirled in the dust they kicked up as they trotted to the branding fire. The ropes were sometimes visible and sometimes not, but the calf was always at least partially hidden by the golden dust. The remaining herd consisted of partially visible cows and bawling bovine faces amid the giant cloud of dust. It lent a mysterious appearance to a commonplace task.

The dust also had a gritty, not-so-mysterious effect on us spectators. It settled in the creases at the base of my daughter's nose, lined her neck, and gave her a dirt mustache. Without looking in a mirror, I knew I must look the same. I periodically wiped my face with my hand, which was also streaked with dirt. I wasn't sure how effective my efforts were, but I felt better for at least having tried.

Milo remained strapped to my back throughout the branding. He seemed to enjoy watching his dad and the other two cowboys ride and rope. I swayed and gently bounced when he got fussy until he fell asleep with his round cheek high on my shoulder. I adjusted the fabric so it covered his head and face for sun protection and kept snapping pictures.

Between shots, I covered the Nikon's lens with the long tail of my back wrap. I didn't want dust to get on the glass and ruin an image. After standing on the back of the truck for a couple hours, I noticed Grace's face looked red. She was drinking plenty of water, but her only shade was the bill of her ball cap. It was getting hot, and I knew I should head back to camp soon. There wasn't much shade at Summers, but at least the kids would be out of the swirling dust.

But Grace was still playing and having fun watching Daddy. It was a big treat for us to see him, and this was my only chance to take photos to run with my magazine story.

Around noon, I switched off my camera and snapped the lens cap into place. Grace's face was a darker shade of red and she was no longer playing with empty water bottles and watching the action. Milo had started to wake up. He twisted and cried on my back, straining against the wrap. I took my camera strap off from around my neck, untied the wrap, and swung Milo around to the front.

I looked at my baby and instantly regretted staying so long in the heat and dust. His face was bright red and his eyes were bloodshot. He cried and rubbed his eyes with his little hands. All that time I'd thought he was secure and content on my back while I snapped away like the hard-workin' mama I wanted to be, when in fact he'd been exposed to way more dust than was appropriate for an infant.

I drove back to camp and washed Milo's eyes with a water bottle and a paper towel. They were still bloodshot and puffy, but he no longer cried and pawed at his face. I was glad I had enough pictures to file with my article, but I felt guilty because I knew I had placed my paid job over my kids' welfare. Making money was nice, but taking care of my kids was more important.

The spring works ended in mid-July. The calves weren't all branded, but the cowboss threw in the towel because it was just too darn hot.

"We should live at a cow camp one day, a really remote one where we have to pack salt with mules," Jim said one evening as we sat in the living room after the kids were asleep.

I looked at him in surprise. It seemed like most of the places we'd lived during our three years of marriage had been pretty remote. Yet he wanted to go even farther into the least civilized parts of America?

"I always wanted to work in Arizona, but I never did when I was younger," Jim continued. "One of these years—I don't even know, it might be five or six years, maybe more than that—I'd like to find some remote, off-the-grid camp in Arizona and work there for a while."

I mulled the notion over in my mind. It reminded me of a journal entry from when I was about twelve or so. I'd written that I wanted to spend an entire year living in a cabin in the Alaskan wilderness by myself, truly alone with only the land and animals for company. I wanted to see if I could survive without help from the modern world and all its conveniences and people.

I nodded at Jim. "Sure, that would be a great experience. But what about the kids? They're too young to do something like that right now."

"I'm not saying we should leave tomorrow. I just think that would be a really great lifestyle for us to have as a family, for the kids to have a chance to live with no TV, no cell phones, just be way out there cowboying."

That did sound nice. An opportunity to let our kids experience a simpler, more rustic childhood filled with cacti and logical thinking as they navigated a steep, rocky hillside on a surefooted horse rather than spending endless hours on their cell phones. Plus, God willing, one day we would be eighty years old and sitting in our rocking chairs looking back at our lives. Then it would be too late to do all the things we always meant to do but never got around to. We had to do those things while we could.

But Grace and Milo were only three years old and ten months, respectively. To me, that was too young to make the leap from the security of semi-civilization into the brushy canyons and boulder piles just yet.

"I like that idea," I said. "And I'll be all about it when the kids are older, more like ten and thirteen. Then they can ride all day, and I wouldn't have to worry about them as much."

Jim nodded and we moved on to another topic of conversation.

I looked out the window by the front door at the three men walking down the driveway in front of the cookhouse with Marvin Buhler, the Flying V manager. Two were medium height and stocky, and one was tall and lanky. All three wore cameras strapped around their necks.

"Who's that?" I asked Jim. Traffic at the Flying V was typically limited to tractors, ranch trucks, and hunters. Pedestrians wearing shiny, non-denim jackets stood out.

"Some camera guys. They came out to make a movie or something."

I stared out the window and plotted how I could hang out with those guys. I bet they could teach me how to use my fancy camera whose advanced settings were still largely a mystery to me.

I bundled up Grace in her coat, handed Milo to Jim, and walked outside. Taking my toddler daughter for a walk was a good excuse to get outside and introduce myself to the strangers. They turned out to be videographer Bud Force, acclaimed photographer John Langmore, and freelance cameraman Tito West. They were shooting footage to make a trailer for a documentary about contemporary ranch life. They were smiling and enthusiastic despite having left the Texas heat for a bitterly cold, snow-spitting October day in Nevada.

The next night, I zipped my laptop into its bag and slung the strap across the stroller handles. I pushed it to the cookhouse, where I planned to keep Milo occupied with a sucker while I showed some of my photos to the camera guys.

When I'd introduced myself in the driveway and told them I was an amateur photographer, they'd graciously agreed to provide feedback on my images. Jim had volunteered to do the dishes for me since I was also acting as the third string cook for the ranch that weekend.

I pushed the stroller into the cookhouse and opened my laptop on the table. All three men crowded behind me and peered at the flat screen. I pulled up the first image: a portrait of Connor Leveille catching a gray horse off the ropes.

"This is a good shot, but why did you crop it down to a square?" Bud asked.

"I have no idea," I answered. "I just thought it looked good. No real reason."

Bud nodded, then said. "The human eye seems to find certain dimensions, like eight by ten, more aesthetically pleasing than an exact square when looking at photographs."

Ah, so those standard photo sizes had reasons rooted in science and art. They weren't just arbitrary constraints placed on photos to make art fit into a rectangle. They were carefully considered and meant to enhance the overall effect of the finished piece.

When I started clicking through my images, a voice from behind me asked, "You took all these photos?"

I answered in the affirmative, took the surprise I detected in his voice as a compliment, and sat up a little straighter on the hard wooden bench. I also wondered why someone might think I would show off a bunch of photos I didn't take.

During my impromptu twenty-minute photography lesson, John told me that ensuring there was separation between subjects in a photo usually enhanced the image's quality. His photographs, mostly black-and-white images shot with 35-millimeter film in a Lecia camera, were renowned and appreciated by art critics and lay people alike. Bud, a storyteller who worked with both videos and photos, informed me that a picture could indeed have more than one subject. Tito didn't say much. I took his silence to mean he was more of a video guy than a still-image maker, but I later learned that his black-and-white pictures had an emotional depth and layered texture that made a person fall right into them and get lost for a while.

My mind was blown. Maybe this was basic photography knowledge, but it was news to this isolated ranch wife who snapped pictures while handing out snacks and rocking babies.

Milo began screeching and pulling at the stroller tray. He twisted and clawed as he tried to escape his plastic throne on wheels. Grace had picked up all the saltshakers and syrup bottles on the table at least twice and was wandering farther around the cookhouse, investigating drawers potentially hiding sharp knives and a washroom that contained several varieties of chemical cleaners. Jim was almost done washing skillets. It was time to go.

I thanked the guys for their advice. People usually had to pay to attend a workshop to receive the kind of feedback I'd been fortunate enough to get right in my front yard, free of charge. I shut my laptop, knowing my photography skills were about to improve. I was slow to hang the bag on the stroller and say good night to the crew. My mind had felt free, focused, and uncluttered by dirty diapers and spilled juice cups for nearly half an hour. It was heaven.

CHAPTER 20 ✳ **Upheaval**

Jim walked through the front door one cold November morning.

"Looks like I don't have to go to work tomorrow," he said.

"Oh, you have a day off?" This was a surprise.

"Well, I have to go to work somewhere, just not here, because I don't work here anymore."

A familiar sinking feeling dropped through my chest.

"You got fired? What happened?" I was experienced at asking these questions, but hearing the answer and confirming that my family had just lost half our income and our home never got any easier.

"Tom wanted to take the cows one way around the hill and down the draw, and I knew it wouldn't work. I told him we should go the other way. He got mad and said if I didn't agree with him, I should go find another place to work. I said fine." He shrugged.

"Really, you got fired over which way to take the cows?" That seemed petty, even for a cowboss.

"I'm sure there's more to it than that. He hasn't liked me ever since I quit drinking. I'm no fun to be around anymore."

He had a point. The whole cowboy crew was still drunk all day and congregated at Tom and Chandra's most nights. Jim was the odd man out.

"Well, it'll be okay," I said. I stepped forward and hugged my husband. His arms wrapped around me almost as a reflex. "The important thing is that you don't start drinking again. We can handle anything as long as you stay sober."

Jim nodded. He took off his boots and coat, then set about the doubtful task of finding a cowboy job at the end of the busy fall season. Most ranches were cutting back the crew size and laying off guys as they headed into winter.

Steve Brown met us at the shipping corrals mid-morning. We'd spent the night before in Kingman, Arizona, then finished the drive to the Mill Iron S Ranch headquarters at first light. Steve was tall and wore a white straw cowboy hat like all cowboys do. He smiled and shook our hands warmly like all ranch managers do when meeting a potential employee. Cowboys are a dime a dozen, but that doesn't mean they want to scare any away.

Steve had good reason to be extra welcoming that day. He was interviewing Jim for the Roca Camp, the roughest, most remote cow camp in Arizona, and possibly in the Lower 48. It was located twenty-five miles from headquarters, a drive that took three and a half hours due to the primitive road. From there, it was another hour to town. Nicknamed "The Moon" and "Camp Far Far Away," it took a special kind of person to seek out that lifestyle.

Jim wanted to move to Roca as soon as we heard it was open. I was not excited at the prospect of living four and a half hours from the nearest town with two kids under the age of four, but I had to put aside the reservations I had voiced when Jim and I first talked about Arizona because it looked like our only option at the moment. Jim hadn't been able to find another ranch job in northern Nevada in the three weeks since Tom fired him. We'd been living at the Flying V as non-employees for nearly a month and starting to feel like squatters. It was time to go somewhere, anywhere—preferably a place with a paycheck and a roof over our heads.

"I'll drive you up to camp and kinda show you the ranch so you guys can check it out," Steve said. "My boy, Tyler, is gonna ride along with us, too."

"Sounds good," Jim said.

Jim's politeness irritated me. He had slipped into easy-to-please, go-with-the-flow mode. Don't want to rock the boat when you're desperate for a job and a home for your family. Or—and this was far more likely—he was just an easygoing person and I was bitter because it looked like I was going to have to leave my friends and home in northern Nevada years before I wanted to.

Steve and Jim climbed into the front seat of a white crew-cab company pickup. I got in the back and claimed a window seat, as did Tyler. We'd left the kids at the Flying V with Gayle, who lived across the driveway. The fourteen-hour drive was much easier without a preschooler and a toddler in tow. We bounced along the rutted red dirt road that headed toward the mountains south of headquarters. I raised the Nikon to my eye and snapped pictures of a group of horses with a Mill Iron S freeze brand on their left hip. I didn't care if I looked like a tourist. It might be the only time I was on this historic Arizona cattle ranch, and I wanted to make sure I took advantage of the photographic opportunities. The cowboys would just have to deal with it.

Several minutes after we left, Steve pointed to a turnoff that led to the cow camp closest to headquarters, called White Cliff. A married couple, Ned and Ramona Hendricks, lived there. Both were well-known Arizona cowpunchers and both drew wages from the ranch. An hour later, Steve pointed to the driveway to the Diamond L Camp. A young family with kids the same age as ours lived there. If we moved to Roca, they would be our closest neighbors at two hours away.

We continued on the dusty, one-track road and bumped through the rocky bottom of a dry creek bed. It was the fourth such crossing we'd made so far. I wasn't sure what these Southwest guys had against bridges, but up north, we used them to cross creeks. They were made of wood or metal and kept the undercarriage of your automobile from coming into direct contact with moving bodies of water. They were convenient and often aesthetically pleasing.

Then I remembered flash floods. Bridges probably just washed out when a heavy rain sent a torrent of muddy water tearing through a canyon bottom.

"How do you cross the creeks when the water is high?" I piped up from the back seat.

"Oh, you can just about always get across," Steve said. "But if the water's real high, you might have to wait a day or two."

So, being stranded on one side of the creek was indeed a real possibility. I began to feel uneasy. What if I got caught on the side of the creek without grocery stores and doctors—you know, the side we would be living on?

"What about snow? Do you ever get snowed in out here?" Coming from northern Nevada, I was more familiar with snowstorms than flash floods.

"We get some snow out here, but nothing to worry about," Steve said. "You won't get snowed in at Roca."

His words made me feel better during that first drive up the mountain, but they would be proven false roughly one month later when a big storm struck and we couldn't leave camp for a full three weeks.

We drove for over two more hours. We covered the fifteen miles between the Diamond L and Roca in record slow time. Steve drove as fast as the road allowed but as slow as common sense dictated. He stopped at the top of the steepest descents to shift into four-low, then crept down the side of the canyon, bumped over the rocks in the unbridged creek at the bottom, then slowly crawled back up the other side. We repeated the process countless times. Steve told Jim the name of each canyon we crossed, and Jim committed them to memory like a good cowboy always does. I instantly forgot all the canyon names and tried to suppress the feeling that we were making a mistake in even coming to interview for this job.

I could hardly believe that an actual house, where people actually lived full-time, existed at the end of this road that was scarcely more than a trail. It was hard to distinguish the road from the surrounding rocks in several places. I lost count of how many boulder-strewn creek beds we crossed. I looked out the window at the cedar trees and prickly pear cactus. There were rocks, rocks, and more rocks scattered everywhere. I'd grown up on a dirt road and had lived down a few with Jim, but this was extreme, even for me.

The white ranch truck started to overheat just before we reached Roca. Steve checked the instrument panel and saw that the temperature gauge was near the right-hand side. He looked back up at the road ahead.

"The truck's about to overheat and I don't know why," he said. "But we're almost to Roca, so hopefully we can make it there and put some water in it."

I saw tendrils of steam escape from beneath the hood. Steve drove faster, the truck lurching over rocks and ruts. The temperature gauge redlined and the steam tendrils merged into one thick stream of smoke trailing behind us in the wind. The diesel engine roared loud to new, heat-fueled heights as it powered us up the final hill through the green gate and into the yard of the Roca Camp.

Steve braked and popped the hood, then jumped out and grabbed a garden hose. He appeared proficient in Cowboy Mechanics 101, which stated you should always pour cold water on anything emitting smoke from beneath the hood of a vehicle.

I was glad to see a garden hose. Those were commonplace in more populated areas. I'd frequently used them myself. They reminded me of filling horse troughs, growing a garden, and running through the sprinkler as a little kid. Where there was a garden hose, there must be electricity.

But there were no power lines on the ranch. The homes back at headquarters were powered by huge diesel generators that sat in a big shed near the owner's house, which was in between the lodge and the manager's house. The scenic desert vistas I'd seen out the truck window for three and a half hours were unbroken by a single stark pole or swooping power line, and that, of course, meant Roca was off the grid.

But I took the garden hose as a good sign, a flash of watery comfort in the arid desert. I got out of the pickup to stretch my legs and check out our potential new home. I vaguely wondered what we'd do about the broken-down truck situation, but I didn't spend any time brainstorming actual solutions. I had no idea how to troubleshoot an engine. Besides, Steve seemed like he had it handled. He had a garden hose.

I was more occupied with imagining actually calling this Godforsaken place home.

"Looks like this thing's gonna be broke down. We'll have to leave it here and come get it later," said Steve. "I'll walk up the hill behind the house and call Jimmy to come get us, I think there's a little bit of cell service up there."

Jimmy Crawley was the Mill Iron S cowboss. Steve strode toward the hill with Tyler walking quickly behind him. They went through the horse pasture gate by the front yard and hurried up the base of the hillside. It was midafternoon and would be evening by the time Jimmy came to rescue us. I knew it'd be well after dark by the time we'd finally get back to headquarters.

"Well," Jim said after the Smith men had traipsed out of earshot, "what do you think of it?"

"I don't know. This is way the heck out there."

"Well, we don't have much other choice right now, do we?"

I didn't reply. I knew Jim felt tremendous pressure to find another job. He was the "man of the house," the provider, the main breadwinner. He knew his family's housing was directly tied to his ability to find employment, and he wanted to provide us a home and start earning a paycheck again ASAP.

But I had a sinus infection, had left my nursing baby overnight for the first time, and was stranded at a cow camp with uncertain contact with the outside world. My body was sore from bouncing over rocks for over three hours in a pickup. If all went as planned, I would be saying goodbye to my friends and power poles and striking out for this unpopulated desert outpost with two small kids in less than a week.

We walked up the hill to the house. Might as well poke around and see what we were getting ourselves into.

The house was small with thick walls and what appeared to be a basement area for storage at one end. We walked up the concrete steps. Somebody had commemorated the modernization of the front porch in large scrawling print letters while the concrete was still wet. "4-7-1970" was etched on one side of the bottom step. Mill Iron S was written on the other side.

I imagined the pack mule trains that had hauled in every bag of concrete mix, every two-by-four and roll of insulation used to build that square tan house. The road had only been drivable for the last few years. Before that, residents of Roca had to ride in on horseback and pack all their groceries and supplies using mules and panniers.

We opened the screen door, then the main door, and walked directly into the kitchen. The room was about ten by fifteen feet and contained a small propane fridge, a gas cook stove, an old wooden table with mismatched chairs, a sink, a propane water heater, and the original wood-fired cookstove. It was a huge steel beast, black with fancy lettering on the door. Bread warmers curved above the cooking surface. A tank attached to the back provided what had been the only source of hot water for the house until the recent addition of a propane water heater.

"Can you imagine packing that stove in with mules?" Jim wondered aloud. "They had to do it piece by piece."

The stove was impressive, both in sheer size and reliability. It had outlasted a number of cowboys as a permanent resident of Roca for decades and promised to provide warmth and hot meals even if the electrical system went out and the propane tank was empty.

We walked through the remainder of the house. Adjacent to the kitchen was a small living room furnished with two grimy recliners and a boxy TV placed directly on the floor. Straight through that was the main bedroom. It, too, came furnished with someone else's well-used furniture. A queen-sized bed was pushed against the middle of one wall. Built-in shelves ran along a recessed section of wall and an ornate antique dresser faced the foot of the bed.

Off the other side of the living room was another bedroom. This one had no bed, but a small table in the corner held a three-CD stereo with "Roca" written on it with a permanent marker. I wondered who they thought would venture way out here to steal an old boombox.

A tiny room, more like a shed, looked like a recent addition onto the hallway between the second bedroom and the kitchen. It had solid walls but an unfinished floor and held a top-load washing machine. There was barely enough room to fit a laundry basket and a person at the same time.

Across the short hallway from the add-on laundry room was a small bathroom. I looked at the dirty pedestal sink and cracked wooden seat on the toilet. I tried to imagine curling my hair in there and helping my kids brush their teeth with bubblegum toothpaste. My hopes for a new family home sank to half-mast.

I pulled back the stained white curtain and looked in the shower stall. It appeared to be made of concrete. Large, uneven sections of waterproof paint were peeling all over the bottom and up the sides. I thought of all the single cowboys who'd lived at Roca before us and what all single guys did in the shower. I couldn't imagine bathing my babies in there.

I let the curtain fall back over the opening and breathed deep to keep from crying. I didn't want to be caught crying when Steve and Tyler came back down the hill to report if they'd succeeded in finding enough cell phone service to call for a rescue vehicle. I forced myself to breathe through the tightening of my throat and walked back into the kitchen with Jim.

The floors throughout the house were made of the original wooden planks, full of character and slivers. The kitchen floor had been covered with linoleum tiles at some point, large squares in a tan pattern that were more chipped and split than not. The last resident had sewn and hung curtains made from cotton fabric with a cowboy print.

"I like it," Jim said. "This is a good camp house."

I looked at the floor for a long moment.

"I like the stove," I managed.

We went back outside and toured the barn. It was a metal garage-like building with a concrete floor and the usual bins for grain and dog food. Panniers and britchings for packing salt blocks on mules or horses leaned against one wall.

Outside the barn, a shiny, dark blue solar panel was installed near the cedar stay loading chute, the flat faces of its panels pointed optimistically toward the southern sky. A behemoth of a generator sat close to the house. It looked nearly as old as the house.

We walked to the back yard. Stout, metal poles held three strands of thick clothesline. All were stretched taut, and some had clothespins attached at random intervals. This clothesline meant business. It wasn't some flimsy modern farmhouse statement piece that a suburban housewife used once a year to dry a set of bed sheets when she felt like being rustic. It was the only way occupants of Roca had to dry their laundry, come sunshine, sleet, freezing cold, or monsoon rain.

Just behind the triple-strand clothesline (or "solar clothes dryer" as I would come to call it) was a chicken coop and fenced run. The thin woven wire was tight and looked coyote-proof.

"I don't care how nice that chicken coop is, I'm not raising chickens," I declared.

"Good," agreed Jim. "I hate chickens."

Once the poultry matter was settled, I inspected the garden plot. It had a rabbit-proof fence and indentations of rows from seasons gone by. I didn't have a green thumb, but I was willing to give the scientific art of growing things a try. I liked fresh salad greens. Besides, the garden space was already fenced and looked so tidy and inviting. Growing vegetables in Arizona had to be easier than in northern Nevada.

A homemade swing hung from a huge walnut tree just outside the garden gate. A wild green bush of some type unfurled behind it. Late afternoon light shone like liquid gold through the ropes and over the thick seat plank. It invited me to sit down and sway in the sunshine.

Then I realized that if I lived there, I would never have an unexpected visitor drop in just because they were passing through the neighborhood. Not a single one. Never. Nobody went to Roca by accident, and hardly anyone ever went there on purpose.

I looked down the hill toward the road to headquarters where it crested over the first hill, then disappeared sharply off the canyon on the other side. There were no other signs of human life in any direction. I felt like I was in an alternate universe, or maybe a low-budget reality show. *Survivor: Ranch Wife Edition.* I wanted to vote myself off the island before the cameras even started rolling.

Jim walked around the horse pasture and climbed the closest rolling hill. He stood at the top and surveyed the canyonland, not quite a king but a man satisfied with all he saw. I hung back several feet and snapped pictures so he could remember the view. I hoped we would never be there again.

CHAPTER 21 * **A Displaced
Nevada Ranch Wife**

We stayed in the bunkhouse for our first night at the Mill Iron S as an officially hired cowboy family. We could no longer crash in the guesthouse like we had on our interview trip, that long wooden lodge with professionally cleaned bedrooms and trophy bucks mounted on the walls. Those accommodations were for hunters, paying customers who wore camo and drove pickup trucks that cost more money than Jim made in two years.

We left our heavy furniture in storage in Elko and brought only what we could fit in a small U-Haul trailer that I towed behind my Jeep.

Jim hauled the horses in the trailer and stashed our guns, a few framed pictures, and other breakables in the back seat of the Dodge. We planned to sleep in bedrolls for a couple months while we test-drove our Arizona plan. We (mostly me) suspected we might hate it and hightail it back to Nevada the first time a decent job came open. If we liked the Southwest, we'd drive back north at some point to retrieve our belongings. My boss at the *Nevada Rancher* agreed to let me work remotely for three months. After that, it would be decision time: stay in Arizona and quit my job or move back to Nevada and continue writing for the magazine.

The bunkhouse was steeped in Arizona ranching history, much of it visible since it looked like it hadn't been cleaned since John Wayne changed his name from Marion Morrison and started making movies. I turned the kids loose to play on the long porch and overgrown front yard while Jim unloaded our suitcases. The cold weather soon drove us all indoors to explore our temporary dwelling.

Immediately through the front door, a common area held two pleather couches, a gigantic boxy TV, and a mountain of DVDs nearly as huge as the television set. The room's central and best feature was an enormous stone fireplace. Off to the right were two bedrooms. The kitchen was straight ahead. The bathroom was to the right of that, and the largest bedroom sat next to it in the corner.

The bunkhouse smelled greasy and dank. The stone walls kept it cool, which was probably more of a benefit during the summer months. But it was December and the interior temperature was icy. Jim lit a couple of strategically placed propane heaters that Jimmy had brought over before we arrived. He poured diesel from a five-gallon can onto a stack of logs in the fireplace and soon had a roaring fire.

I tried not to touch anything as I cooked hot dogs for dinner in the grimy kitchen. I walked into the bathroom to start a bath for the kids, then walked right back out.

"There's no way I'm putting our kids in that bathtub," I announced. "If that's my only option, I'll take the kids up to the lodge to give them a bath."

I looked up the hill in the darkness toward the lodge just over the rise, with its clean white walls and fresh-smelling carpets. Jim stepped inside the bathroom to check it out.

"Give me thirty minutes," he said. He grabbed a bottle of bleach and a pack of sponges, then headed back in.

The sound of running water alternated with scrubbing, first at one end of the bathroom, then the middle, then the other end. I watched the kids play and kept fourteen-month-old Milo from falling into the fireplace while wondering if Jim could get the bathroom clean enough. The plastic shower curtain was coated in mildew at the bottom, and I just knew my son would put it in his mouth. Who knew what kind of urinary tract infection my daughter could catch from sitting naked in a tub that was more colorful rust and dark stains than original porcelain white?

"Aright, come check it out," Jim called after a while. "See if you approve."

I walked into the bathroom. It smelled like a public swimming pool, but in a good way. The soap scum was gone from the bottom and sides of the tub and the urine stains that surrounded the base of the toilet had disappeared. Even the floor in front of the sink looked safe enough to stand barefoot.

"Alright," I said as I looked around one more time. "I'll bathe the kids here. It looks amazing. Thank you for your hard work."

After bath time, I put clean jammies on the kids and tucked Grace into her narrow bedroll with hot pink Minnie Mouse sheets. I laid Milo down on the oversized bedroll I shared with Jim, since that's where our toddler would end up anyway. We all slept in the big corner bedroom so we could share a propane heater. As long as we pulled our bedrolls away from the ancient single-paned window and snuggled at least one family member at all times, we'd stay warm through the night.

Jim would stay at headquarters for a few days before taking his supplies and heading up to Roca. "Taking his supplies" sounded like a prospector heading into the Yukon, and the notion wasn't that far off. He had to haul two big eighty-gallon tanks full of propane to run the camp house's stove, hot water heater, and refrigerator. He loaded the ranch pickup high with hay bales. The horse pasture didn't produce much grass in the dead of winter. He brought salt blocks for the cattle and all the groceries he'd need for a couple weeks.

"Have fun," I said. Jim knew I was not crazy about the idea of moving our kids to Roca, so we'd agreed I would look for a place to rent in Prescott. From there, I could drive up to Roca and visit Jim for a few days each week or two. In the meantime, Steve was letting me stay at the bunkhouse while I searched for available rentals.

Jim headed up the mountain loaded down with rations for livestock and himself, and I set about making the old bunkhouse livable for myself and two small kids.

I walked through the front door after taking the kids for a walk around headquarters one morning and found Jimmy and another cowboy reinstalling the stovetop grill in the kitchen.

"When you got here, I realized how dirty this place was," he said. "Sorry it was such a mess. We took the grill out and pressure-washed it."

"Thanks," I said with surprise and gratitude. I hadn't realized the grill was so dirty, what with all the other dirty things to notice. It must have been bad if a group of cowboys felt the need to pressure-wash it. It was nice to have help with the move-in cleaning, though.

Jimmy showed me how to light the portable propane heaters before he left. I thanked him for his help and wiped off the old wooden kitchen table. The fridge and its suspicious smells were more than I was willing to tackle for a temporary living situation, but I swept the floor and pulled up the blankets on our bedrolls.

I stopped to study a framed collage of sepia-toned photographs on a wall between the kitchen and the common area. The pictures showed men with taco-shaped hats riding stocky Quarter Horses and working horned Hereford cattle. Hat shapes, horse conformation, and boot styles had evolved over the decades, but the grins on their faces and ease with which they sat in the saddle were interchangeable with those of today's cowboys.

I wondered how many of the cowpunchers pictured on the wall had sat around the wooden table I'd just cleaned with a paper towel and eaten some type of beef, maybe drunk whiskey and played cards. I wondered how many of them had warmed themselves in front of the big stone fireplace before letting the screen door snap shut behind them and tromping down the wooden porch to turn left into one of the bedrooms that ran in a neat row alongside the porch.

I was willing to bet none of them thought a displaced Nevada ranch wife would feed her kids Kraft Mac 'N Cheese in the kitchen and shove a plastic tub of blocks and blankets behind the couch before banking the fire for the night because she was calling the bunkhouse "home" while figuring out her next step.

The flames leaped and jumped in the big stone fireplace. The fire glowed orange and red, sending sparks and thin rifle shots of noise across the bunkhouse. Grace snuggled beside me on the pleather couch in her footie jammies and I held Milo on my lap as he nursed to sleep. *Soul Surfer* played on the giant TV next to the fireplace as the kids settled into slumber before I carried them to bed. I was tired of watching the cute blonde girl get her arm bitten off by a shark, then overcome the odds to surf in competition once again. We'd watched the movie almost daily since coming to the Mill Iron S. I wondered if I'd traumatized my young daughter by repeatedly letting her watch the attack scene with all the blood swirling in the water, but she kept asking to see the movie, so what the hell. It did have a positive, uplifting message, after all. At least it wasn't rated R like most of the films in the giant stack.

That evening, we cozied up under the handmade lap quilt I'd bought at a thrift store in Prescott. The fabric was burnt orange and brown with a pieced calico back, tied with yarn. The colors matched the warmth of the fire, which I'd come to think of as a friend. It was a living thing, something that needed to eat and breathe. It cheered the room with its light and warmth, crackling and snapping in a language with syllables and a cadence all its own.

I had officially quit looking for a cheap place to rent in Prescott. Now that we had been in Arizona for several weeks, I already knew I'd have to leave my job with the *Nevada Rancher*, despite having the three-month grace period from my editor. We'd then lose half our monthly income and have no way to pay for a second residence. The only reason a cowboy family could afford even one residence was because it was free.

I'd come to terms with leaving my job because, to begin with, there was no cell phone service at the Mill Iron S headquarters. I could only talk to my editor, family, and friends when I drove up the road a ways toward White Cliff and parked by the cedar tree on the right-hand side of the road, the one with the giant trunk. If my best friend or mom didn't pick up during my limited window of cellular connectivity, I drove back to the bunkhouse even more aware of my isolation. At least I had the fire for company.

There was also, of course, no internet at the bunkhouse. Through all five of our previous moves and temporary lapses in phone and internet coverage, I'd managed to relocate my household while writing and filing all my articles by deadline. I hadn't admitted defeat until I finally called my editor from the "phone tree" and told her I'd need to cash in my vacation days to account for filing only half of my regularly assigned stories. It was just too hard to research and write about the goings-on in the Nevada ranching industry from a remote ranch in a different state with no Wi-Fi.

But we were almost one month into our "Southwestern Project" and Jim had already nested at his rugged cow camp home. I knew he loved packing salt on the mules, Whiskey and Ted. He could happily live without cell phone service, internet, or TV. Give that man a stack of Zane Grey paperbacks and a few scratchy FM radio stations and he was set.

Jim told me he'd cleaned the camp house and hung pictures. All that was left was for me and the kids to make the move up the mountain to join him. Losing half our income felt like less of a risk than it used to since Jim had quit drinking.

Grace fell asleep before *Soul Surfer* ended. Milo had long since conked out with his head in the crook of my arm. I listened to my friend the fire crackle and pop for a few minutes, then carried my children to our shared bedrolls on the cold floor of the big stone room in the corner.

CHAPTER 22 ✳ **It's Up to Me**

I chained the green panel gate shut and walked back to my Jeep, my bulky canvas bedroll tied to the roof rack. Surrounded by southwestern desert with a backdrop of distant mountain ranges, the whole scene looked like an ad for off-brand camping gear. I hoped my granny knots stayed tied. If my heavy canvas bed packed with homemade quilts fell off the roof and rolled down any one of the several steep canyons I was about to traverse, I wouldn't be able to drag it back up the mountainside by myself.

I opened the driver's side door and sat down behind the steering wheel. Behind me, Grace looked out the window and chattered happily in barely understandable gibberish. Milo sat strapped into his car seat next to the other window.

I looked at the road ahead. It was red dirt and wound invitingly into a thicket of evergreen trees. It looked like the kind of road you'd take on a long weekend when you wanted to get away from the city, maybe bring the family along for a Sunday picnic. But it was my new way home, and I wasn't at all excited about it.

Beyond the pine trees, Cedar Mountain rose sharply out of the desert like a mighty watcher of all things that happened on the ranch. I knew that once I drove past the base of the huge mountain, the road climbed a steep hill and then grew increasingly primitive with each passing mile. I'd need four-wheel drive for sure to get up the hill. I was never the type to go four-wheeling for fun, and I didn't look forward to possibly spinning my tires on the loose gravel of a steep road every time I wanted to go to town and buy groceries.

"Everybody ready to go see Daddy?" I called into the back seat as I shut the door and shifted into drive.

"Yeah! Daddy!" Grace squealed.

Milo threw his chubby toddler arms up into the air and smiled. I took that for a yes and began to drive farther onto the ranch. The kids didn't know how anxious their mother was about living four and a half hours from the nearest town. They had no clue what a generator was or that I didn't know how to use one but would now depend on one to make the lights come on during cloudy spells. They didn't understand what propane was or how useful it was for cooking and heating hot water for their baths, so they weren't the least bit concerned that it was difficult to obtain and haul each eighty-gallon tank up to Roca.

The road required a four-wheel drive vehicle with high clearance on a good day. It was impassable if one of the creek crossings was running high or the road was slick with deep mud. I wasn't an experienced off-road driver, but I had three hours in front of me to practice my skills. I drove increasingly slower as the road wound farther through the wild Arizona desert country, stopping at the top of each canyon to shift into four low. I crept down the steep path carved out of the mountainside and tried not to look over the drop-offs that lay just beyond the shoulder. At the bottom of each canyon, I followed the switchback road up the far side only to repeat the process again all too soon.

Finally, the Roca Camp came into view. I could see the small house, square and tan. The metal barn with a solar panel on the roof sat across the driveway from a larger solar panel. A handful of horses meandered around the mostly dirt pasture behind the house. Our green Dodge pickup was parked out front. Smoke drifted from the chimney for warmth against the chill of the mid-December day.

The Jeep crawled down the final stretch of rock-strewn road just in front of the entrance to the camp. I turned into the yard and parked next to the Dodge. Jim stood in the yard. He was smiling.

"Hey, you guys made it," he said.

"Yep, just barely," I replied. "That road takes forever."

I unstrapped the kids and grabbed the diaper bag. Grace and Milo ran to jump on their daddy in a volley of hugs. After he kissed his kids, Jim embraced me with long arms that wrapped all the way around. Then he carried my bedroll and our suitcases into the small camp house. I followed him with bags of groceries and half-eaten road snacks. I was impressed as soon as I walked through the front door. The last time I'd seen the house, the floor was covered with grime and loose dirt. The walls were coated with smudges and fingerprints. All the windows were streaked with rain-driven mud and spotted with fly specks. I'd refused to sit down on the cracked wooden toilet seat and cringed when I touched the knobs to turn on the water in the bathroom sink.

But now, the floor was freshly swept and free of filth. The windows still provided only limited visibility, but the walls were clean. In the bathroom, the seat was still cracked but the toilet was scrubbed.

"Wow, you have been busy," I said.

"I wanted you guys to feel at home," he said.

"Well, it worked. You did a great job."

I walked through the small house and examined my husband's handiwork. I could feel how much he wanted us there with him. A signed and framed William Matthews print hung on one wall. It had been a gift from the owner of the hunting and fishing store I'd worked at while in college and what I considered one of my "fancy" wall hangings. An Arnold Rojas print titled "Jaquima to Freno" hung on another. I'd given it to Jim as a Christmas gift two years before. While the bed at the far end of the house wasn't ours, the denim quilt with cheetah print flannel backing that I'd sewn for Jim was neatly draped over it. Everywhere I looked, I saw a few more pieces of us in the house that I didn't want to live in.

Maybe I did belong there after all.

The kids explored the dirt front yard within the loose confines of its falling-down fence while I went inside. The road was too rough to transport furniture very often, so residents of the Roca Camp just used the dresser that was already there. The legs were hand-carved from dark brown hardwood. It was topped with a mirror in a matching frame. One side had a door that opened to a single cupboard, and the other side held a few drawers. Its elegant yet small design reflected a time gone by when people had fewer material possessions and everyday items were individually handcrafted. It had been there for years, most likely packed in with mules like the big cook stove in the kitchen.

Or maybe someone picked it up in Prescott, bought it for cheap at a moving sale when someone else was in a rush to get out of town. It seemed I was always dropped in the middle of historic homesteads without an explanatory placard in sight. The backstories were mine to imagine and the future was up to me.

The kids played outside until afternoon quickly gave way to early evening and a winter sunset. Inside the house, a low fire burned in the cook stove. I began unpacking our folded clothes into the antique dresser in the bedroom. I didn't know how long we would live there, but this was our home for now.

ACKNOWLEDGMENTS

'd like to thank my husband, Jim, for his support and encouragement from the very beginning of this book project. He was my first reader as I struggled through early drafts of separate sections and never once told me I should leave the book writing to the pros. He read the first full draft and didn't suggest a single change. This is especially impressive when you consider many parts of this book are hardly a flattering portrayal of his past behavior.

I'd also like to thank Jim for taking me on the big adventure that has been our marriage. Without his dedication to me, us, our children, and the cowboy way of life, this book would have been much shorter—more like a pamphlet, with fewer stories about outlaw horses.

Filmmaker and family friend Bud Force was the second person I told about my book idea. His words echoed in my mind whenever I felt discouraged: "I've never heard of a book like this before. This is definitely a book I would read." He and his wife, Megan, read early drafts of select passages and provided the just-right combination of critical feedback and friendly encouragement to keep me writing.

I'm grateful—and amazed—that Rebecca Didier and Martha Cook at Trafalgar Square Books read a half-finished manuscript and bought the book on the spot. Who does that? People with faith and vision, that's who. Thanks for believing in my story and my ability to tell it.

An extra big thanks to Rebecca for her masterful editing. Her suggestions were just what this book needed, and I'm grateful for her straightforward feedback. I also appreciate her support and encouragement throughout the emotionally taxing task of bringing such a personal story from rough draft to finished product.

Thank you, Crystal Brennan, for giving me the sage advice to never burn my moving boxes. Embracing that mindset helped make our big-outfit cowboying years feel like an adventure instead of a slow but steady train wreck.

Many thanks to my blog readers, especially those who have been with me since 2010. I so appreciate all your support and especially your words of encouragement over the years. Writing is a solitary pursuit, but connecting with you fine people (and even you unsavory types) has been a satisfying reward.

I can't forget my kids. Grace, Milo, and Levi—thank you for dreaming big dreams and reminding me that childhood aspirations do come true. I'm so glad you think it's cool that your mom is an author, something I have dreamt of since I was nine years old. Thank you for being full of hope and joy. Never lose that.

The biggest thanks of all to the good Lord for giving me the desire and ability to write this story and others. He sure has blessed me with more than I ever would have thought to ask for.